THE DE-ROMANIZATION

OF THE

American Catholic Church

THE
DE-ROMANIZATION
OF THE AMERICAN
Catholic Church

Edward Wakin and

Father Joseph F. Scheuer

GREENWOOD PRESS, PUBLISHERS
WESTPORT, CONNECTICUT

Library of Congress Cataloging in Publication Data

Wakin, Edward.
   The de-Romanization of the American Catholic Church.

   Reprint of the ed. published by Macmillan, New York.
   Includes bibliographical references and index.
   1. Catholic Church in the United States. 2. Ca
2. Catholics--United States. I. Scheuer, Joseph F.,
joint author. II. Title.
[BX1406.2.W3 1979]   301.5'8   78-10157
ISBN 0-313-21238-4

Reprinted with the permission of Macmillan Publishing Co., Inc.

Reprinted in 1979 by Greenwood Press, Inc.
51 Riverside Avenue, Westport, CT 06880

Printed in the United States of America

10 9 8 7 6 5 4 3 2 1

Contents

Preface

To MANY this book may seem irreligious, if not antireligious, possibly because of a popular fear that social commentators and social scientists threaten religion with natural
curiosity about what is supposed to be entirely supernatural.
This leads to the assumption that books about religion
preach, indoctrinate, defend—or attack religion.

Rather than persuade in any way, the authors have set
out to present American Catholicism and American Catholics in the perspective of the available data, without a supernatural reference point. Here are the particular and general
patterns of people living within institutionalized forms in
specific settings. The dimensions include the social, cultural,
economic, political, and intellectual. The Catholic Church
is both an institution and people; in depicting both, our
intention is to convey understanding rather than to evaluate
—either negatively or positively.

We are *not* depicting the transcendent Catholic Church,
that mystery of faith which is eloquently set forth in the
Constitution on the Church, one of the most significant
documents issued by the Second Vatican Council. We are
treating the empirical American Church and its members
—that Church of the here and now out of which the supernatural phenomenon of transcendence arises.

The book's title emphasizes a process of change which is
being described and analyzed. In the course of our research,

organization and writing, the theme of de-Romanization and Americanization was not imposed on the material. It emerged from the material, determining both analysis and conclusion. Our final chapter formulates in theoretical and conceptual terms the theme that runs through the individual chapters.

We have drawn on many sources and various disciplines, particularly the social sciences, but we are not writing a formal academic treatise or following any particular theoretical model. We have used many studies by social scientists without necessarily accepting the theoretical framework in which they are presented. However, in the background there are elements from Parsonian theory, Weberian analysis, psychological forms, and political trends of thought. The presentation is not tied to any side in the controversies involving Catholicism, though the attackers will find ammunition for attacking and the defenders occasion to defend. That is a risk without being an intention.

Both authors undertook with enthusiasm this task of presenting a wide-ranging view of American Catholics when Mr. William Birmingham was prescient enough to see the need for such a book and the possibilities in using material that has never before been brought together. The authors owe much to him and to the many colleagues and friends who enriched our perceptions with information and insights that otherwise would be lacking, as also to the many others who have advised, admonished, and at times harangued us.

PART I

Past and Present

CHAPTER 1

◇◇◇◇◇◇◇◇◇◇◇◇◇◇◇◇◇◇◇◇◇◇◇◇◇◇◇◇◇◇◇◇◇◇◇◇

Double Identity

THE LABEL *American Catholic* expresses ambivalence and implies conflict. *American* and *Catholic* are two demanding identities, each supported by an environment of values, attitudes, and relationships which surround the individual. Though the pressures of each identity often reinforce each other, they can also be centrifugal, sometimes pulling the American Catholic away from his Catholicism, sometimes drawing him away from the mainstream of American life. As an American he reflects his Catholicism and as a Catholic his Americanism. Each makes a difference; each has consequences for the other.

While Catholics are an inextricable part of American society, they are also *apart* from it. This is more than a play on words. Their apartness is evident in a kaleidoscopic system of organizations and institutions that range across their spiritual, social, educational, professional, and personal lives. Catholics can be found apart in hospitals, schools and colleges, charitable and welfare agencies, and even in their dating behavior. Their doctors, lawyers, journalists, historians, social scientists, war veterans, policemen, firemen, and social workers cluster in Catholic organizations and meet in Catholic conclaves, listening to scholarly lectures on biblical exegesis and speeches on the dangers of dirty books.

There are some Catholics (though a small minority) who don't leave their group even when they go to work. This is the small but formidable army of "professional" Catholics—largely priests and nuns, supplemented by brigades of laymen and -women—whose thought, action, socializing, income, and influence derive from functioning as twenty-four-hour Catholics. American Catholicism thereby has the makings of a separate community which can encircle its members from the cradle to the grave.

Yet most Catholics seem indistinguishable from their fellow Americans. On the surface they have blended into the national landscape at home, work, and play, in their habits, attitudes, and style of life. Then on Sunday morning Catholics become those Americans who attend a Catholic church as part of the traffic jam on Main Street. On Monday morning you cannot tell them apart.

Catholics, who as a group constitute a Church of immigrants, are adjusting to the disparities and conflicts between American pressures and Catholic demands, between the values and attitudes of the former and the rules, regulations, and ideals of the latter. This two-way pull ranges from the trivial to the transcendental, and not all the circumlocutions, Americanizing platitudes, and ecumenical rhetoric conceal them.

The adjustment and the conflict can be as ordinary as the case of a Catholic storekeeper with customers who want to shop on Sundays, including some fellow Catholics. An Indiana supermarket owner told of being congratulated after Sunday mass by a fellow parishioner for closing on Sunday, unlike his competitors. That afternoon he saw the same lady walking out of a competitor's store with an armful of groceries.

Or the conflict can be as atypical as that of a Catholic in the Central Intelligence Agency who conceivably may have to square his Catholic conscience with such cloak-and-dagger activities as lying, aiding assassins, and committing suicide.

Or the conflict can be as publicized as the birth control

issue. Mobile, aspiring Americans who are also Catholics want to limit their families, but they confront a Church ban on artificial contraception. For conscientious couples, the choice can be agonizing.

The American Catholic can confront such predicaments by ignoring them, arguing them away, or reconciling them. Some take the uncomplicated path of rejecting their Catholicism or retreating from the American life around them. One example is the political boss of Plaquemines Parish (or county), Louisiana, Leander Perez. He conformed to his local segregationist environment, and for his outspoken opposition to the desegregation of Catholic schools he was excommunicated in 1962 by the late Archbishop Joseph F. Rummel of New Orleans.

The most famous American Catholic adjustment was made by President Kennedy, and its most elegant exposition was in his pre-election appearance on September 12, 1960, before Protestant ministers in Houston, Texas. In his statement, which was worked on by a key behind-the-scenes adviser who is a dean of intellectual Catholic journalists, Kennedy said:

Whatever issue may come before me as President, if I should be elected—on birth control, divorce, censorship, gambling or any other subject—I will make my decision in accordance with these views, in accordance with what my conscience tells me to be in the national interest, and without regard to outside religious pressure or dictate. And no power or threat of punishment could cause me to decide otherwise.

But if the time should ever come—and I do not concede any conflict to be remotely possible—when my office would require me to either violate my conscience, or violate the national interest, then I would resign the office, and I hope any other conscientious public servant would do likewise.[1]

It was a brilliant, thoroughly American, pragmatic response for a Catholic to make. By assuring his audience that any issue would be settled in the national interest, Kennedy opted for the American side of his commitment. But Catholics also had the assurance that he would never violate his conscience, while both Catholics and other Americans were reassured that no conflict was even "remotely possible." He thus made both possible choices and dismissed the need for any choice.

The statement was no fussy, theoretical approach to the persistent historical and philosophical tension between the sacred and the secular or the sociological double identity of American Catholics. Kennedy spoke in the pragmatic here and now, the way things are and would be resolved in the existential world in which he lived.

Yet double identity—the social conflict of pluralism—remains a reality, producing competing pressures. Of course the problem of adjusting to different demands and modes of behavior is not uniquely Catholic. Americans are pushed, pulled, and prodded by a variety of commitments, some held lightly, some felt strongly. From antivivisectionists, teetotalists, and vegetarians to Christian Scientists, Mormons, and Hasidic Jews, Americans experience conflicts between their environment and their commitment to particular codes and creeds. American society is a monumental reconciliation of all these varied commitments.

Catholics, constituting one out of four Americans, are the largest single element in this national reconciliation. In examining Catholics in America, it is necessary to range from the classroom to the church pew, from the dinner table to the ballot box, from the civil rights picket line to the chancery office. For in his lifetime as an American, the Catholic plays many roles—as parent, pupil, businessman, union man, athlete, soldier, voter, consumer.

Each role is influenced to some extent by the duality of Catholicism and Americanism. Even in the religious role, as churchgoers, laymen, joiners, or clerics, Catholics reflect the influence of their American identity. There are conflicts, compromises, choices, and just plain differences in all these roles. And when Catholics differ from non-Catholics and from one another, the reasons are not simply religious or theological. Historical, cultural, sociological, and ethnic factors are involved.

In a social and psychological sense, a Catholic is anyone who says he is. In a religious and formal sense, he is anyone who is baptized a Catholic. The first depends on conscious choice; the second is predominantly a matter of birth and ancestry. The Church counts its Catholics and buries them on the basis of baptism, and only formal and public withdrawal from the Church will keep a Catholic out of consecrated burial ground. According to Church law, a Catholic must make his Easter duty, telling his sins in confession and receiving holy communion once during Lent or within the sixty-day period following Easter. In some dioceses at certain times, he may also have to send his children to parochial school. These are minimum standards of performance.

In describing American Catholics, the statistics, surveys, and their interpretations may vary, but it is always clear which definition of a Catholic is being applied. Those who can be classified as Catholics are readily identified, and both their differences and their similarities in regard to other Americans are well documented.

Within their Church as a formal entity, Catholics are involved in a formal institution which has a hierarchical bureaucracy and a bureaucratic hierarchy. The Church and its members constitute a social institution and community like any others. When they are examined from that viewpoint, anxiety and change are evident behind what appears to be a monolithic façade. An accelerating process of Americanization is overtaking Catholics and their church. The term *Roman* has become so imbedded in the Catholic identity as a catchall description that the present process of change constitutes de-Romanization. There is an evolution —more rapid in some areas than in others—from *Roman*

Catholic to *American* Catholic. As a result, there is tension between the inertia of an institution and the pace of changing times, between conserving and overturning. It is the tension of the double identity facing America's largest minority, those Americans who are Catholics in one way or another.

CHAPTER 2

◇◇

The Ethnic Accent

IN THE WINTER of 1938 the papal desk of His Holiness Pius XI contained papers designating the successor to Patrick Cardinal Hayes as archbishop of the flagship of American Catholicism, the Archdiocese of New York. But the name on those papers was, by reliable report,* not that of the famous incumbent who would emerge as the most powerful Catholic churchman in the New World. Listed for the appointment was an archbishop, John T. McNicholas of Cincinnati, who would, as it turned out, languish in Midwestern obscurity.

Pius XI died before he could make his appointment and was succeeded by Eugenio Cardinal Pacelli, a close friend of a Boston bishop who had been counted out as a possibility for archbishop of New York. The bishop's diary entry for March 20, 1939, summed up his slim chances: "Am feeling relieved to know what the serious reasons were that prevented my appointment to New York. The reasons are good ones and there is another good one—I don't want to go myself. Am informed there are three Cardinals against my

---

* In addition to the information available to the authors directly, this was confirmed in the authorized biography of Cardinal Spellman by Rev. Robert I. Gannon (see Note 1 for this chapter): "There were solid grounds for thinking that Pope Pius XI had always regarded Bishop Spellman as the logical successor of Cardinal O'Connell [of Boston], and that on the other hand he had been deeply impressed by the zeal and scholastic accomplishments of the Dominican prelate of Cincinnati. It has even been said on good authority that the papers designating Archbishop McNicholas for New York had reached the Holy Father's desk" (p. 129).

going to New York. That is one reason why I should think I might go."[1]

The Boston bishop did go to New York in 1939 after all, by appointment of Pius XII, formerly Cardinal Pacelli. He was Francis Joseph Spellman, seven years later a cardinal, the cherubic-faced churchman who came to represent so much of both the successful and the controversial in American Catholicism.

Spellman became a cardinal for all kinds, and more—a churchman who pleased the many and antagonized the few —the epitome of Roman Catholicism in America. He was more than the beneficiary of hierarchical friendship; his appointment constituted a seal of approval for the conservative, Irish, pragmatic, centralized style of the Catholic Church in America.

The intellectual Dominican from Cincinnati who had so impressed Pius XI with his zeal and scholarship was in many ways representative of a different tradition. As a member of a religious order, he did not belong to the predominant secular clergy. He also came from the Midwest, where German Catholics are a major bloc. Both geography and nationality support were against him. Moreover, the Church in New York, as in the rest of America, was at the takeoff stage; the hand that held the crosier had to direct a vast physical expansion and a spreading bureaucracy. There would be little time to stop and intellectualize.

On the other hand, the Boston bishop had family roots in Tipperary, Limerick, and Cork, too, and grew up in the flowering fields of Irish-American Catholicism. According to his Jesuit biographer, Robert I. Gannon, he also had the benefit of a father's opportunistic advice: "Always go with people who are smarter than you are—and in your case it won't be difficult to find them"[2] The advice understates Spellman's intelligence, but it does single out the political and pragmatic stress that runs through his career. He is cut from the American cloth. He gets things done and does not consume his energies in just planning them. The Spellman approach, carried to an extreme, is epitomized by his protégé, James Cardinal McIntyre of Los Angeles. In a remarkable exposé of conditions in the Los Angeles Archdiocese published in the summer of 1964, the crusading Catholic magazine *Commonweal* cited Cardinal McIntyre's "ability as a fund-raiser and construction foreman," and quoted one of his priests: "Social action, no—but concrete and cost estimates, those he understands!"[3]

It is a practical ecclesiastical style that has long prevailed in America and was so nicely pointed up by De Tocqueville in his nineteenth-century observation: "The American ministers of the Gospel do not attempt to draw or to fix all the thoughts of man upon the life to come; they are willing to surrender a portion of his heart to the cares of the present; seeming to consider the goods of this world as important, though secondary, objects."[4]

Cardinal Spellman is a child of the American Church, whose sons brought their dreams and their faith to the New World and watched many of the dreams come true and the faith flourish. It was a faith that they transplanted in their distinctive style, mixing nationality and religion. Each did this: the English, French, Irish, Germans, Italians, Spanish, Scandinavians, Poles, Czechs, Bulgarians, Lithuanians, Lebanese, Greeks. And many more. But it was the Irish who imposed the dominant ethnic brand. More than anything else this side of eternity, American Catholicism comprises a church of immigrants, with its lingering accent a brogue.

It is impossible to talk with meaning about 50 million American Catholics today* without establishing these roots,

---

* The estimate of 50 million Catholics is computed from the finding of the United States Bureau of the Census, which reported from a representative sample in 1957 that the U.S. population is 25.7 percent Catholic. The percentage has been applied to the 1965 U.S. population of 194 million, assuming that all things are equal and that no great Catholic migration or mass defections have taken place. The 1965 *Official Catholic Directory* (New York, Kenedy, 1965) lists 45.6 million Catholics.

bearing in mind that as late as 1908 they were regarded by Rome as well as by themselves as members of a missionary church. Much of their "other-worldly attitude," their aloofness and tendency toward separateness are related to their immigrant experience. Many times even now they "just don't fit" or exaggerate their pride in having "arrived." In 1965, it was still possible to read a full-page advertisement in the *Catholic Press Annual* offering mailing lists of Catholic ethnic groups: "If your well of Catholic contributors is running dry, why not test our reservoir of Catholic ethnic groups?" The company offered this assurance: "Many millions available. These have been tested and reordered by many fund raisers."[5]

Immigrant roots in the American soil have produced the American Catholic hybrid which has been called the finest flowering of practicing Catholicism in the world. It has also been dismissed as a theological backwater, as an anti-intellectual, unenlightened, bricks-and-mortar religion. Regardless of the rhetoric of the apologists and critics, American Catholics today can hardly be seen in perspective without a preliminary examination of the immigrant roots.

In the beginning Catholics were very few in number, perhaps 25,000 in the colonies at the time of the Revolution. For the most part they had no clergy, much less organization. Many of their numbers—an estimated 250,000—strayed from their Church in a country where Protestants predominated. At that time, the only Catholic immigrants of consequence were the French. Their clergy, coming after the French Revolution, soon predominated; by 1817 all United States bishops except one were French. In the late seventeenth and early eighteenth centuries, Catholics comprised a secure, well-established community. Never has American Catholicism been so socially acceptable or so unimportant as it was at that time.

The French clergy, many of them cultivated aristocrats fleeing libertarian democracy, were ill equipped to face the waves of Irish and Germans arriving after 1820. They were unable to cope with the rough-and-tumble and, to them, irresponsible immigrants who called for their own churches and native-language liturgy and clergy. Except for the order of the French Sulpicians, who carried on a tradition of training American (and other native) clergy, the French influence was washed away by nineteenth-century immigration. In the face of the growing desire of American bishops for their own seminaries and faculties training priests in a distinctive regional style, even the seminary influence—stern, authoritarian, and Jansenistic—is waning.

When the Irish came, they literally shocked the established clergy, laity, and Americans in general. This was not just one shock but a series, extending over the first half of the nineteenth century. By the 1850s the Irish had established beachheads of power and influence whose consequences are still felt. When European liberals were taken aback by the relative theological conservatism of American prelates at the Second Vatican Council, they would have understood better had they considered the history and emergence of the Irish in America over the past hundred years. When a hurrah is sounded for Irish ward politics, it recalls the arrival and the impact of these rambunctious, cohesive, aggressive immigrants of the early and middle nineteenth century who fought the French clergy, fought among themselves, fought the German immigrants, and have fought many others since. Their hierarchical posture in the 1960s is rooted in this pugnacious past. The siege mentality lingers, favoring the status quo and making the American hierarchy both subservient to Vatican bureaucrats and sensitive to any threat to the status quo.

The Irish immigrant had to fight to survive, almost every step of the way. First of all, as the Irish immigration began, the cry in America was that "Europe is casting upon us the refuse of her Almshouses and her prisons."[6] And again, "There are so many paupers at the Almshouse in Bellevue

Hospital that they have to be lodged in cells and garrets, in the chapel, even in the morgue."[7]

Paupers, but militant ones. Riots and outbreaks were commonplace items in both American and European newspapers.

On the 29th and 30th ult. it was known that a contractor on the 3rd division of the Baltimore and Ohio railroad about 25 miles from the city, had absconded, leaving his laborers unpaid, and that they (as too often happens in Ireland, the country which, in general, they had recently left) had taken the law into their own hands, were wantonly destroying the property of the company, because their employer had wronged them! They were between 200 and 300 strong, and, with pick axes, hammers and sledges, made a most furious attack on the rails, sills, etc., and whatever else they could destroy. The sheriff of the county, and his posse, were resisted by these ignorant and wicked men—and a requisition was made on Brig. Gen. George H. Steuart for a detachment of the volunteers under his command —and, although it rained very heavily, a sufficient number of patriotic soldiers started in the cars from the depot at about 10 o'clock in the night of the 30th of June, and reached the scene of violence before day-light next morning, fully prepared to put down such outrageous proceedings, but those who had resisted the civil officers so rudely and violently, suffered themselves to be arrested by the military, without opposition or precipitately fled—and none of them were personally injured.[8]

The fighting Irish had to fight. Or nurse their frustrations and deprivations both here and in the home country. Striking back at both real and imaginary opposition became a reflex action. So did the habit of favoring their "own kind." The reflex action has been evident in Catholic militancy, and the habit of favoritism is reflected by the Irish predominance in the American hierarchy.

When the Irish immigrant arrived, he was greeted by his own kind, particularly his Irish priest. Like the newcomer, the priest was often the youngest son of an Irish family, who left home to go on mission, poor, with a second-rate education, and without much of a future in his own land. In

America he and his countrymen had to learn to live side
by side with the analytical New Englander, who had been
bred in a theological atmosphere where intellect had been
sharpened by controversy on "fixed fate, free will, fore-
knowledge." Such religionists felt little sympathy for the
Irishman and his priest, who had never discussed a point of
doctrine in their lives.[9] But in the end the righteous Yankees felt a responsibility for the new immigrant's condition,
and gradually the old traces of Puritan contempt for the
"Irish papist" would disappear.[10]

Another view of the Irish newcomer helps explain his
situation and his devotion to his Church:

The great mass of the Irish people of the class that emigrates
to America live in Ireland chiefly on potatoes, oatmeal, butter-
milk—on a simple and almost entirely vegetable diet. They
have not the means, if they had the inclination, to drink much
whiskey, or use much tobacco. They land in America with clear,
rosy complexions, bright eyes, good teeth, and good health generally. They are as strong as horses. They find themselves in a
land of good wages, cheap provisions, cheap whiskey and tobacco. Flesh meat they have been accustomed to consider a
luxury of the rich, and they go in for it accordingly. They eat
meat three times a day, rudely cooked, and in large quantities.
Whiskey, of an execrable quality, is plentiful and cheap; so is
tobacco, and they drink, smoke, and chew abundantly.[11]

These were also the people

who have dug the canals, built the railways, and done the
rough work of the cities of the North and West. They are
settled in hundreds of cities and villages, on those great works
of internal improvement, and wherever they have gone of
course their priests have accompanied or followed them. They
have had good wages, and are always liberal and open-handed,
especially for anything connected with their religion. The result
is that there are everywhere Catholic Churches, convents,
schools and colleges.[12]

Whatever else, the Irish were uncompromisingly loyal to
their Church and their clergy. Unlike the French, German,

and some other nationalities, they had no tradition of anti-clericalism.

This solidarity was reinforced by the Irish woman who migrated. Loyalty to Church was refracted through loyalty to family, which is the root of much of the twentieth-century mystique of family that pervades middle-class American Catholicism.

> The great ambition of the Irish girl is to send 'something' to her people as soon as possible after she has landed in America; and in innumerable instances the first tidings of her arrival in the New World are accompanied with a remittance, the fruits of her first earnings in her first place. Loving a bit of finery dearly, she will resolutely shut her eyes to the attractions of some enticing article of dress, to prove to the loved ones at home that she has not forgotten them; and she will risk the danger of insufficient clothing or boots not proof against rain or snow, rather than diminish the amount of the little hoard to which she is weekly adding, and which she intends as a delightful surprise to parents who possibly did not altogether approve of her hazardous enterprise.[13]

While such acts and the attitudes upon which they are based are not necessarily rooted in theological virtues, they are easily raised to a dignity worthy of medieval knighthood and incline bishops and priests to define women as the "heart of the home." (Men are the head.) Thus home and Church, family and clergy were the great balance wheels of the Irishman's passion and loyalty. Whatever else he might desert, to these he cleaved.

Moreover, it was through family and clergy that the Irish took advantage of opportunities for power that they did not have in their homeland. They brought to the New World, particularly the large cities, an almost tribal solidarity, a loyalty to their counties rather than their numerous towns of origin, so that unity was easy to achieve. The priest provided leadership. Carrying vestiges of undisputed tribal authority as the man of schooling and importance in rural Ireland, he consolidated a nationality consciousness which made Church and country synonymous. To be Catholic and Irish-American became practically the same thing, expressed in the widespread practice of displaying American flags inside Catholic churches.

And they had numbers on their side. Between 1820 and 1865 about 1.9 million Irish immigrants arrived, practically all of them Catholic,* while the Church in the United States expanded from 650,000 to 1.6 million members in the single decade 1840–50. With such numbers the Irish could face up to the antagonisms they encountered, and the antagonisms increased their unity.

Inevitably, the Irish were committed to tribally organized parishes established on a territorial basis, with the pastor as a relatively absolute head. Their flirtation with trusteeism in the early nineteenth century was brief. To have the laity as trustees controlling their churches' secular affairs and property was to them the Protestant way and out of tune with the traditional clerical role. Moreover, this led to a demand that the laity select their own priests, even their own bishop. The demand passed as soon as the dominant French clergy, whom the Irish resented, were replaced by their "own kind." Then the Irish reverted to type. It was up to the laity to pay and the clergy to rule. With the defeat of trusteeism, Irish hegemony in the Church was established, a hegemony that placed power in the hands of the Irish hierarchy, set an Irish brand upon American Catholicism, and established an authoritarian image. In the middle of the twentieth century, that victory still seemed secure.

It was already too late to turn this trend when the Germans arrived, close on the heels of the Irish, to escape poverty and to seek their fortunes. Their situation was a familiar one:

The chief emigration to America at present is from the Upper and Middle Rhine, the Grand Duchy of Baden, Wur-

* In 1800 there were hardly more than a million people in all the original thirteen colonies.

temberg, the two Hesses and Bavaria. In Bavaria especially, whole village communities sell their property for whatever they can get, and set out, with their clergymen at their head. 'It is a lamentable sight', says a French writer, 'when you are travelling in the spring or autumn on the Strassburg road, to see the long files of carts that meet you every mile, carrying the whole property of the poor wretches, who are about to cross the Atlantic on the faith of a lying prospectus. There they go slowly along; their miserable tumbrils—drawn by such starved, drooping beasts that your only wonder is, how they can possibly hope to reach Havre alive—piled with the scanty boxes containing their few effects, and on the top of all, the women and children, the sick and bedridden, and all who are too exhausted with the journey to walk. One might take it for a convoy of wounded, the relics of a battlefield, but for the rows of little white heads peeping from beneath the ragged hood'. These are the emigrants from Bavaria and the Upper Rhine, who have no seaport nearer than Havre. Those from the north of Germany, who are comparatively few in number, sail mostly from Bremen. The number of these likewise is increasing. From 1832 to 1835 inclusive, 9,000 embarked every year from Bremen; from 1839 to 1842, the average number was 13,000; which increased to 19,000 in the year 1844.[14]

That was how they looked in Europe. In American eyes, the German immigrants were an intensely loyal people, but with loyalties divided among city-states and county principalities. If Ireland was the land of saints and scholars, theirs was the land of rulers and universities. While the Irish headed for the cities and ward politics, the Germans—with their crafts, their love of farming, and their learning—headed for the rich agricultural regions running through mid-America: Pennsylvania, Ohio, Indiana, Illinois, Iowa, Missouri, and Kansas, with spurs running north into Wisconsin, Nebraska, and the Dakotas.

There was no single spirit among them. They were split into numerous religious bodies and into political factions. There were many attempts to establish new little empires, new little kingdoms. And the German clergy were commonly the spokesmen for factions rather than the whole.

Where there were no churches, the Germans proceeded to build their own in their own factional image. Where the Irish were already ensconced, there was a clash, particularly in the large cities, notably Baltimore and Philadelphia. The German clergy even protested to Rome that the Irish regarded German parishes as subordinate and were eager to do away with them.

It was out of German dissatisfaction with Irish hegemony that a daring and revolutionary proposal was advanced in 1890 in the Lucerne Memorial by Peter Paul Cahensly. Worried about the fate of his fellow German Catholics, Cahensly suggested that Catholic dioceses be established in the United States on the basis of nationality rather than geography. The traditional territorial divisions, about seventy-five of them at that time,* would be abolished and replaced by ethnic divisions. Irish, German, and Italian dioceses would then offer a familiar religious setting for the immigrants, and American Catholics would be united in a federation. The Irish hierarchy obtained Vatican condemnation of the proposal on the ground that it would undermine the Church's catholicity, though they blinked at local violations of this same catholicity.

Though the nationality-based dioceses were denied, nationality-based parishes multiplied. The effects can still be seen in American cities. A noteworthy example is the Diocese of Gary, Indiana, where twenty-five out of forty-five urbanized parishes cater to the spectrum of ethnic groups that have settled since 1900 around the steel mills and oil refineries of Lake County. The national parishes have done at the grass roots what Cahensly wanted to do at the top. In the long run, the victory of the hierarchy ensured Irish predominance and Church solidarity and strength, at least officially and formally. While new national parishes can no longer be established (as in the case of the Puerto Rican

* In 1965 there were 148 archdioceses and dioceses.

migrations), a bishop still needs special Vatican approval to close down a national parish or convert it into a territorial parish.

In the post–Civil War period, the Italians, the pope's own people, were added to the influx of Catholics, and they disappointed their coreligionists. From the viewpoint of the Irish and Germans, the Italians presented a second-rate form of Catholicism, arriving poorly instructed in their faith and indifferent toward the building and support of Church institutions. Their numbers became great, increasing from 27,000 immigrants in the decade ending in 1880 to 130,000, 390,000, 802,000, and 275,000 in the ensuing decades to 1920.

The Italians were mainly poor and rural and came from central and southern regions of agricultural poverty: Abruzzi e Molise, Campania, Apulia, Basilicata, Calabria, Sicily. They came from a Catholic country where the historical urge toward unity was complicated by anticlericalism expressed in freemasonry, where the abuses of the state often were blamed on the church. To the Italians, church and state were not one and the same in Utopia. They had unpleasant memories of the days when the Papal States dominated Italy.

While the Italian women displayed ostentatious religious fervor, their men were notably nonconformist religiously. The Irish and the Germans disapproved on both counts, particularly since they were such militant supporters of their churches. To them, the Italians were poor practitioners of their faith, and worse—in a practical, success-minded culture—they were poor supporters financially. The Italians were not welcomed in the Irish and German parishes, and they themselves wanted their own parishes.

They formed "Little Italys" in the large American cities, for their migration was personal, intimate, and clannish. Sicilians from Cinisi concentrated in midtown Manhattan, while Calabrians concentrated on Mulberry Street in lower

Manhattan. In Utica the majority came from Laurenzana and the adjacent province of Basilicata. In Stamford, Connecticut, the Italians were drawn from Avigliano, in Cleveland from Termini Imerense, in Chicago from Altavilla Milicia, Bagheria, Vicari, and Monreale. Little Italy in Detroit reputedly grew from a single immigrant and his family who persuaded others to follow.

Their national parishes were tight-knit enclaves that reflected the strong neighborhood focus of the Italians. They emphasized neighborhood clergy, neighborhood churches and schools, and neighborhood customs. Unlike the Irish and Germans, the Italians seldom came with their *padrone;* he was imported later or commissioned to come by formal hierarchical appointment. Italians arrived with little religious motivation and without a tradition of social structures tying them to their Church. Ever since, the drift of Italians from the Catholic Church has been a problem. Of an estimated 6 million Italian Americans in 1939, it was estimated that 2 million were fervent Catholics, 1 million lost, and 3 million "doubtful."

The Italians arrived in a booming America. It was a time when economic empires were rising in rails, oils, steel, wheat and other grains, cattle, and sheep, a time of westward sprawl and urban explosion, an age of robber barons and social Darwinism. The American profile, with its prominent immigrant features, was being drawn. The Poles, largely Catholic by tradition and sentiment, also belong to this period, and their strong backs and hard muscles built the automobile industry in Detroit, the steel mills and railroad yards in Buffalo and Lackawanna, New York, the steel and Pullman industries in Gary and on Chicago's South Side.

The Poles were strongly individualistic, and they, too, built their own parishes, churches, and schools. Against the formidable array of Irish hierarchy, they practically created their own church within the American Church and created cities within cities like Hamtramck, Michigan—completely surrounded by Detroit but politically and ethnically as distinct as their native Poland from the rest of Europe. On the pages of the Catholic directories of the late 1890s and early 1900s, auxiliary bishops named Plagens, Wosnicki, and Zalencki emerge next to Irish ordinaries like Foley, Gallagher, and Mooney. In diocese after diocese in the Midwest, the Poles showed they were as militant and as loyal in support of their clergy and their national parishes as the Irish and Germans.

After World War I, two more waves of European immigrants augmented the ethnic accent in American Catholicism. Basically, the first was only a ripple because of the change in immigration policies early in the 1920s which produced the quota system. Since the overwhelmingly Catholic southern Europeans were the most affected, this was cited as an instance of American anti-Catholicism, though the policy was also anti-Asiatic. But Catholic immigration continued through the back door as Puerto Ricans and Mexicans settled in the United States. The Puerto Ricans, Catholic in tradition, represent a mixture of seven or eight different strains, running from black to white, from Indian to Castilian Spanish. A Mexican is also Spanish, as well as French, American, and several kinds of Indian. Mexicans and Puerto Ricans speak Spanish, but seldom do they speak it to one another. They are Catholic, but they don't always speak, even as Catholics, with their Irish, German, Italian, or Polish coreligionists. Social distance makes close contact almost impossible.

The second wave of immigration since World War I involved about 300,000 people fleeing the Nazis and Fascists between 1933 and 1945 and millions entering the U.S. after World War II under the Displaced Persons Act (1948) and the Refugee Relief Act (1953). There were enough Catholics among them to add a new dimension to the ethnic accent in American Catholicism. These newcomers were middle-class, educated, usually skilled, and often professional people. They embodied a set of characteristics different from those typically associated with American Catholics. They were less downtrodden and defensive and more mobile than the nineteenth- and early twentieth-century immigrants. For those who would notice, they personified the cultural and social variability of Catholics and Catholicism.

The current chapter in American Catholicism has developed from the adjustment to America by this continuing stream of newcomers. As ethnic groups and as individuals, they are still Americanizing, reshaping attitudes, actions, and religious involvement. Meanwhile, the variety of backgrounds has prevented the emergence of a single community of American Catholics and perpetuated residual conflicts between the dominant Irish and other groups.

Overall, generalized traits have resulted from this social-historical-cultural matrix. In adjusting to America, Catholics have been characterized by defensiveness, parochialism, and inflexibility. These traits, more than any others, have placed the accent on *Roman* in Roman Catholic and these traits, in particular, are under growing pressure. The parallel American tendencies of liberalism, openness, and innovation are producing an Americanizing—or de-Romanizing—process as Catholics respond to their environment and to their national ambiance. In each role played by Catholics in their church and in the larger American community, the two cultural orientations collide. The various collisions are analyzed in the subsequent chapters—collisions that are largely social and cultural, though dogma and dictum can also be involved.*

Defensiveness, parochialism, and inflexibility all stem

---

* The compelling pattern, which emerges in Parts I, II, and III, culminates in the concluding chapter where the conflict is traced to the confrontation between the diametrically opposed Roman and Anglo-Saxon traditions.

from the militancy of the immigrant struggling for his place in America. Most striking in the Irish Catholic milieu, the traits have been evident throughout American Catholicism. The defensive tone, deriving from the constant Catholic suspicion that there is an enemy all around, has created a reactionary image. The Know-Nothing movement and the American Progressive Association in the nineteenth century and the POAU (Protestants and Other Americans United for Separation of Church and State) in the mid-twentieth have singled out Catholics as antidemocratic. The popular stereo-typing has been reinforced by episodes like the Coughlin movement and the witch-hunting of the McCarthy period and by the rantings of such antediluvian Catholic publications as the Brooklyn *Tablet*.

Meanwhile, in a self-imposed ghetto of Catholic aware-ness and activity, parochialism was nurtured in the ethnic enclaves. Catholics tended to view the world exclusively in terms of how it affected them. Their range of interests and spectrum of sympathies were usually circumscribed by the Catholic context. Certainly this was the abiding impression created by the public, the official, and the visible in Catholic life before the *aggiornamento* of Pope John XXIII.

The defensiveness and the parochialism fostered inflexi-bility among Catholics, particularly concerning their reli-gion. Strength being the goal, uniformity was paramount and authority unquestioned. Flexibility was interpreted as weakness and individualism as a threat—both were tinged with Protestantism, which until recent years was the enemy camp.

Catholics suffered from theological and intellectual myopia in approaching their religion because they failed to see that religion is subject to cultural and social influences. These influences affect the form in which religion is deliv-ered to the believer; no reputable scholar any longer doubts this. But popularly, Catholics failed to distinguish between the principles of their religion and the practices which emerge in a particular time and place. The many accidentals became mixed with the few essentials. As historical perspective and the notion of cultural relativity were lost, Catholics in America seemed more Roman than the Romans.

Yet Catholics hold to a faith that was originally spelled out by simple people devoid of the sophistication of philosophy and symbolic logic and far removed from the accumulation of modern empirical science. It is a faith which in the ensuing centuries became imbedded in particular systems of thought, schools of philosophy, and methods of formulation. These were the manner, not the matter of the Gospel message, but they achieved almost equal prestige and sanctity. The clerical bearers of Catholicism to the New World were imbued with the ethnocentrism of Europe; they carried with them the nationality-bound, culturally dominated religion of their homeland. And an uneducated constituency of immigrants sought them out as guides and intermediaries between them and their faith.

A historical pattern of inflexibility developed. One glaring result was the anguish among conscientious Catholics as they confronted reappraisal of the Catholic stand on birth control. They were thrown into shock by the prospect of personal decision-making on a matter of faith and morals. They wanted the priest to tell them what to do.

Meanwhile, the inflexibility of the immigrant tradition is compounded by the inflexibility of any large bureaucracy— the Church bureaucracy included. Consequently, adaptation and change, accompanied by the appearance of novelty, appear as threats. Nonetheless, a pragmatic, changing, innovating America is dictating the terms of adjustment and adaptation for its Catholicism.

CHAPTER 3

◇◇

Until Death Parts Them

THE YOUNG COUPLE sit in a cleanly painted room with bare walls, except for a crucifix and pictures of the local bishop and the pope in Rome. They face a man dressed in black, some years older, but a man who has never married and has learned about life between the sexes from books, teachers, parents, perhaps a brother or sister—and the sterile, structured intimacy of the confessional. He sits at an uncluttered desk as he instructs them on the holy sacrament of matrimony and the mutual obligations they will face as husband, wife, parent. The instructions are a required formality, and a cold encounter at a time of heightened romance for a man and woman who are about to possess each other. There is no inclination to hold hands.

With the exception of the few dioceses with marriage preparation courses or enterprising Christian family groups, the encounter is typical. The dish being set before the couple is Catholic marriage in all its chill logic and idealized state. The essential phrases are familiar: You are about to unite freely to form a home and to help each other save your souls by fulfilling your respective duties. . . . Marriage is an indissoluble contract. . . . What God has joined, let no man put asunder. . . . You marry for better or worse, to have and to hold each other, to be faithful to each other. . . . Never let the sun go down on your anger. . . . There must be authority in the home; the husband is the head. . . . The wife is not a slave, but a companion. . . . The greatest happiness in marriage comes from children. . . . Remember, the school of schools is the home, but send your children to a Catholic school; make sacrifices for this. . . . Let your home be a truly Catholic home.

What the couple usually want and probably need most is a frank, intelligent discussion of sex. They seldom get it. After the antiseptic instruction, a typical question is, "Can we have one more bridesmaid?" Ironically, the question suits the level of instruction. Meanwhile, the priest-instructor is tired after a long day and he still must finish reading his daily office before midnight. He trudges back to his solitary room, and the courting couple, having been separated from both romance and reality, leave.

Almost a third of a million American Catholic marriages are launched annually in such "instruction" sessions whose tone and direction are illustrated by the following guidelines taken from a typical instruction sheet used in the Midwest:

Remember God makes the laws and regulations for marriage as He is also the Author and Institutor of marriage—not man. If you don't want to live according to God's law, you have no right to enter marriage.

Contraceptives are always sinful and injurious to the health of the woman. Doctors will tell you this—it's a goldmine for the doctor's pocketbook [sic].

All parents want good children; but remember that good parents will have good children.

To not only beget children but to educate children—as children of God—both father and mother must cooperate in this all-important work.

In the background are the facile pulpit and parochial school descriptions of the Holy Family's virtues as set forth in the New Testament: Jesus, the only child, is obedient, submissive; Joseph, the humble carpenter, is the model husband, guardian, and protector; and Mary, the Virgin Mother, is the loving, kind, understanding, and patient wife. If priest-instructors and Catholic couples stopped to

think about the anomaly, they would realize with a jolt that
this is not a realistic working model for the twentieth-
century's urban, technological society. Fewer brides-to-be
are virgins in the first place; husbands have become aggressive organization men and distracted fathers; children can
be an expensive burden.

Actually, no signal specific formula has been established
for Catholic family life. It has always been set in a social and
cultural context throughout history—a fact too often passed
over in the rigid statements of American Catholic spokesmen. In its official theology and canon law, the Catholic
Church never has and never can delineate any single family
structure as the ideal for all times and places. The family
exists in the concrete, not merely in a neat syllogism.*

In addressing delegates to the International Conference
on the Family during the summer of 1965, Pope Paul made
this point in noting that "it would be vain to close one's
eyes to the adaptations that must come about even in the
most stable and traditional institutions." He viewed "with
satisfaction the positive side in many innovations . . . such as
the freer and more discerning choice of the marriage partner, the deeper solicitude for the development of husbands
and wives, the more lively interest taken in the children's
education, and the many other factors still being studied by
specialists."[1] A brief historical flashback will demonstrate
the changing specifics of Catholic marriage and place it in
focus against the blurred background of the version presented publicly by a clerical congeries of diocesan bureaucrats assigned to marriage and the family.

Cultural and social influences have always been at work,
since the early days of Christianity, through centuries of
stress on traditional ties of kin, clan, and tribe. Moreover, a

---

* The pendulum of the theorists has swung between the Augustinian
view of *fides, proles* (loyalty, children) and the Thomistic view of *proles,
fides*. While modern moralists tend to bring the views together, most
favor the marry-and-multiply emphasis over the marry-and-love.

constant complication has been the mystique of virginity and celibacy, which runs counter to the Old Testament admonition in the first chapters of Genesis: to "increase and multiply."

In the context of the classical culture of his time, Saint Paul displayed antifamilial attitudes, extolling virginity and only tolerating marriage while discouraging its use "as the time is short." Early Christians believed in an immediate *parousia*, or second coming, and directed their energies toward personal perfection in anticipation of the event. In his more positive statements, Paul counseled more a status quo than a new image or an evolution in family life.

When the Roman Church encountered the extended families of the Franks, Goths, and Anglo-Saxons, among others—all tribal, largely nomadic, and patriarchal in structure—a clash ensued as the Church sought to impose its authority over marriage and family. Carle Zimmerman's *Family and Civilization* documents in detail the course of the maneuvering to limit kinship matches and the power of the clan and tribe. Laws "forbidding marriage within 12 degrees of consanguine relationship, difficult then to enforce, and very frequently violated, tended over time to break up and dispel kinship linkage."[2] The all-encompassing father authority had to be weakened since it even included power over life or death. The Church encouraged marriage outside the clan and tribe and worked to reserve authority over marriage to itself or the state. The stress on marry-and-multiply stems from this early Christian contact with the large tribal groupings of Catholics, and persists in both European and American Catholicism.

But there were always cultural accommodations. Members of the Spanish nobility have intermarried for centuries in defiance of both the spirit and the letter of the law and have maintained extended families both within and outside official Catholic precepts. Ireland, with its old maids, bachelors, and delayed marriages, has in effect practiced population control. Puerto Ricans accept as a matter of course and without religious scruples the present-day consensual marriage (also called a companionate marriage or a common law marriage in U.S. civil law). This particularly scandalizes the strict and often Jansenistic Irish and German clergy.*

Catholic scholars have noted that the essentials of marriage remain unchanged, but the actual cultural expression should and must vary. While this may succeed as an intellectual answer, it is completely lost in the web of social realities and experiences confronting a young couple who receive marriage instructions at a rectory.

Rapid social change, mobility, urbanization, industrialism, and technology are transforming family life, and American Catholics find themselves without a view of the family appropriate to their time and place. Many Catholics are trying to pick up the pieces of the broken nineteenth-century images of marriage and family life. And they persist in mistaking the variable cultural and social aspects with the religious essentials.

The ethnic pressures engendered by the national groups comprising American Catholicism are disappearing and can no longer maintain their power over marriage and family. However, they still exert residual influences on the attitudes and actions which produce the modern American Catholic family, and are therefore the starting point for an examination of the changes in contemporary Catholic family life in America. Each has had a distinctive effect.

The Irish, in particular, have contributed a mother mystique that centers the family's emotional ties around the mother, particularly since male alcoholism became wide-

* Actually, marriage licenses in the United States did not come into vogue until the middle of the last century. Much of Catholic canon law in regard to marriage was not formalized, except as local law, until 1918. In many respects man's sexual drives are no more institutionalized than his economic and political drives. Even today the Catholic Church recognizes consensual marriages where no clergy is available.

spread among Irish immigrants. It remains a pronounced problem. In a post–World War I study, alcoholism was reported 74 times "as important" in causing psychoses among the Irish as among Jews. As recently as 1947, a study of first admissions in New York state for alcohol psychoses showed that the Irish rate per 100,000 population was 25.6 compared to 4.8 for Italians and 3.8 for Germans.[3] Drink, indeed, has been deeply embedded in the family framework of the Irish, and invariably it has been the father's problem, reducing his family role and strengthening the mother's position.

By contrast, the German family, like almost all European families, was father-centered in an atmosphere where heroes were men or had male characteristics, like Wagner's operatic heroines. The man of the house was provider, disciplinarian, and administrator, with diffuse authority. In her subsidiary role, the *hausfrau* was meek, mild, and subordinate to the unquestioned authority of the husband and father.

With Americanization, the German ideal became corrupted by a number of deviations, ranging from male submission and withdrawal to unabashed adultery and uninhibited extramarital sex. The Germans were often well-educated or skilled craftsmen and they were a hard-working lot. When they confronted American pluralism and its permissive atmosphere, their family mores and structure—sustained in their homeland by a stable culture and clearly defined religious identification—underwent severe strains.

The Poles, arriving with a later wave of American immigration, brought deeply ingrained family commitments which resembled the German more than the Irish style. As Warner and Srole found in their study of "Yankee City," the immigrant father was king. When the American environment challenged his old-country authority, the Polish father refused to yield. Instead, "The evidence from the new ethnic groups, Poles and Russians, Greeks and Armenians, is that the father reasserts his authority through direct controls with an even greater vigor than before."[4]

The Polish family became a vehicle for maintaining apartness in America. It was tied by language and custom to ethnic community and national church. Like the Russian, Greek, or Armenian family, it tended to become self-contained. Warner and Srole reported that in these families the father appropriated the children's earnings, expressing his authoritarian role through economic controls. And the children submitted. The Poles remain one of the most resistant groups to assimilation, and political candidates still woo them with campaign pledges to free their homeland from Communist tyranny.

Italian Catholics generally exhibit family pressures involving intense emotional ties to the mother and strong respect, even fear, for the father. For the son of the Italian immigrant, success is tied to his family, and a son is prized for keeping close to the family and marrying his own kind. The Italian success story is rooted in family and neighborhood: the ideal man is competitive in the American marketplace without losing a clearly recognizable Italian style. As Glazer and Moynihan point out, a prime example is Frank Sinatra, renowned and famed in the larger society but "still the big-hearted, generous, unchanged boy from the block."[5]

The residual force of these ethnic backgrounds in the American Catholic family outweighs any theological factor. The Jesuit sociologist and marriage expert, John L. Thomas, points this up in a revealing analysis of cases that came before the Chicago archdiocesan Marriage Court.[6] By canon law, Catholics must go before such courts to receive approval for separation or civil divorce, though of course they may not remarry. The records reveal the tensions in Catholic marriages and also show different patterns for different nationality groups.

For instance, Father Thomas found that mixed marriages were more prevalent among German couples than among

Irish. The Irish courted longer before marriage and married at an older age. Drink and mental breakdowns were more pronounced in the Irish marriages, while among the Germans adultery was more frequent. Among Poles and Italians, whose ethnic neighborhoods were still intact and whose national churches were thriving, there were almost no mixed marriages, in either religion or nationality. The Italians had a large number of brief courtships in contrast to the Irish and Poles. Poles had few marriages involving a short courtship; their engagements, like those of the Irish, were long. Italians married much younger than Poles, but like the Poles made relatively fewer adultery complaints. Drinking was often a problem with the Poles as with the Irish. Both Poles and Italians, particularly the latter, had in-law difficulties, reflecting their strong family pressures.

Yet America intrudes surely and steadily upon these ethnic family patterns, though the process varies according to nationality background and the newness of the immigrants. Inevitably Americanization does occur, as all ethnic families move in the same direction from different starting points in place and time. This can be illustrated in the changing tone and style of the southern Italian peasant family over three generations.[7]

The metamorphosis of southern Italians in America begins in a small Italian village where the family encompasses the life of the individual as he works and worships, plays and studies, loves and lusts, confronting his environment. In the first generation, America traps the family between the old country and the New World. Old customs and traditions no longer fit, though there is nothing else to do but try to make them fit. The second generation, born in the New World but taught to respect the Old, faces the inevitable contradictions and strives to accept the new while clinging to the old. Sometimes the old can be given the appearances of the new; more often it cannot, and must be rejected. By the third generation, a familiar pattern is emerging:

The father, once feared, retains respect and possibly admiration, but he is no longer the patriarch. Autocracy to democracy is a long road, involving lifetimes.

The mother, once the dominant love figure, must now learn to share her emotional position with the father and sometimes also with an in-law.

The sons, once the unchallenged preference, still tend to maintain their superiority, but suddenly find their sisters competing for status.

The parents discover that they are no longer the center of the home. Their children are. And the older they get the more likely this is to be the case.

Parents no longer choose their children's mates. Sons and daughters were first completely obedient, and then began to select their own spouses with parental consent. Now the bond is completely broken. They choose alone, with or without consent.

Marriages once within village, group, and Church, now occur outside all three.

The community consent was solemnized in a Church ritual. This gave way to exceptions, and a few second-generation Italians were married without the "blessing." But a new blue suit, a marriage license, and the judge soon replaced the community and its complicated rituals and personal involvements.

Children are born in hospitals instead of homes, with obstetricians in attendance instead of midwives, and prescriptions have replaced old folk remedies.

Adultery is more readily solved by court divorce than by family blood feud. And sex is no longer shrouded in the secrecy of the sacred but is discussed openly.

The family, once dictator of life choices, surrenders to individual decision, and the individual is drawn more and more away from the family circle. The family style becomes less ethnic, more American.

Neither Church nor its fading ally, nationality, could withstand the pressures of Americanization. Nationality, in keeping with the melting-pot process, was the first to weaken. *Intermarriage* once referred mainly to mixed nationalities; it now means mixed religions, as the romantic ideal and free choice in love and marriage have come to be applied over a wide range of choices. Only a few decades ago, free choice was often limited to the girl next door or a boy from the home town, but now the choice is broader and will continue to expand as society changes its scale. Geographic and social mobility have increased at an unprecedented pace, particularly in the large cities where most Catholics live.

The national trend toward intermarriage includes Catholics. Studies made in various dioceses since 1910 reveal a constant increase in mixed ethnic and religious marriages. Between 1940 and 1950, an estimated one out of every three Catholic marriages was mixed religiously. The actual number would undoubtedly be much larger if it included mixed engagements culminating in conversions before marriage and the many Catholics who marry outside the Church. Forty percent of Catholic marriages in Connecticut were religiously mixed in 1949, and when all factors were reconsidered, the total figure was interpreted as probably 50 percent. Marriage experts Judson and Mary Landis reported in 1961 that from one-fourth to three-fourths of the Catholics in some dioceses marry non-Catholics.[8]

In national parishes, the wife is usually the Catholic partner in a mixed marriage, reflecting the social fact that women cannot choose their partners so readily as can men. Where there are fewer Catholics, the number of mixed marriages is much greater, as would be expected. In cities like Raleigh, Charleston, Savannah, Atlanta, Nashville, and

Little Rock, where Catholics were only 2 percent of the population, mixed marriages ranged from 56 to 76 percent. Where Catholics were about 50 percent of the population, as in El Paso, Corpus Christi, Providence, and Santa Fe, mixed marriages ranged from 17 percent down to 8 percent.[9]

Personal factors are also at work. Catholics who marry persons of another faith tend to have less religious parents and greater early family strife and to be more dissatisfied with their parents when young and more emancipated from their parents at the time of marriage. This was borne out in the Midtown Mental Health Project in New York City when case studies of the intermarried Catholics (21 percent of the total) were analyzed.[10]

Acceptance of intermarriage is taken for granted among Catholics. Three out of four Catholics have no serious objection if a son or daughter marries a Protestant.[11] The acceptance is even higher among the college-educated. A study of 3000 University of California students revealed that the Catholics were willing to marry outside their faith much more frequently than were the Protestants and Jews. A recent national survey of colleges and universities found that 95 percent of the students—whether Catholic, Protestant, or Jewish—dated outside their religious group.[12] Even within Catholic schools in the survey, 82 percent dated outside their religion. When priests at Newman Clubs at thirty-seven colleges and universities were polled, seventeen replied that interfaith marriages were increasing and thirteen said they were occurring at a steady rate, but none said they were decreasing.[13] The implications on the college level are far-reaching, since more and more Catholics will attend secular colleges in the coming decades. They represent an important source of leadership and strength for the Church, and their continued commitment to Catholicism is of major significance.

The trend toward more mixed marriages will undoubt-

edly continue to gain momentum, propelled by the ecumenical spirit and the relaxation of Church regulations. It
is predicted that before long one out of two valid Catholic
marriages will be mixed. The number of invalid mixed
marriages, also on the rise, will increase the figures even
more. It is estimated that the loss of parents and children to
the Church because of valid and invalid mixed marriages
"must be at least 25 percent."[14] Moreover, the mixed marriage has a cumulative effect: the children are less likely to
be brought up as Catholics and more likely to intermarry.[15]
This also means there will be more and more personal confrontation between those who are Catholic and those who
are not, and at the most intimate level. The threat to Catholic solidarity is self-evident.

In marriage, perhaps the most forceful and intricate
problem involving Catholic sex life is that of birth control.
But it is not the only one. Few other religious groups face
such a complex of factors: an Irish puritanical influence
dominating through the clergy, the weight of inhibitions
created in parochial schools where family ideals are taught
by priests and nuns who do not have the reinforcement of a
personal family life, the apparent tension in Catholicism
between standards of chastity and the stress on producing
children, the conflict between the American emphasis on
sexual enjoyment and the Catholic demand for self-
control.

The Catholic problem in sex was summarized by Msgr.
John C. Knott, director of the Family Life Bureau of the
National Catholic Welfare Conference, at a 1963 meeting of
the Catholic Physicians' Guild in Chicago. He said that the
secular person "sees the physical aspects of sex not only as
something good" but "goes to the other extreme of seeing it
as the only good." By contrast, the average American Catholic finds it difficult to "accept sex not only naturally, as
something good, but also totally, as something more than
physical."

Msgr. Knott argued persuasively that the source of this Catholic attitude is the "shotgun marriage of American Puritanism, which suggests that sex is shameful, and the Jansenism of Irish or French Catholics, which held that sex was an evil, but a necessary one because of the need to procreate." Added to this was Catholic conditioning "to some extent" by the secular attitude. He urged a better understanding of sexuality as distinct from sex and the positive values which Christianity places on it. "Sexuality is made by God and therefore it is good. It is sacred because it is concerned with life—either with initiating it as in the infant, or with perfecting life as between husband and wife."[16]

But the vestiges of the old milieu still inhibit the formation of a realistic model of Christian sexuality, especially in all the areas where Catholics are socialized. In some parish schools boys and girls still have separate entrances; they are seated apart and often instructed apart. Nuns run the high schools for girls, priests and brothers the high schools for boys. The same situation often obtains on the college level. Even when social exchanges like conferences and dances take place, a chaperon is always prominently on location lest "something happen." And general canon law, as well as most local synodal law created in its likeness, discourages if it does not forbid coeducation. The symptoms of the inhibited attitude toward sex actually range across the spectrum of Catholic life—from Sunday sermons and simplistic pamphlets on church racks to pietistic articles in the Catholic press and a morbid concern over pornography.

But birth control is the explosive sex issue, epitomizing the conflict in the American Catholic identity and reflecting the influences of a society openly in favor of birth control. While the differences between Catholic and non-Catholic attitudes testify to the strength of Catholic teaching on marriage, the teaching is being violated more and more. This is evident in the near-hysteria in official Catholic circles. One expert on family and fertility statistics, Paul C. Glick, has commented that the differences in the views on fertility among the major religious groups reflect differences in age, sex, color, geography, and socioeconomic factors perhaps as much as or more than do differences in religious doctrine.[17] In other words, Catholics are becoming more and more like non-Catholics. The convergence is an uneasy one from the Catholic standpoint. The zealous efforts to sell the rhythm method reflect this apprehension, and the description of the method as "Vatican roulette" reflects the resistance among Catholics.

While the Catholic acceptance of family limitation is still markedly different from the non-Catholic, signs of change are evident. In 1955 a national sample of wives between eighteen and thirty-nine, the child-bearing age, found 85 percent of the Protestants and 45 percent of the Catholics in favor of family limitation. Among Catholic wives capable of conceiving, four-fifths had exercised birth control, and over half of them had used some method considered immoral in formal Church teaching. In a 1959 survey, 33 percent of Catholic wives gave "unqualified approval" to family limitation, along with 12 percent who gave "qualified approval." (Among Protestant wives the "unqualified approval" was 72 percent, and among Jewish wives 88 percent.)

The Americanization of the Catholic attitude on birth control is unmistakable. The gaps between Catholics and Protestants and Jews have narrowed dramatically, and now approach a national consensus. One example is the issue of making birth control information available in the United States. In June, 1953, a Gallup poll found 53 percent of Catholics in favor of making the information available; by January 5, 1965, the figure was 78 percent. The national figure was 81 percent. In June, 1965, a report of a Gallup poll in *Look* magazine stated that 63 percent of Catholics felt most of their coreligionists wanted the Church to change its birth control position.[18]

A *Catholic Digest* survey found that about half of the Catholics did not accept their Church's teaching on the morality of contraceptive practices. The finding was startling. It is one thing to violate a rule but acknowledge its validity; it is another thing to reject the rule outright. Father John L. Thomas, in his analysis of the survey findings, accurately outlines the implications for official *Roman* Catholicism in America:

The Roman Catholic faith includes belief in a divinely established teaching authority concerning matters of faith and morals; for a Catholic to reject an explicit, clearly stated, serious moral directive of the church is tantamount to rejecting the faith, though a considerable number of Roman Catholics are apparently not aware of this obvious implication.[19]

Nonetheless, the Church's position has had a measureable impact on Catholic attitudes concerning fertility. Catholics both expect and want to have more children than non-Catholics. A nationwide study reported in 1959 that Catholic wives expect 3.4 children, Protestant wives 2.9, and Jewish wives 2.4. And the higher the educational background, the more children expected.[20] Catholic couples also want more children (3.6) than either Protestant (2.8) or Jewish couples (2.9), with white-collar couples wanting more children than do blue-collar.[21] The outlook of Catholic couples is evident in fertility rates; in 1958, Catholic wives over 45 had the largest number of children born per 1000—three, as compared with 2.75 for Protestants and 2.2 for Jews.[22]

The few available individual studies bear out the greater fertility of Catholics. Among 40,766 urban couples studied in Wisconsin between 1919 and 1933, the fertility of Catholic couples was consistently greater, though Catholic fertility declined at a faster rate than that of non-Catholics. A 1941 Indianapolis study showed that Catholic couples had 18 percent more children than did Protestant couples, and similar findings have been reported in a comparison of Catholic and non-Catholic sections of Louisiana. However, the statistics conceal the differences among Catholics according to social class; generally, the higher the class, the greater the resemblance of the fertility rate to the non-Catholic. In addition, as far as Catholic religious behavior is concerned, studies have shown that there is no direct correlation between large families and faithful religious observance.[23]

Meanwhile, the Catholic establishment has officially encouraged the large family as the ideal. For instance, the Family Life Bureau of the National Catholic Welfare Conference has been selecting a Catholic Family of the Year since 1961. The choices are revealing. A rural Missouri couple, married fifty-three years, were selected in 1961. They had eight children, three of them Divine Word missionary priests and three of them nuns. In 1962 a suburban Chicago couple with eight children were selected. They had been married sixteen years and the ages of their children were fifteen, fourteen, eleven, nine, eight, six, five, and three. A Minneapolis couple were honored in 1963 for their eleven children, who included two priests and two nuns. They also had sixteen grandchildren.

The Catholic Mother of the Year averaged ten children during the twenty years she was selected by the National Catholic Conference on Family Life. The number of children ranged from fifteen in 1946 and 1948 to five in 1961, the final year of the award, with three-fifths of the Catholic Mothers of the Year having ten or more children. In 1945 all ten children of the chosen mother were either priests or religious; over the twenty years an average of three children per family were in the religious life.

The applause for these versions of Catholic life as the ideal is no longer automatic. Nor is it altogether enthusiastic. In the summer of 1964, while he was teaching the sociology of religion at the University of San Francisco, Father Raymond H. Potvin of Catholic University sounded a significant caveat which was quoted in both the secular and the Catholic press. Referring to his examination of Catholic education to see whether it encourages a "fertility cult," he commented, "If the fertility cult theory proves true, then we will have raised an even bigger issue for the Church's moral theologians to chew on." He suggested that "perhaps we should stop pinning medals on the parents with the most children," and that it might be time rather to "start applauding the heroism of those who limit their families for the sake of building a better society for all concerned."[24] A year later Father Potvin wrote in the *Homiletic and Pastoral Review,* "It is important, therefore, that couples understand the responsibility of parenthood in all its dimensions, societal as well as familial, and not leave family size to chance."[25]

Indeed, the present ban on artificial contraception may be to American Catholicism what prohibition was to American society: honored more in the breach than in the observance. Some recent studies even suggest that as many as 70 percent of married Catholics in this country may be using one form or another of contraception forbidden by the Church.[26] The problem is forcing a painful debate, accompanied by the expected cries of doom from both sides. Dr. John Rock's provocative argument for oral contraceptives in his 1963 book, *The Time Has Come,* threw down the gauntlet in America.

When asked about oral contraception by *Newsweek* magazine in the summer of 1964, Msgr. George A. Kelly, head of the Family Life Bureau of the New York Archdiocese, replied, "My Irish is getting up." This is beside the point of contraception, but it is at the heart of the problem: the elevation of the historical and social role of the Irish American to the theological level. Mounting the strongly defensive ramparts of American Catholicism, Msgr. Kelly warned, "If the pill is accepted, anything can happen." Among the possibilities he mentioned were fornication, abortion, and adultery. And then he added; "You must stifle discussion of certain things."[27] But the pressures confronting the American Catholic made discussion unavoidable; for whether or not Catholics agreed with Dr. Rock, time had indeed come for facing the conflict between practice and principle.*

Divorce presents an issue undermining Catholic solidarity on another fundamental tenet of marriage—its indissolubility. A study conducted in Philadelphia in the early 1950s confirmed an acknowledged national trend: divorce among Catholics is increasing. The report of the researchers indicates that the "sizable proportion of divorces among Catholics . . . is surprising," and goes on to point out that while Catholics still had less than their share of divorces, they were overrepresented in desertion cases.[28]

In his analysis of divorce using a selected sample in the Detroit area, William J. Goode found that "the contribution of Catholics to the total divorced population is not much less than their proportion of the total population." Because of greater pressures against divorce, he found Catholics seeking marital counseling more often than non-Catholics, but once having made the final decision to divorce, the Catholic wife stuck by the decision without reconsidering 85 percent of the time. He reasoned that the devout Catholic "has already crossed the divide when she makes her 'first' final decision." After divorce, more of the Catholic wives fell into the "high trauma" group, but not in dramatically larger numbers, while the rate of remarriage was "somewhat higher" for the Protestant compared to the

* The intricacies of the birth control controversy are worth recounting in the social context. Msgr. Kelly's comments would be unimaginable in most Western European countries, where the climate is very different from what it is in the United States. In a subsequent issue of *Newsweek* (July 27, 1964), Msgr. Kelly commented in a letter to the editor: "And so as not to appear too much of a 'heavy' to your readers, let me say that while I would be the last one in the world to stifle discussion (the Irish could never last under that kind of practice), I do say with St. Paul: 'Keep a watch on those who are causing dissension and doing hurt to conscience without regard to the teaching which has been given you' (Romans 16:17)."

Catholic divorcees.[29] The *Catholic Digest* survey came up
with the surprising finding that half of the Catholics did not
feel that those who remarried after divorce were living in
sin.

For Catholics, separation and desertion are functional
equivalents of divorce, making it difficult to analyze family
disorganization and disintegration where Catholics and
Catholic teaching are concerned. Knowing that divorce and
remarriage are out of the question religiously, many Catholics choose to leave the Church or desert their families. A
conservative estimate is that more than half of the divorced
Catholics remarry and leave the Church. Desertion is more
common among lower-income groups.

Nationally, an estimated 55,000 Catholic marriages break
up each year—about one out of five. Citing the figures, an
article in *The Sign* magazine dramatized the failure of the
Catholic Church to meet the needs of these members: "The
divorced Catholic who remains faithful to his marriage vows
and does not remarry often lives like an outcast."[30] The
neglect of the divorced and faithful Catholic by his Church
is a striking example of unrealism in facing American realities.*

One conclusion appears painfully clear, and it touches
American Catholicism where it lives: in the home. The
more Catholic couples conform to the pressures of America,
the more they will move away from traditional and religious
ideals. The more recognizably American, the less ethnically
Catholic. Losing the protection of an isolated minority,
Catholics are winning acceptance and risking the loss of
their Catholic commitment as it has been expressed in the
past.

In the modern context, the struggle must be waged
mainly on an individual basis without strong community

---

* However, behind-the-scenes discussion of changes in Catholic regulations
on marriage and divorce has begun.

support. As Msgr. Kelly has written, echoing the views of many modern Catholic commentators on marriages:

> Today there is no religious solidarity among Catholics. Each couple faces the hostile culture alone. Whereas they followed the Catholic crowd, now they must make individual choices, oftentimes in the face of strong social pressures. . . . Modern couples need a greater intellectuality, deeper spirituality, and more solidarity than their forebears.[31]

This loss of solidarity results from a typically American emphasis on experience. Abstract systems create unity; modes of thinking based on experience tend toward pluralism. Recently, various articulate and informed Catholic laymen have stressed the importance of the marriage experience for each couple and their particular adjustment rather than blanket *a priori* formulas for duties and obligations. The result has been controversy where once there was apparent unity. [32]

The pervasive impact of the American environment means that the Catholic family must search for an identity compatible with beliefs and belonging. The search is most difficult for the middle-class American Catholic, the urban-suburban mobilite striving to get ahead for himself, his wife, and his children. In his social context, children are expensive hostages to the future, and an unhappy marriage is a burden that Americans are not supposed to bear. For his wife, often working, equality is not a gift from her husband as lord to vassal but a personal right, and inalienable.

In the context of current realities, the nuptial blessing completes the cycle of unreality with which Catholic couples are officially launched into marriage:

> Let her [the wife] follow the model of holy women: let her be dear to her husband like Rachel, wise like Rebecca, long-lived and faithful like Sara. Let the author of sin work none of his evil deeds within her; let her ever keep the faith and the commandments. Let her be true to one wedlock and shun all sinful embraces; let her strengthen weakness by stern discipline.

Let her be grave in demeanor, honorable in her modesty, learned in heavenly doctrine, fruitful in children.

The wife described is hardly recognizable in marriage, American style. Clearly, the Catholic marriage must be dressed in modern clothing, freed of older fashions from other times, other places, and other patterns—while retaining its essential principles.

CHAPTER 4

◇◇◇◇◇◇◇◇◇◇◇◇◇◇◇◇◇◇◇◇◇◇◇◇◇◇◇◇◇◇◇◇◇◇◇◇◇

"Near Each Church a Parochial School"

B Y T H E S E A at Atlantic City, New Jersey, 17,850 Catholic educators assembled during the 1964 Easter Week
vacation as in sixty other years. Teaching sisters, the traditional core of Catholic education, were particularly visible.
Some walked along the seashore sprayed by ocean waves, but
most strolled on the boardwalk in little groups of black and
starched white. Hotels and restaurants were crowded with
convention business; dinner tables were filled with priests,
brothers, and nuns in animated conversation. The mammoth Convention Hall, where the Democrats later nominated their candidates for 1964, was overrun with religious,
but there were few laymen and -women, though they have
become a major component of Catholic educators. Roman
collars and religious habits dominate the annual conventions of the National Catholic Educational Association,
which are a combination of junket, reward, and professional
refresher for the participants.

Downstairs at Convention Hall, textbook publishers,
school bus salesmen, and school supply and visual aid pur-
veyors were displaying wares and taking orders. They gave
away inscribed pencils, brochures, shopping bags, and
rulers, and talked to anyone who stopped to look at their
exhibits. Upstairs in the main hall and meeting rooms,

there was talk of modern math and French in the early grades, of programed learning and teaching by team and by TV, of teacher-student ratios and ungraded classrooms, of vocations and vacations, and, of course, of challenge and response.

It was almost an NCEA convention like the many others in various cities that had gone before it, except that the center of attention, Mary Perkins Ryan, was missing and under attack. A Manchester, New Hampshire, mother of five who had a modest reputation as a writer about the liturgy in Catholic publications; her eight books had such unassailable titles as *How to Pray, Key to the Psalms,* and *Perspectives for Psalms.* But her recent book *Are Parochial Schools the Answer?* had turned her into a controversial subject at the convention. She had become to Catholic education what Dr. John Rock and his book on oral contraception were to birth control. She had opened the door of debate on what was supposed to be a closed issue, the Catholic commitment to parochial schools. The immediate response of the parochial school educators was defensive and inflexible.

Mrs. Ryan had ended her book by declaring that Catholics are called upon to give witness to Christ in his Church and in our society in every possible way:

And we can only carry out this work, first, by putting ourselves, and by helping to put one another, in as close contact as possible with the Christ who speaks to us and acts on us in his Word, in the sacrifice and sacraments of the Church, and then by putting ourselves in contact with our neighbor, sharing his interests and concerns, working with him for the welfare of all men. It is hard to see how, under present circumstances, the continuance or extension of the Catholic school system can be anything but an obstacle to the pursuit of these aims.[1]

Mrs. Ryan and her book dominated the convention, not only in the corridors but on the speaker's platform. Either direct answers were addressed to the challenge of her book or, if the speaker's topic did not provide an opportunity for rebuttal, references were made to "armchair educators," "New England pundits," and "self-styled experts," bringing chuckles from the audience. A full-dress press conference was called to rebut the book, and at its very first meeting the NCEA elementary department approved a fund to publish a book in support of the concept of the parochial school. The fund, which could total $40,000, would also "publicize in popular terms the remarkable success story of the American parochial school." The Catholic educators had closed ranks at the challenge posed by the lady from New Hampshire.

They were rising to the defense of an immense enterprise, educating 4.5 million children in 10,731 parochial elementary schools and more than a million in 2477 high schools. The total is approaching 6 million and involves more than 170,000 teachers.[2] The physical size of Catholic education facilities is reflected by a 1960 nationwide estimate made by the magazine *Catholic Building and Maintenance* that their replacement value then was more than $7 billion. The system, which consistently grows in numbers and size each year, saves U.S. taxpayers an estimated $2 billion annually.

With characteristic American energy, all this has been wrought in response to the Third Plenary Council of Baltimore which decreed in 1884, that "near each church, where it does not exist, a parochial school is to be erected within two years from the promulgation of this Council, and is to be maintained *in perpetuum,* unless the bishop, on account of grave difficulties, judge that a postponement be allowed."

At the time, there were Catholics who made the same challenge that so upset Catholic educators eighty years later. Dr. Edward McGlynn argued for his fellow "liberals" that the work of the Church was apostolic, not pedagogic, and that it was supposed to help the poor and provide for the spiritual life of its adherents "rather than to sacrifice these great things and to entail upon the people the expense of parochial schools."

The Baltimore Council, which made the crucial commitment of Catholics to their own separate schools, stood between two significant events in the history of American Catholics. In 1792, John Carroll, the newly consecrated first bishop of Baltimore, who had jurisdiction over all American Catholics, had called on the country's first President, George Washington, and asked him to put a Catholic priest on the government payroll. Congress thereupon allotted a small annual salary for a priest who would Christianize and educate the Indians. Early in 1963, the first Catholic President sent a bill to Congress for federal aid to education that excluded parochial schools. Kennedy called such aid unconstitutional, and while many dispassionate onlookers agreed with him, the Catholic hierarchy denounced the Kennedy bill as discriminatory.

Much to the surprise of many American Catholics, support for their case came from such opinion makers as educator Robert Hutchins, the liberal *New Republic* magazine, and columnist Walter Lippmann. Hutchins was emphatic: "In fact, the Constitution says nothing of separation [of church and state] and makes no mention of a wall. . . . My conclusion is that Federal aid to parochial schools is not a constitutional issue. It is a political issue, a real and important one."[3] When Lippmann was asked in a CBS television interview whether he regarded federal aid to education as so important that he was in favor of aid to parochial schools, he replied, "I am. I think it's so important that we cannot afford to postpone the improvement of education any longer."[4] Public opinion was also shifting in the Catholic direction. In March, 1961, a Gallup poll found 36 percent in favor of federal aid for parochial schools. Two years later 51 percent were in favor, a majority finding that was repeated in March, 1965.

The articulate and knowledgeable executive secretary of the NCEA, Msgr. Frederick G. Hochwalt, repeated in private what he told congressional committees and journalists inquiring about the Catholic stand on federal aid: "The NCEA feels that federal aid to the schools is a decision for Congress to make. But if there is going to be federal aid, we want a sense of justice in positive legislation enacted by Congress. We want equity. We don't want total support. We want aid in nonreligious areas."[5]

Early in 1965, President Johnson did what a Catholic President might not have been able to do. He provided aid for Catholic schools—though it was roundabout. His comprehensive education program utilized the shared-time principle by which students from Catholic schools attend public schools part-time. One of us wrote of it, "President Johnson has opened a new era of cooperation between public and parochial schools that can revolutionize American education. The federal government is now officially out to encourage local partnerships between public and parochial schools."[6] In offering federal aid aimed at the student and designed for a sharing of services between public and parochial schools, the President offered a measure of the "equity" called for by Catholic educators. It was enough of a step in their direction to prevent the "Catholic veto" of federal aid to education by sympathetic congressmen.

An overlooked irony was concealed behind the Catholic demand for federal aid to their schools: they were asking for assistance that they had not wanted a century ago and espousing a point of view that Protestants had held at that time when they fought for government support of schools. Actually Catholics had opposed government help as much to protect the identities of their various ethnic groups in separate schools as to protect the faith.

When Bishop Carroll met with George Washington, the states contained "established" churches, sometimes several in a single state. The schools upheld the denominational interests they served, and when state and local governments took over the financing, the fires of their interdenominational and sectarian rivalries were banked. However, these public-supported schools had a Protestant orientation which Catholic immigrant groups came to regard with suspicion. The dominant Irish, in particular, were sensitive to a "Protestant threat." The presence of the King James version of the Bible in public schools was a red flag to them, and they saw an antipapist plot.

The Germans agreed. Whether Lutheran or Catholic, they established independent schools to preserve their German identity through their language and customs. What they would not permit the Irish clergy to take from them they would not surrender to public schools. Had not the great benefactor and patron of German-American Catholics, King Ludwig I of Bavaria, sent out the first group of German Catholic sisters with the promise and the admonition, "I shall not forget you, but stay German, German! Do not become English"?[7] German bishops like Joseph Dwenger of Fort Wayne, Indiana, linked the future of the faith to the preservation of German identity in the schools: "No schools now means empty churches later," he said repeatedly in the mid-nineteenth century.[8] In 1964 the Catholic Central Union of America, founded in 1855 by German immigrants and now the oldest Catholic lay organization in this country, still was loyal to this viewpoint, expressing "deep concern" at its annual meeting over parochial school criticism which "cast doubt on the worth and efficacy of Catholic education."

The Baltimore Council put a seal of approval on the desire of the immigrants to protect their various ethnic identities. The Catholic school system which the Council set in motion remains unique in world Catholicism, besides being the world's largest single private system of education. It was not the only possibility but was primarily a response to the American situation.

Like any large decision-making assembly, the Baltimore Council was pragmatic, decreeing no more than was already being done. Actually, it gave ecclesiastical status to the ethnic cleavages among Catholics by placing the schools in parish hands where nationality groups would be in control. The local pastor was made responsible for establishing the school, for maintaining and administering it, and for deciding on the curriculum. While giving the surface impression of unifying Catholics with a body of schools, it fragmented the system, dividing the schools into dioceses and then into parishes. As late as the 1964 NCEA convention, the fragmentation was manifested in a prediction by Msgr. O'Neil C. D'Amour, then an NCEA official and a leading spokesman for Catholic educators, that within ten years the finances of parochial elementary schools in heavily populated areas would be handled by a central diocesan office instead of by individual parishes. It was intended as a proclamation of progress: eighty years after the Baltimore Council, there was a prospect of some unification on a diocesan level.

The Baltimore Council followed a traditional pattern in distributing responsibility at the local level and retaining authority at the top. The pastor faced the task of carrying out the dictum on schools, but the bishops retained all the power. Often it seemed that the pastor, like the Jews in ancient Egypt, had to make bricks without straw. The frantic drives for funds and the strong pressures upon parishioners for support have continued unabated ever since, ranging today from monster bingo evenings to monthly collection envelopes.

The goal of putting every Catholic child in a Catholic school is clearly beyond the realm of possibility, despite the enormous expansion that has taken place. Msgr. D'Amour, a pronounced optimist, has said, "The question is: 'What is our potential?' We now educate about 45 percent of the Catholic elementary school-age children. I think there is only another 25 percent who want to get in."[9] A much smaller proportion of Catholic children of high school age—one in five—are in Catholic schools; and by 1967, it is estimated, two out of three Catholic children will be in a public elementary school. Despite its size and continuous expansion, the parochial system serves only a minority of Catholic children. While the number in Catholic schools increases, the percentage of Catholic children attending them shrinks dramatically. The birth rate is against Baltimore.

In many ways, the Catholic school crisis repeats the crisis that faced the Protestant denominational schools in the mid-nineteenth century. It is a crisis in supply and demand. The schools then were inundated by an expanding population swollen by the European immigration. Today Catholics cannot keep pace with the demands of a booming school-age population. This lies behind the Catholic concern about any federal aid that is limited to public schools. It could be a death sentence for the present Catholic enterprise, which strives to parallel the public schools in scope, variety, and size.

The New York archdiocesan system exemplifies the ambitious nature of the Catholic school commitment. It probably has been Cardinal Spellman's major achievement, evident in a review of his twenty-five-year school-building record. In 1939, when Cardinal Spellman took over the New York Archdiocese, 117,907 students attended 130 elementary and secondary schools; 222,232 students attended 429 schools in 1964. The number of religious and lay teachers increased from 3871 to 7120. In that quarter-century 361 school projects were undertaken, including ninety-two new elementary and thirty-eight new high schools. New York City's Catholic schools constitute the second largest school system in the state, topped only by the city's mammoth public school system.

For New York Catholic schools and those throughout the country, a grant of federal aid to the public schools alone would mean that Catholic schools would fall hopelessly behind the public schools. They would have to retrench and surrender any attempt to run a parallel system. They would be hopelessly outmatched in resources and would fall even farther behind in teacher recruitment.

NCEA's spokesman Msgr. Hochwalt described the threat implicit in "discriminatory" aid, support limited to public schools: "It is entirely possible that in such an event we may be priced out of educational effectiveness."[10] The prospect of retrenching and limiting the role of Catholic education horrifies the Catholic establishment. Msgr. Hochwalt's former colleague, Msgr. D'Amour, has warned that "the very existence of the Catholic school system as traditionally conceived is threatened." Admission standards and tuition rates would restrict enrollment, and then Catholic schools "will become not public schools for the many but private schools for the exclusive few."[11]

The supply of nuns and brothers cannot meet expanding classroom demands and the pressure to reduce teacher-pupil ratios—thirty-eight to one on the elementary level and twenty to one on the high school level in 1965. Both the numbers and the proportion of lay teachers have been increasing steadily until now one-third of the teaching staffs are laymen. Catholic schools are barely able to maintain salary levels at a respectable distance behind those in the public schools; one-sided federal aid would place them at an insurmountable disadvantage. Chicago's assistant superintendent of Catholic schools, Father Robert Clark, has pointed out, "Our problem is the recruitment of adequate and competent personnel. The competition for lay teachers is ferocious. It's much tougher to keep a school open than it is to get it built."[12]

The academic quality of many Catholic schools has been seriously challenged on the grounds that teacher-student ratios are high and that teachers hold lower qualifications than their public school counterparts. Nationally, academic evaluation is complicated by wide variations in quality from diocese to diocese and by the fact that the conventional criteria—size of classes, teachers' qualifications, and dollar support—do not take into account the intangible assets of the Catholic classroom. They exclude the motivation of the teacher and the discipline of the students, which are a source of pride to Catholic educators.

A favorable report was given by Dr. William H. Conley, who directed the opening phase of a national study of Catholic schools, financed by the Carnegie Corporation and sponsored by the University of Notre Dame. According to data gathered in the 1962–63 school year, he reported that in every area except natural science Catholic elementary and high school students outscored public school students. However, he cautioned that the statistics must be qualified because Catholic schools tend to be more selective and expel troublemakers. The pupils, supported by their parents, are well motivated and attend the schools by choice, while public schools must take everyone, including pupils with language and behavior problems. In tests of reading achievement, the crucial skill in elementary schools, the results were also favorable. In various dioceses, Catholic school pupils who began to learn reading in first-grade classes of sixty to seventy pupils were tested at the end of the sixth grade. They equaled or exceeded their potential, according to standardized measures.[13]

Nonetheless, despite the political strains and financial stresses, the colossus of American Catholic education remains a monumental accomplishment that, for better or worse, bestrides American Catholic life. It defies safe generalizations because it is divided into 17,637 parts—each part a parish. The larger parts, 148 archdioceses and dioceses, usually have limited control over the parish units, where the Baltimore dictum is fulfilled. The Catholic system of schools is really 148 systems, some well organized, some chaotic behind the façade of a single commitment to the Catholic education of Catholic children. A nationwide look at the

beginning of a typical Catholic school year (1963) drama-
tizes the variety, the complexities, and the confusion within
the Catholic school situation.

In Saint Louis nine new suburban schools remained
closed until the teaching staffs could have a ratio of three
religious to one lay teacher. Yet in the Diocese of Rockville
Centre, Long Island, two elementary schools had been
opened with only lay teachers on the staff. One diocese's
stumbling block was another's solution.

In Chicago suburban parishes, some Catholic parents
were advised to send their children to public school for the
early grades. In another diocese, farther west, parents were
instructed in no uncertain terms to get written permission
from the bishop before sending their children to public
school. One diocese's necessity was another's anathema.

In Abilene, Texas, a new Catholic high school opened on
a "coinstitutional" basis, using the same premises with
separate faculties of religious and classes for boys and
girls. In Bay City, Michigan, some Catholic high school students were attending public school part-time for language,
mathematics, and vocational courses. One diocese innovated
within its own four walls; another reached out to the public
schools.

In the Rochester, New York, suburb of Fairport, a pastor
who had decided not to build a parochial school was operating a school of religion for released-time instruction of
Catholic children attending public schools. The parish next
door was heavily in debt and running a newly built parochial school. Two adjacent parishes formulated different responses to the education of Catholic children.

In many heavily Catholic areas, a large number of Catholics were teaching in the public schools while the Catholic
schools, faced with a teacher shortage, were using non-
Catholic teachers. According to the nationwide Carnegie
study, "a significant number of non-Catholics" were em-
ployed in Catholic schools.

In some large urban centers, downtown schools were half empty and fully staffed by nuns while suburban schools had waiting lists and teaching staffs dominated by the more expensive (though underpaid) lay teachers. In Oklahoma City and Providence, laymen were playing a major role on Catholic school boards, but in most other dioceses the school boards were clerical monopolies.

In Saint Louis the superintendent of Catholic schools, Msgr. James T. Curtin, asserted that "our schools must be controlled by religious in order to implement total Catholic education." In Rockville Centre the Catholic school superintendent, Msgr. Edgar P. McCarren, felt that an all-lay Catholic school "can be just as good a Catholic school as one taught by nuns."[14]

Meanwhile, back in Washington, D.C., the National Catholic Educational Association stands as a helpless shepherd for Catholic schools, trying to bring the sheep into one educational flock. But only the bishops of America can call the flock to order, and they say not a word, except to look outside their internal school problems and denounce federal aid programs that exclude Catholic schools. Yet it is not unreasonable to suggest that the fragmentation of Catholic education makes across-the-board federal aid a practical impossibility. One Catholic expert, Father Neil G. McCluskey, S.J., has remarked, "Without this illusion of massive federal aid, Catholic energies and imagination could be channeled into more profitable ways of solving our problems."[15] He urged more central planning, more sharing, more cooperation.

"A general examination of the entire Catholic school system"—urged by among others, the perceptive Catholic layman Donald McDonald in the Jesuit magazine *America*—has been long in coming. He wrote with unquestionable validity:

The more I think about it, reflect on it and experience its reality, the more convinced I become that the Catholic school system—which certainly came into existence in response to a need—has become what it is today not so much through an organic, intelligently and rationally ordered growth as through accidental accretions, the cumulative weight of layers of random decisions which may well have been ordered to particular local needs, but which failed to take into consideration questions of total educational resources, the most effective deployment and employment of these resources, the economic limitations of the layman, the establishment of a priority of educational needs, and a realistic, objective appraisal of the educational resources of the secular school.[16]

The fundamental question concerning Catholic education remains unanswered: is it worth the financial and human investment? Mary Perkins Ryan at least raised the question in its proper context—the contribution of Catholic schools to the Catholic Church in the mid-twentieth century. She answered that Catholic schools are not the most effective way to use the resources involved, though her argument was built more on rhetoric than on evidence. Her book upset the 1964 NCEA convention simply because her posing of the question received attention. But when 28,000 people attended the 1965 convention in New York City, "There was a feeling in the speeches and discussions that in the interval since Atlantic City the evidence had come in and that 1964's charge that the schools were outdated and their days numbered had been disproved."[17] Actually, the Catholic educators had only proved the merit of outwaiting the critics, and they could take satisfaction in the passage of President Johnson's education bill which provided aid for parochial school pupils. Even the proposed $40,000 defense fund of 1964 receded into the background.

As one of the 1965 convention speakers noted in drawing a moral from the rumble over Mrs. Ryan's book, "There are too many Catholic educators who are too sensitive to criticism."[18] At least Mrs. Ryan had left the door slightly ajar for candid self-appraisal, which was a notable feature of the convention speeches in 1965. The unusually direct remarks ranged from a bishop's criticism of money-raising projects in parochial schools to a philosophy professor's concern over academic freedom. The NCEA closed its 1965 convention with unintended irony by electing Bishop Ernest J. Primeau of Manchester, New Hampshire, as its president general. He had written the foreword to Mary Perkins Ryan's book *Are Parochial Schools the Answer?*

When Catholic educators hesitate to face this fundamental question, it is understandable. The pyramids being already there, should you question whether the stones and the manpower might have been better utilized elsewhere? Moreover, can you ask for and expect massive support and enormous sacrifices while you question the place of Catholic education? Finally, the educators can take refuge in the fact that definitive evidence is lacking on the success or failure of Catholic education and on the potential merit of alternatives for providing religious schooling. The Catholic educator is making his version of Pascal's gamble—believing in parochial schools to avoid the risk of rejecting them and being wrong.

Nonetheless, the available data provide some indications. Catholic schools do strengthen Catholic identity, and their graduates tend toward greater religious participation. But the cause of this apparent effect may be the Catholic home and the Catholic environment rather than the Catholic school. Pupils in Catholic elementary and high schools are likely to have more committed parents in the first place. The most ambitious attempt to study the effects of Catholic education, begun in 1963 by the National Opinion Research Center (NORC) at the University of Chicago, makes a serious and startling point. The study "did not substantiate the idea that the apparent vitality of Catholicism in the United States is the result of the parochial school system; indeed, one might almost suspect the opposite—that the schools are the result of the vitality. . . . It seems quite probable that were there no parochial schools, Catholicism in the United States would not be overwhelmingly different—quantitatively—from what it is today."[19]

Moreover, the success of Catholic schools in imparting values and deepening spiritual commitment is open to question. This is a matter of considerable concern to Catholic school superintendents, as has been confirmed in conversations with a number of them. One superintendent expressed a consensus when he said that Catholic schools do bring about formal religious participation but do not succeed nearly so well in instilling the natural Christian virtues. A striking example was the finding that only 53 percent of those who had gone to Catholic elementary and high schools agreed with the statement that "Love of neighbor is more important than not eating meat on Friday," compared with 60 percent of those who had had no Catholic education. This finding in the NORC study prompted the suitable reaction of outrage in *Commonweal* magazine:

> This is a shocking figure. A parochial school system which cannot manage to get over to its students an essential part of what Christ called the "greatest commandment" deserves hardly any Christian respect whatever, regardless of how much it may impress a sociologist. To go one more step: a Catholic school system which leaves the slightest doubt in the graduate's mind about the relative value of a minor Church law and the most essential teaching of Christ constitutes a major danger to his religious life.[20]

Theoretically, Catholic education is "permeated" with a value system, evident in such obvious places as religion courses and in such intangible areas as the attitudes of religious and lay teachers. In a typical pamphlet on Catholic education, Father William J. McGucken, S.J., makes the familiar statement that there is a hierarchy of values in Catholic education: "Supernatural values are obviously of more importance than the natural; spiritual values of greater import than the bodily; and eternal of more significance than temporal."[21] Pope Pius XI said in his encyclical *On Christian Education,* "Christian education takes in the whole aggregate of human life, physical and spiritual, intellectual and moral, individual, domestic and social, not with a view of reducing it in any way, but in order to elevate, regulate and perfect it, in accordance with the example and teaching of Christ."

Catholic educators have long wrestled with the concept of permeation; on the elementary and even on the high school level, it has led to the traditional attitude that there is a Catholic way of teaching everything. The attitude still lingers, as was illustrated by the report of a working committee on Aims of a Catholic Language Program at the NCEA convention in 1963. The committee stressed that even languages must be taught differently in a Catholic school: "If then the Christian influence is to be evidenced in education, it should be foremost in the area of language." The committee report went on to state, "The aim of a foreign language program in Catholic education cannot be limited to a course in linguistic gymnastics. The very human values hidden in the literature and culture of the new idiom constitute the 'pearl of great price' which we must aid our students to find."

An obvious result has been the "baptized textbook" where blatant preaching is inserted into reading, writing, and arithmetic. However, this is changing, as textbook publishers confirm. One publishing representative summed up the current approach: "Nothing is included just because it is Catholic, but neither is it left out because it is Catholic."[22] Ideally, Catholic textbooks can even be superior to public school textbooks, which tend to leave out significant Catholic material in an attempt to be neutral.

Because the approach to permeation varies so widely and is subject to so many uses and abuses, it is not possible to generalize about its application. Yet, since it figures prominently in the philosophy of Catholic education and its goals, some judgments on its effects must be attempted. In spite of this education philosophy, there is no compelling evidence of major differences in values between parochial and public school children. The studies which have been made indicate little difference; the Catholic school pupils share American values with their public school counterparts.

In his 1958 study of a typical Midwestern parish school, Saint Luke's in Chicago, Father Joseph Fichter, S.J., found virtually no difference in a comparison with pupils at Taft Public School by using the California Test of Personality: ". . . both accept and demonstrate in about the same proportions, the virtues of honesty, obedience, gratitude, self-control and kindliness. As may be expected in their sport-centered milieu, they have an abhorrence of cheating in games or of appearing to be 'poor sports.' "

Both groups of students showed the impact of popular culture. When asked to name their favorite movie stars, the parochial school children picked Tab Hunter, John Wayne, and Debbie Reynolds; the public school children differed only in their third choice, Rock Hudson instead of Debby Reynolds. Both groups had the same choices as the greatest persons in history: George Washington, Abraham Lincoln, and Christopher Columbus. The Catholic influence was evident in naming the "greatest men living today": the parochial students chose Pope Pius XII, President Eisenhower, and Cardinal Mindszenty; the public school students chose President Eisenhower, Vice President Nixon, and Elvis Presley.[23]

In an analysis of various studies made of Catholic school children, Joshua A. Fishman has concluded that the child arrives at parochial school already formed and that the school does not overcome outside influences. He comments:

Thus it seems that the child arrives at the Catholic parochial school with already established attitudes and needs in relation to his total American environment, and that the school itself is not strong enough to change these attitudes, even when it regards change as desirable. . . . The tireless efforts of Catholic leaders to employ parochial education to transmit the deep philosophical and religious differences which separate Catholicism from American Protestantism and from secularism have been most consistently embarrassed by the strivings of Catholic parents, young people, and children.[24]

Indeed, the parochial school has been a vehicle of social mobility for the immigrant children who have passed through its portals. What parochial schools once did for the Irish, they now are doing for the Negroes and Puerto Ricans. For the lower-class Catholic in particular, the parochial school is a place where neatness and discipline—familiar Yankee traits—are imposed with a passion. Even superficial observation of a parochial school confirms this.

A "white-collar" tendency has been noted in sending children to parochial schools.[25] Middle-class Catholics tend to send their children to parochial schools more than do lower-class Catholics, and this is especially evident in the surge of Catholic schools in the suburbs. For instance, a religious census in Saint Augustine, Florida, found that 66 percent of parents with twelve years or more of education sent their children to parochial schools, compared with 49 percent of those with less than eight years of school.[26]

Critics of Catholic schools will be surprised to learn of the favorable profile of social attitudes among the students. In the "Bay City" study, the parochial school students scored consistently higher than public school students on economic liberalism and prolabor opinions.[27] The Fichter study, using specially devised tests and measures, found parochial school children consistently "better" in their attitudes toward foreign aid, Negroes, refugees, voting, and labor unions than the public school children, whether Catholic or not.[28] But as the Rossis note, this probably reflects the social position and political attitudes of Catholics by comparison with Protestants rather than the content of the school curricula.[29]

The Rossis, after reviewing several studies of adult Catholics, summarized what appears to be the limited impact of the parochial school:

> We have been unable to find strong evidence that parochial-school Catholics are very different from other Catholics. The influence of the school is shown most dramatically in areas where the Church has traditionally taken a strong stand, for example, on support for religious education, or on the performance of ritual duties. In other areas of life the parochial-school Catholic is only marginally differentiated from other Catholics.[30]

On balance, the parochial school emerges as a reinforcer, particularly of religious participation. The authors of the NORC study on the effects of Catholic education found that it made a high level of religious practice higher. Judging from the impact on religious behavior and attitudes, the Catholic schools are described as "moderately successful," with this qualifier: "Whether this success has been worth the time, money and effort expended is beyond the research analyst's province"—again the unsolved question on whether Catholic schools are the answer. There was no evidence that the Catholic school has veto powers over the American influences on race issues, other domestic matters, and international problems. There was one expected difference—a stricter sexual code among the Catholic school products.[31]

The sociological term *system maintenance* applies to the network of Catholic schools, for as a system it supplies and maintains itself. Studies consistently single out the Catholic school, particularly the secondary school, as the strongest single influence after the family leading to religious vocations. At the 1963 NCEA convention, Father Richard Madden, O.C.D., of Youngstown, Ohio, described Catholic high schools as "the nurseries of vocations." He cited Philadelphia, where in a recent year 500 out of 10,000 graduating high school students went into seminaries, monasteries, or convents. "Therefore," he commented, "the better a Cath-

olic school system in a diocese, the more the vocations."[32]
In the case of religious educators, the need is created by the
very system which is supplied with teachers. This school
contribution to Church manpower is evident from the hierarchy down. A 1957 survey showed that 61 percent of the
American hierarchy was educated in parochial schools and
78 percent in Catholic secondary schools, many of them
minor (high school) seminaries.[33]

Undoubtedly the parochial school strengthens the Catholic identification of its pupils, and from the standpoint of a
large organization like the Catholic Church, this is an important consideration. Parochial schools keep Catholic children in close association with their churches and with other
Catholics. The point was made dramatically when Fichter
compared the "three best friends" of Catholics in a public
and a parochial school. Among those in the parochial
school, 50 percent had Catholics as their three best friends
and another 31 percent had two Catholics among the three.
Only 2 percent of the Catholics in public schools said all of
their best friends were Catholics; another 11 percent said
two of the three were Catholics. The contrast is significant:
over 80 percent of parochial school pupils had Catholics as
two of their three best friends; the comparable figure for
Catholics in public schools was 13 percent.[34]

Moreover, Catholic parents generally want to send their
children to parochial schools and have demonstrated their
willingness to make sacrifices to do so. A national opinion
poll found 45 percent of American Catholics "very satisfied"
with parochial schools, while most Catholic parents whose
children do not attend parochial schools said the reason was
inaccessibility or unavailability—not disagreement with
their goals.[35] A certain amount of social status surrounds
the parochial school, besides the fact that parents judge the
quality of their parish—rightly or wrongly—by the vigor of
its school program. A school superintendent illustrated the
demand by describing what happened when a Long Island

suburban pastor announced he would accept first graders on a first-come, first-served basis. On registration day, one parent rose before dawn, filled a thermos, put a blanket under his arm, and headed for the parish school expecting to be the first on line. He arrived at five A.M. to find a hundred parents ahead of him!

In this context, Mary Perkins Ryan's challenge to parochial schools faces strong resistance. She argues from a viewpoint that is ecumenical and not pragmatic, liturgical and not educational. What she asks is that the Catholic Church turn itself over to the Holy Ghost, who operates in a strange and distant fashion better suited to the Trappist monk than the ecclesiastical organization man in the suburbs. Her view of a pristine Christianity belongs to earlier and simpler times and places, not to a modern Church struggling to give witness in an urban, technological, pluralistic society. Mrs. Ryan would like the American Catholic Church to take a mystical gamble at enormous risks, a gamble on the vast structure of a partially successful educational enterprise. She upset the Catholic educators by challenging their educational colossus, but the challenge was outside their context. The appropriate answer must come from within the context of the Church's situation today, its resources, the effectiveness of Catholic schools, and the practical alternatives.

The average Catholic pastor needs something tangible around which to rally his parishioners, and he finds it inconceivable that he should close down his schools and retrench. For better or worse, the parochial school has become a rallying point, and certainly one that the predominant majority of pastors and parishioners is unwilling to surrender. There is little likelihood that the American Catholic school—oversold in the past—will be discarded in the future, though it may eventually wither away.

◇◇

CHAPTER 5

Catholics on Campus

H E I S A C O L L E G I A N in his early twenties who is from a sizable Northeastern city and is likely to think of himself as "good-looking, idealistic, and witty." His parents graduated from high school; his father is in a managerial or professional position and earns more than $7500 a year. The collegian goes to church every Sunday, and regards himself as religious and conventional but also as liberal. His main worries concern money and future plans. His vocational goal is a job with a large company or possibly teaching; his most important future satisfaction in life is a family. He is more likely also to mention religion as a source of satisfaction than are Protestant and Jewish collegians.

He is a Catholic in college. In only one out of three instances is he in a Catholic institution. He closely resembles the Protestant collegian, though Catholic, Protestant, and Jewish college students all share the American dream of the good life as they climb the social stepladder of a college education. Father Andrew Greeley, who extracted this profile of the Catholic collegian from a national survey of 1961 college graduates, observed that "Catholics were different from their fellow graduates only in their church attendance and their valuation of religion as a source of life satisfaction."[1] Father Greeley found that Protestant and Catholic collegians had:

A similar view of the intellectual value of college; only one-third stressed its vocational value.
Similar academic achievement.

Relatively little difference in choice of studies, and a highly
favorable opinion of their colleges.

Of course, there were differences in degree. Catholics
were less likely to attend "top"-quality schools than Jews
and less likely to attend "low"-quality schools than Protestants. Catholics chose schools nearer home than did Protestants and were more likely to commute to school. Less likely
to live in sorority and fraternity houses, Catholics were less
likely than Protestants to have their closest friends on
campus.

Catholics also joined the parade to graduate school, falling in between their Protestant and Jewish counterparts: 28
percent of the Protestants and 47 percent of the Jews had
graduate study plans, compared with 34 percent of the
Catholics—16 percent planning on professional schools and
18 percent aiming at arts and sciences. A year later the
Catholic dropout rate from graduate school was about the
same as the Protestant, though higher than the Jewish.[2]

These findings, limited to a fixed point in time, captured
the Catholic collegian in the early 1960s, when changes
were already affecting the composite profile. Particularly
significant is the drastic and accelerating decline in the proportion of Catholics attending Catholic colleges and universities. By 1985 four out of five Catholic students will
be attending non-Catholic undergraduate and graduate
schools. As in Catholic elementary and secondary education,
demand is overwhelming supply.

This has taken place in spite of the impressive expansion
of Catholic college facilities, which are largely a twentieth-
century phenomenon. Although Catholic higher education
dates from 1789, when Georgetown University was established, more than two-thirds of the almost 300 Catholic
junior colleges, colleges, and universities were founded in
this century. In 1900 there were only seventy Catholic colleges. Expansion and increases in enrollment have been

dramatic ever since: 16,000 enrolled in 1908, 103,000 in 1940, a third of a million in 1961.[3]

With Catholics attending college in proportion to their numbers in the population (about 25 percent), they comprised 1.07 million out of the 4.5 million enrolled for American higher education in 1963–64. In 1985, when nationwide enrollment is expected to reach 12.6 million, the Catholic share is estimated at 2.9 million. Of these, 2.4 million, or over 80 percent, as noted, will be on non-Catholic campuses.[4] More and more, the American college campus reflects the pluralism of American society.

Catholic commentators who confront the challenge of the non-Catholic campus are concerned about its influence, not because the atmosphere is antireligious but because it is neutral. Father Richard Butler, a leading spokesman for the Newman movement, which serves Catholics on secular campuses, writes of the problem from the Catholic viewpoint:

> But the doctrine of secular humanism is widespread enough on our campuses to influence a large percentage of students who later on will create the dominant attitudes of our society. The simple core of this doctrine is that man himself is the ultimate value in life and he is confined to a material universe which produces him and ultimately destroys him. Meanwhile, progress consists in the constant improvement of his condition, both personally and socially. And that's all the reality there is.
>
> Implicit in this doctrine, usually made explicit only by insinuation and inference, is the denial of the existence of a personal God, divine law and providence, the eternal destiny of man and consequently his religious obligation and responsibility based on a transcendental sanction. The social consequences of such a doctrine are multiple and complex, but they are certainly far removed from our cherished notions about "life, liberty and the pursuit of happiness."[5]

Whether the campus is Catholic or secular, the problem and the challenge still have a common denominator: the Catholic role in higher education. Since the role is being worked out primarily on the Catholic campus, that is the place to begin, bearing in mind the admonition of a leading Catholic college president, Father Paul C. Reinert of Saint Louis University, that Newman centers on secular campuses "should definitely be considered as part of the total Catholic higher educational system in the United States."[6]

Yet even within institutions under formal and direct religious control, the Catholic role is ambivalent, caught between the intrusive influences of American society and sporadic Catholic militancy. Catholic higher education not only projects two images of itself but actually leads a double life. On one hand, Catholic colleges and universities stress their special denominational role as the apex of the world's largest system of private education. On the other hand, in their drive to enter the academic mainstream and in their bricks-and-mortar campaigns, they are imitating and sometimes emulating secular higher education.

Watch the Catholic college president in action. When his listeners are Catholic, particularly when they are potential alumni donors, he stresses the importance of Catholic higher education to the future of Catholicism in America. His accent is on the Catholic. When his audience is non-Catholic, particularly when it is composed of philanthropists and foundation executives, he stresses his institution's role in American higher education and its importance to the future of America; its role becomes hardly distinguishable from that of the secular campus across town. His accent is on education.

The professional image builders who are growing in importance on the Catholic campus epitomize the dilemma. Father William J. Dunne, S.J., a former college president who became associate secretary for the College and University Department of the National Catholic Educational Association, pointed in their direction in a July, 1961, address to representatives of Catholic institutions: "In some of your university relations offices the question is being discussed with regard to the emphasis to be placed or not to be placed

upon the religious nature of our colleges and universities."
He added later in the speech:

We have been speaking of a certain perplexity over the national image of Catholic education. It is not altogether surprising, then, to find in these times a kind of "shying away"
from the religious character of our colleges and universities.
You can observe this in many brochures and publicity pieces.
There is an obvious "playing down" of the religious side of our
institutions. Whether this be done to enlarge the green pastures
of the fund raisers or to broaden the field of student recruitment I do not know. Whatever the motives are, I simply say
that it is bad.[7]

The image is blurred because the role is unclear, despite
conventional curtsies toward Newman's *Idea of a University,* which stresses "integrity" in intellectual and university
life. As Catholic colleges and universities enter the mainstream of American education and share in its fragmentation and specialization, the main principles summarized by
Newman appear more and more out of reach:

The view taken of a university in these discourses is the following: that it is a place of teaching universal knowledge. This
implies that its object is, on the one hand, intellectual, not
moral; and on the other, that it is the diffusion and extension
of knowledge rather than the advancement. If its object were
scientific and philosophical discovery, I do not see why a university should have students; if religious training, I do not see
how it can be the seat of literature and science.
Such is a university in its essence, and independently of its
relation to the Church. But, practically speaking, it cannot fulfill its object duly, such as I have described it, without the
Church's assistance; or, to use the theological term, the Church
is necessary for its integrity. Not that its main characters are
changed by this incorporation: it still has the office of intellectual education; but the Church steadies it in the performance of that office.[8]

A well-publicized attempt to update Newman was made
when Father Theodore M. Hesburgh, president of the University of Notre Dame, urged the role of "mediator" upon

Catholic higher education. As Father Hesburgh expressed the role in terms of Catholic educators,

> We are men committed to Truth, living in a world where most academic endeavor concerns only natural truth, as much separated from supernatural truth, the divine wisdom of theology, as sinful man was separated from God before the Incarnation. If these extremes are to be united, a work of mediation is needed. The ultimate pattern is before us in the Incarnation and in the mediatorial work of redemption that follows the Incarnation.
>
> The mediator, the university or the university person, must somehow join in his person the full reality of the two extremes that are separated. This means that we must somehow match secular or state universities in their comprehension of a vast spectrum of natural truths in the arts and sciences, while at the same time we must be in full possession of our own true heritage of theological wisdom.[9]

Such mediation or integration depends on the emergence of Catholic Harvards (a very remote possibility at this time) and the emergence of a modernized Catholic theology of our times (still being formulated both theoretically and educationally). Even on Father Hesburgh's own campus, his faculty seems uncertain about the actualities of mediation, particularly since it implies a mastery of theology as well as an individual's academic specialty. In practical terms, the aim of mediation is undermined by the avowed hiring policy of Notre Dame and other leading Catholic institutions; they are out to "hire the best in the field," regardless of religious affiliation. When Father Hesburgh convened a committee of prominent psychologists to recommend a scholar to head the psychology department which has been embarrassingly absent from his university, he told the committee that their choice did not have to be a Catholic!

As a matter of fact, the Catholic campus lacks both intellectual integration and an educational rationale that is distinctly Catholic. Given the Catholic involvement in contemporary intellectual life—which is diffuse, complex, and inchoate—it is not surprising that a unifying ethos has not emerged for the educator or the scholar. The energies and resources of Catholic higher education are devoted to the pursuit of excellence as defined by the secular mainstream of higher education.

Meanwhile, as Professor John Donovan points out in his recent study *The Academic Man in the Catholic College,* a nineteenth-century definition of the Catholic college still has a powerful influence: "The transition to a new conception of academic functions and roles is still to be fully realized. The problem of the objectives of Catholic higher education in the twentieth century is still unresolved."[10]

In the tension between the sacred and the secular, the trend is toward accepting the demands of each academic discipline without systematic reference to a Catholic approach. The notion of a Catholic physics or chemistry is, of course, laughed out of the laboratory by Catholics as well as non-Catholics. Moreover, in such potentially value-laden fields as English literature, history, and sociology, the primary emphasis of Catholic specialists is on the rigorous demands of the discipline, not on a Catholic orientation. In stressing the importance of leaving the Catholic ghetto, the influential avant-gardists of Catholic scholarship are horrified at suggestions that they "baptize" their teaching and research. Even theology is being taken out of denominational confinement and subjected to universal standards of scholarship, as was pointedly noted by an influential Catholic educator in the field of theology: the priest-professor of comparative religion said the highest compliment he could receive for his scholarly articles was the reaction that his religious faith is not obvious in what he writes.[11]

This educational approach was evidenced during an unsuccessful taxpayers' suit challenging Maryland state aid for buildings at four church-affiliated colleges, two of them Catholic. During the 1964–65 school year, Sister Margaret Mary, president of the College of Notre Dame in Baltimore, testified that she was not aware of any significant areas in which Catholic doctrine would interfere with what is taught in liberal arts courses. When Sister Maura was asked whether she used the Bible as a model in her English literature and writing classes, she replied, "It's such a fine piece of literature that I think we probably should, but we don't. As a matter of fact, we use *The New Yorker*." Sister Mary Alma, a biology teacher, testified, "If anything comes up about the theology of the beginning of life, I refer them to the philosophy department. I've been trained as a scientist, and my knowledge of Catholic doctrine and philosophy never enters into my teaching. If it did, I shouldn't be in science."[12]

Professor Donovan discusses the efforts, as yet ineffective, to resolve the tension between the supernatural commitment of Catholic educators and the demands of scholarship in the natural order of things:

> Education, viewed as moral and as conserving, sought and still seeks an acceptable pattern of accommodation to the more secular climate of the dominant educational scene. Theology as a science rather than an apologetic, the behavioral sciences as independently valuable rather than as "proofs" of social philosophy, philosophy as a discipline rather than as an ideology, these and other developments illustrate the attempts of Catholic higher education to achieve a dynamic equilibrium in which the sacred and the secular are each accorded a respected place. So far the equilibrium has not been attained—if indeed it can be without major institutional changes.[13]

The indeterminate state of Catholic higher education is complicated by the free-enterprise character of the colleges and universities. Founded mainly by, of, and for religious orders as appendages to their apostolates, as part of their supernatural mission in the City of Man, Catholic colleges have never been official Church enterprises. It is true that American higher education in general originated in the foundation of seminaries. But while secular institutions have shed these denominational bonds, the Catholic college continues to nurture them in contexts that are influenced by religion and religious order.

The consequences are shattering to unity in Catholic higher education and inimical to a primary commitment to advanced study in and for itself. The clerical administrators who run the colleges and the clerical professors who teach in them are caught in a conflict of roles between a religious and a scholarly commitment. For the most part, commitment to their particular religious order comes first.

Nationally, "chains" of colleges and universities are operated by religious orders. In one such chain, a furtive hiring policy prevents a professor from changing schools within the group without the approval of his original institution. If approval is refused, the job application is turned down and the professor never discovers why. In an instance in the Midwest, a cardinal became so outraged by this practice that he urged the secular priest involved to sue the order. Instead, the priest changed university "chains."[14]

Meanwhile, lay faculty members—now in the majority—have a growing sense of professionalism which makes them more independent and more mobile in a sellers' market. They are demanding and receiving more professional treatment in tenure and salary. They are beginning to demand and to receive academic freedom. In numbers alone, the lay professors have increased from half of 13,000 faculty members in 1940 to about three-fifths of 25,000 faculty members in the 1960s. Since Catholic higher education is still adjusting to their emergence, clashes are inevitable, as was demonstrated during the 1964–65 school year at Georgetown University and at St. John's University, the largest Catholic university in the country (13,000 students). In both well-publicized instances, the faculty talked back to the religious order running the university.

When Jesuit-operated Georgetown fired a thirty-three-year-old English professor, Dr. Francis E. Kearns, he charged (and the university denied) that it was because of his articles and speeches criticizing Georgetown and other Catholic colleges on the questions of academic freedom and racial justice. Thereupon seventeen faculty members criticized the dismissal, saying it infringed upon "his academic freedom and therefore on ours." His faculty defense committee said Dr. Kearns should be promoted, not dismissed.

At St. John's the revolt involved about half of a lay faculty of 600, protesting against the paternalism of the school's fifty Vincentian priests. The common complaint was that the administration treated the faculty as "children." Besides adjustments in a much-criticized salary scale, the faculty was promised a voice in running the university after the president of New York City's Hunter College, Dr. John B. Meng, was hired as a "special consultant for educational planning." After threatening to quit en masse, the faculty returned for the school year 1965–66 mollified, and St. John's had a new president.

But an overnight change could not be wrought by a religious order that operated St. John's as an appendage—a very prosperous one whose enrollment had mushroomed in ten years from 800 to 13,000 students. When demands for academic freedom and professional status persisted and several faculty members continued to challenge the administration, the Vincentians struck back just before Christmas, 1965. Some two dozen faculty members were fired, including Msgr. John J. Clancy, associate professor of theology and canon law and a former member of the Vatican Secretariat. The monsignor's pointed comment underlined the ambiguity of Catholic higher education as dramatized at St. John's: "There is no sinister plot being undertaken by the administration; it is simply lack of comprehension of what is meant to have a university be a university. It cannot be a catechetical extension of a parish."

Ideally, academic freedom on the Catholic campus is

easily defined: a professor operates freely as long as "his teaching does not threaten the official dogmas of the Church or invade the areas of faith and morals."[15] In theory, the limitation is no more stringent than the one faced by a state university professor who cannot advocate anarchy or free love. But in practice the naïve, the ignorant, the authoritarian, and the nonprofessional administrator erects barriers to academic freedom. Religious like these, chosen because of the monopoly maintained by the order operating the university, regard higher education as a subsidiary enterprise operated for the sake of their order.

To a large extent, the adjustment between lay and religious on the Catholic campus mirrors the larger adjustment of the layman in the Catholic Church and reflects the tension between the American environment and Catholic parochialism, inflexibility, and defensiveness. Professor Gerald F. Kreyche of De Paul University, an informed and candid commentator on Catholic higher education, feels that "prospects for the future of academic freedom are bright" as the layman emerges on campus.[16] But the adjustment will be a troubled one, and publicized outbreaks are likely to continue as an American style of criticism and individualism invades the Catholic campus.

Catholic higher education throughout the country emerges as a sprawling kaleidoscope, largely uncoordinated and, by its own admission, wasteful of the available resources. A 1962 compilation by the American Association of Fund-Raising Counsel of campaigns exceeding $10 million reported a total of $575 million sought by only twenty-two of the more than 300 Catholic colleges and universities. Those twenty-two alone had physical plants valued at a third of a billion dollars, an indication of the physical magnitude of the Catholic institutions.[17]

In its current expansionist mood, Catholic higher education shows no sign of consolidating and even few signs of cooperation within its own house. Catholic critics have cited "the large number of third-rate institutions" and of "discredited institutions"[18] as well as the imminent danger of outstripping "the financial and personnel resources necessary for excellence."[19]

For the religious orders founding them, colleges are status symbols, which are particularly irresistible to the orders of nuns responsible for many inferior Catholic girls' colleges. Of all the orders involved, higher education comes most naturally to the Jesuits, by tradition and by training. They are dominant in the field, operating twenty-eight colleges located in every major American city except Pittsburgh and enrolling about one-third of the total student body on Catholic campuses. Their schools are authoritarian, urban, and strongly committed to intellectual values. Overall, their standards are probably the highest, and their schools constitute a close-knit system within the uncoordinated mass of Catholic colleges and universities.

The various styles of Catholic campuses reflect the particular religious order in control. At Notre Dame, the Holy Cross fathers epitomize institutional pride, while Jesuits think first as Jesuits and secondarily in terms of their institution. The Benedictines stress a communal family life, the Franciscans harmony in personal relations, the Dominicans intellectuality. The Sacred Heart of Mary nuns, with their Marymount colleges, have a snob appeal which contrasts with diocesan-sponsored colleges which have an egalitarian atmosphere. The latter schools, lacking the imprint of a single religious order, are largely influenced by regional location and the inclinations of the local bishop.

From the religious viewpoint, these institutions share common externals. There are crosses on the buildings, crucifixes in the classrooms, and a church on location where religious services are readily available to the students. Add certain rituals such as a Holy Ghost mass to inaugurate the

academic year, spiritual retreats for the students and faculty,
and an episcopal blessing at graduation. Also, their school
cafeterias do not serve meat on days of abstinence. But this
combination of externals hardly constitutes a religious
framework which is different from that in a Catholic boys'
camp.

Ironically, the theology department—the distinctive academic component of the curriculum—is in the lowest
repute, though the 1960s have seen vigorous attempts to
raise standards. Philosophy, with its traditional emphasis on
Saint Thomas Aquinas, has also suffered from academic
neglect. Both departments, but particularly theology, have
harbored academic marginals who are members of the ruling religious order. Since the students are required to take
theology and philosophy courses (and pay for them), the
use of this free professorial labor has helped subsidize the
operations of Catholic colleges at the expense of the students. (There seems little doubt that if theology and philosophy courses were made into electives, their enrollments
would dwindle.)

As for the students, differences do exist between those on
Catholic campuses and Catholics in secular colleges. In finding that the more well-to-do Catholics send their children to
Catholic schools, Father Greeley reported "major and 'significant' differences between the Catholics in Catholic colleges and the Catholics who did not go to such schools":

The former group [in Catholic schools] is more female (43
per cent as opposed to 31 per cent), more likely to be from a city
over 500,000 (48 per cent as opposed to 35 per cent), to be
unmarried (81 per cent as opposed to 68 per cent), to have a
college-educated father (40 per cent to 26 per cent) and have a
family income over $7,500 (50 per cent as opposed to 42 per
cent), and to be in the upper half of the SES [socioeconomic
status] measure (57 per cent as opposed to 47 per cent).[20]

Whereas Catholics in non-Catholic schools tended to see

themselves as more liberal, they regarded themselves as less religious; 76 percent of Catholics in secular colleges regarded themselves as religious, compared with 92 percent in Catholic colleges. This was borne out in differences in religious observance during college and one year after graduation: 93 percent of those in Catholic colleges were weekly churchgoers, compared with 77 percent of their Catholic counterparts in non-Catholic colleges. Among the latter, 83 percent of those who were still Catholics at graduation were going to mass weekly or several times monthly a year after graduation. This compares with 96 percent of the Catholic college graduates.

These religious differences are not substantial, and they are by no means proportionate to the heavy investment in Catholic higher education. The differences also reflect factors that have nothing to do with the impact of the college attended; presumably Catholic institutions attract Catholics who are more committed in the first place. Moreover, the relatively low apostasy found among Catholics in secular colleges, 12 percent, seems to be connected with attitudes and decisions that existed before college. Father Greeley concludes, along with Newman Center chaplains, that the secular campus itself does not seriously threaten the faith of Catholic students.[21] Agreeing with Father Greeley, Newman chaplain Father Butler cites "the experience of most university chaplains who usually find that the 'fallen-aways' were already falling before they came to the secular campus."[22]

One of the few systematic studies of the moral orientations on secular and Catholic campuses produced results not altogether flattering to the Catholic campus. An investigation made in 1961 and 1962 by Father Robert McNamara, S.J., compared Columbia and Cornell liberal arts seniors with Notre Dame and Fordham seniors, and found that students on the Catholic campuses were restrained in their sexual behavior (as might be expected for social as well as religious reasons) but relatively unrestrained in academic cheating! At the two Catholic schools, only 14 percent regarded cheating on a semester exam as a "terrible wrong," compared with 44 percent on the secular campuses. And 41 percent of the Catholic college seniors admitted cheating more than once on examinations, compared with 16 percent on the non-Catholic campuses.

On the Catholic campuses the vast majority considered "heavy necking on a date," "sexual relations with your fiancée," "sex relations with a prostitute," and "homosexuality between two consenting adults" as immoral. The majority increased progressively on these four items—from 73 percent condemning necking to 93 percent condemning homosexuality. By contrast, only a slight majority on the secular campuses condemned homosexuality, and 45 percent rejected prostitution as immoral, only 23 percent condemned sex relations with one's fiancée, and a handful—14 percent—necking.[23]

In another study, of 1800 Catholic students at five Catholic and three non-Catholic colleges on the West Coast, Father Thomas Rogalski found resentment at the Catholic colleges against the required philosophy and theology courses and little difference at the colleges regarding sex and drink —"Most of the Catholic fellows try to get as much of both as they can."[24]

While the Catholic campus is strongly influenced by secular values and secular higher education, there are few signs of Catholic influence on the secular campus. Some administrators have expressed interest in the teaching of theology at Catholic colleges, but it is hardly much more than curiosity. At leading secular universities, the Catholic presence is limited to a large handful of scholars who are known more for their specialization than for any impact as Catholics.

The burden of the Catholic influence on the secular campus falls mainly upon the Newman Centers, and it is hardly being taken up. The Newman movement is an exercise in tokenism; its clubs have been regarded "as a place or provision for Catholic ping-pong or a Catholic date bureau."[25] Although 100 Newman Centers have been added in the past decade, there are still only 175 of them, and only 80 of these are considered reasonably adequate. A mere 235 priests are engaged in full-time Newman work. With the aid of another 690 priests serving part-time in conjunction with parish duties, minimal Newman operations of some sort exist at 913 schools. Such as they are, they reach only one out of five Catholics on secular campuses. While Catholic campuses have a ratio of one priest or religious for every thirty-five students, secular campuses have one priest for every 3100 Catholics. The large majority of Catholics on campus—those at secular institutions—have not merely been neglected; they have been abandoned.

The episcopal moderator of the National Newman Apostolate, Archbishop Paul J. Hallinan of Atlanta, stirred comment among Catholic educators in 1963 by reminding them of these leftover Catholics in education. He told the College and University Section of the National Catholic Educational Association, "We should redefine Catholic education as the education of Catholics, wherever they may be." The goals of the Newman movement are clear—to emphasize liturgical participation, leadership programs, mission work, and religious education. A step in this direction has been taken at some forty state schools where Catholics can earn college credits from Newman Center courses in theology, philosophy, Scripture, Church history, and marriage.

A definition of the ideal Catholic center is not lacking, just its realization. A considered description has been presented in a sober appraisal of the Newman challenge published in *America* in the fall of 1964:

> On these secular campuses, the ideal Catholic center would be not merely a social organization, but rather one built around the rapidly developing group-concept of a Catholic center. It

would be staffed by a group whose talents and interests included the faculty-member scholar, the pastor and the counselor as well as the administrator of the center. Such a group could easily include religious, both men and women, and Catholic laity, all devoted to the center's work, which would extend from first-rate academic programs in Catholic thought and theology to full-scale liturgical life. In brief, this type of center would aim at providing educated Catholics on secular campuses with a properly adapted opportunity to know their faith fully and practice it actively.[26]

Meanwhile, an Orwellian Jesuit writing under the prudent pseudonym of Lawrence Shaw has looked into the future of 1984 and described the turning over of a mythical Jesuit university, Georgeham, to complete lay control.[27] Such advanced thinking among Catholic educators fits into the growing needs of Catholics on secular campuses. Shaw's plan would free priests on Catholic college faculties to confront the majority instead of the Catholic minority in higher education.

With the growing demands made upon diocesan priests, the religious orders are the obvious source of Newman clergy. But they look primarily to their own enterprises. The Jesuits, with 4693 priests, had only twelve of their number in Newman work during 1962–63. The Franciscans, with 2507, had sixteen; the Benedictines, with 1939, had eleven; the Dominicans, with 1100, had twenty-three. The six largest religious orders devoted only ½ percent of their clerical manpower (sixty-four priests) to the Newman effort.

Caught in the inertia of bureaucracy and absorbed in the requirement of upgrading their private system of colleges and universities, the religious orders cling to a parochial view of their role in higher education and show little inclination to go where most of the Catholics are on campus. As a result, the next generation of Catholic professionals, intellectuals, and influentials will be produced mainly by institutions where a Catholic presence has not been maintained. Even if these graduates remain steadfast in creed, their style, at least, will be overwhelmingly American and increasingly independent of the Church establishment.

PART II

Inside the Church

CHAPTER 6

Shepherds and Their Flock:
The Parish

INSIDE the rectory dining room Father John, the first assistant, and Father James, the second assistant, stand at their places, shifting from one foot to the other, conducting a desultory conversation on the coming baseball season. It is several minutes since they responded immediately to the six o'clock dinner chimes rung by Mary Finnegan, the rectory housekeeper. Suddenly a swirl of black cassock sweeps into the room. Monsignor has arrived.

Silence. Grace before meals: "Bless us, O Lord, and these Thy gifts which we are about to receive from Thy bounty, through Christ Our Lord." Mumbled amens. Napkins removed from their rings. Before Monsignor can finish shaking a small bell, Mary Finnegan pushes through the swinging doors into the dining room with a tureen of steaming soup. Then the rest of Monday dinner: boiled potatoes, cabbage, and corned beef, cooked for better or worse, followed by an invariably heavy dessert.

It is a family scene of a special clerical kind. The pastor as authoritarian father, the first assistant as an elder and compliant son, the second assistant as the younger and the least influential member of the household. And the housekeeper, like many an immigrant Irish mother before her, feeds the "family." As she swings into the dining room the conversation trails off into vague noncommittal remarks and as she swings out it mounts again. The tone, content, and mood of the dinner conversation is set by the head of the household, an ecclesiastical father who plays his role to suit his personality, a patriarch with almost unrestricted power.

This composite scene, drawn from actual rectory experiences, is enacted daily with little variation in some 18,000 rectories throughout the United States, in the midst of rundown tenements or suburban split-levels. The atmosphere is both intimate and restrained, friendly and formal, subject to the uncertainties of a chemical combination where strangers are turned into a family unit joined by the common bond of clerical commitment.

Mary Finnegan, stout, gray-haired, beyond reproach, is the lady of the house. A loyal parishioner in her fifties, she must give no cause for scandal; a conscientious, unimaginative lady, she must be discreet, closemouthed, and if possible, a good cook. She is chosen with more care than most wives, and treated better. Even if her cooking is in a soggy tradition of meat and potatoes, a priest says his grace before meals and digs in—without complaint. A good housekeeper is hard to find.*

Around the table in this true-to-life rectory sit embodiments of the three stages of clerical life.

The young, energetic priest is full of ideals, dreams, and plans, but devoid of power. He must patiently harness his enthusiasm, enduring frustrations, sustaining the vision of his vocation. Not long out of the seminary, he unburdens his irritations on evenings out with former classmates. Young priests sustain each other, compare notes on the "boss," their pastor, and exchange clerical shop talk. It helps not to be completely alone.

---

* As a sign of changing times, the traditional housekeeper is being replaced by the secretary, a parish lady who runs rectory and office for her clerical boss, whom she serves with an obsessive devotion worthy of any housekeeper.

Celibacy can also be a problem for the young priest, though a muted one in the past. A priest publishing anonymously in *The National Catholic Reporter* raised a touchy point:

> Many young priests, who live with their elders in celibacy, see in twisted and neurotic lives a high percentage of failures, and while sincerely desiring to be Christ's priests, they seriously question the Church law that imposes celibacy on them for life.
> . . .
> There are many priests who undoubtedly possess the gift of celibacy and hence have no problem. But what of the many authentic priests who sincerely desire to continue their priestly work, but who have discovered that they have no such gift?[1]

Undoubtedly, the stress of celibacy, reflected in the problem of alcoholism, contributes substantially to defections from the priesthood. According to reliable reports, there are 4000 to 5000 ex-priests in the United States today, a loss that cries out vainly for serious research.[2]

Then there is the middle-aged first assistant, who long ago learned his place. Unconsciously, he often becomes automated and passive, a good priest who performs his duties in a manner that is above criticism. His ideals and his zeal have suffered from the waiting game—twenty to thirty years as an assistant. He adheres to a prudent operating principle: "Don't rock the boat." In the actuarial process, he will become a pastor someday. He can then stretch his legs at the head of his own table, have his own assistants and his own command post. Tomorrow is his turn.

The pastor, a man in his late fifties, set in his ways, sits at the head of the table. Experience has molded him and parish responsibilities absorb his energies. The idealist who left the seminary some thirty years ago ends up as an administrator, watching ledgers, checking Sunday collections, and hovering over the myriad details involved in running the most important piece of ecclesiastical territory in the Amer-

ican Catholic Church—the parish. He is unequivocally dedicated to the dictum that as the parish goes, so goes the
Catholic Church in America. And one particular parish is
paramount: his parish.

By applying the findings of a 1964 survey of a national
cross-section of parish priests, predictions can be made about
the personal possessions of these three clerics. The chances
are nine out of ten that each owns a car, one out of two a TV
set, and about one out of three a collection of classical
records and a hi-fi set. One in five parish priests is in debt
and one in four contributes regularly to the support of relatives, usually his mother.[3]

The activities of these three ministers of God on a typical
Monday mirror parish life in America. Though each is
highly visible, each lives as a man set apart, a man of
this world but not in it, and he engages in a daily routine
that is little known and too little understood outside the
ecclesiastical establishment.

All Catholic priests share two universal religious duties:
celebrating mass every morning and reading the appropriate section of the daily breviary. With these two timeless
acts, the holy sacrifice and solemn prayer, the priest renews
his commitment to the City of God. Most of his remaining
time is spent in the City of Man, serving parishioners in
duties that are religious, social, administrative, clerical, and
charitable, duties that are elevating, inspiring, personally
gratifying, and also plain boring. By the time they reach the
dinner table, the priests have been stretched and torn,
elated and depressed, challenged and routinized by the daily
round of the "typical parish priest."

The pastor begins his Monday by checking the figures on
the Sunday collections and transferring them to deposit
slips. The packets of fifty $1 bills and the rolls of pennies,
nickels, dimes, quarters, and half-dollars must be put in
order for the trip to the bank. The process, along with the

necessary entries in the parish books, consumes the morning. Then come lunch, a nap, and a visit to the parish school for a chat with the sister-principal. With his frequent visits to the school and the playgrounds, the pastor becomes a familiar though distant father figure to the children of his parish.

In the late afternoon and evening, there are office calls: a couple seeking a separation, a mother who cannot understand why the parish school has no room for her son, an officer of the Ushers' Club or Holy Name to discuss a meeting later in the week, bingo and bazaar committee chairmen to get approval of their plans. Monday is a quiet day. Later in the week meetings will pile up, including talks at the chancery office with the building commission. (Parishes are invariably adding something new to the rectory, convent, school, playground, or church, and plans must be approved "downtown.") Daytime meetings range from discussions of the new liturgy to plans of the Altar Rosary Society to buy new vestments. Social functions take up many evenings. A pastor has little time to reflect, for he is the administrator and decision maker, surrounded by pressures that are familiar to the businessmen in his community. He faces the same threat of ulcers and heart attack.

On this typical Monday, the pastor has probably seen his assistants only at the dining room table. His first assistant, Father John, conducts novena devotions after the nine A.M. mass (to be repeated at seven-thirty in the evening). At the novena, the formalities proceed quickly—prayers "in honor of the Sorrowful Mother," benediction of the blessed sacrament, blessing of religious articles. He doesn't give a sermon or a sermonette, not even a "fervorino." The fifty or sixty people in attendance are mainly older women, and the first assistant realizes that these pious ladies are not in need of his rhetoric.

Much of his Monday is taken up with preparations for

catechism lessons for public school pupils and arrangements with the second-grade sister about instructions for first communion and with the fourth-grade sister for confirmation. In the evening, he moderates a pre-Cana Conference for engaged couples and a Cana Conference for married couples, followed by a personal meeting to give final instructions to a couple before marriage. If the marriage is mixed, the meeting will be longer than usual.

Meanwhile the second assistant, Father James, spends a parallel day with an increment of youthful energy and idealism. He spends more time preparing and giving catechism lessons, caring for the sick, and working on his sermons, and he makes an effort to get close to the youth of the parish. He joins the boys in the playground, moderates the young ladies' sodality, and takes an active part in Catholic Youth Organization athletics and in sodality socials.

For the typical parish priest, life is filled with such established routines and administrative burdens, activities which are not distinctively priestly and could be handled by laymen as well or better. This was borne out in a 1964 survey of parish priests conducted by Father Joseph Fichter. Except for counseling, the three most time-consuming tasks listed by parish priests are directing organizations, administering finances, and overseeing the parochial school. These are also the three activities in which the priests feel least competent and which give them the least satisfaction.[4]

One priest remarked, "What justification do we have for receiving Holy Orders and then dedicating almost our whole life to these secular activities? Is this not our greatest waste of priestly talent and manpower?"[5] Father Fichter points out that the situation is "largely determined by the internal organization of the parochial system. The authority structure is relatively 'flat.' Responsibility and decision-making rest directly in the hands of the priest, while the laity remain in an ancillary position."[6]

Basically, the parish is rooted in its fourth-century origins when the Catholic Church adopted Roman legal and political forms.* Applied to tribal and locally ruled populations, like the Goths in France, the parish reflected the relationship between the chieftain and his people. The pastor as shepherd of his flock directed a local, largely autonomous unit. By the sixth century the parish was a viable ecclesiastical organization and administrative tool.[7] In feudal Europe it developed a congenial link with local lords and barons.

The parish priest was also responsible for the teaching of the young, a responsibility stressed in 789 by Theodulf, Bishop of Orleans, in a letter to his priests:

> Let the priests keep schools in the villages and towns, and if anyone of the faithful shall wish to give his little ones learning, they ought to accept them willingly and teach them gratuitously. . . . And let them exact no price from the children for their teaching nor receive anything from them save what the parents may offer voluntarily and from affection.[8]

In 1070, with the discovery of the long-lost *Digest,* one version of Roman Emperor Justinian's famous code, the study of Roman law was sharpened, laying the groundwork for legal concepts still applied to the parish. *Corporation* and *office* became legal instruments for defining priests as pastors and as holders of a benefice which included the church, school, designated property, and a specified community of people.[9] Twentieth-century canon law still uses the legal language and much of the legal imagery of the first code promulgated by Pope Innocent III in 1210. Canon 215 defines the parish as follows: "The territory of every diocese is to be divided into distinct territorial units; and each unit is to have a special church with a designated people, and a special rector is to be given charge over it for the necessary

---

* The term *parish* comes from the Greek word *paroika* (near the house); the equivalent French transliteration is *paroisse,* from which the English word is derived. Roman missionaries, who used fourth-century Greek, the language of the educated, applied the Greek term to the French context.

care of souls." (The necessary care of souls includes *all* the population.)

This concept of the parish, so compatible with the rural and tribal context of feudal France where it was developed, suits a homogeneous community held together by strong, unifying traditions. The church was an integral part of community oneness. Today that same ecclesiastical unit serves pluralistic communities contained within arbitrary borders which encompass ambiguities, contradictions, and change. A feudal instrument strains to meet the demands of urban and suburban life in contemporary America, and the strain is showing.

At the turn of the century, the United States was divided into 79 dioceses and 7000 parishes; in 1965 there were 148 dioceses and archdioceses and almost 18,000 parishes. As territorial units, American parishes defy generalization. They are as varied as the American context with its contemporary social, economic, technological, and religious changes. The parish reels under the increase and shifts in population, under the impact of urban decay, suburban growth, and the development of the megalopolis. It encounters and becomes the religious focal point for much that is changing in America: age structures, fertility patterns, ethnic affiliations, immigrant pressures, residential mobility.

Three types of American parish can be identified in this picture: territorial parishes, national parishes, and special service parishes.

The last, once thriving neighborhood enterprises, now serve business and financial districts and their transient populations. Adjusting to the time-conscious businessman, professional, and secretary, these churches serve up an hourly round of weekday religious services. They close when the sun goes down and the commuters go home. They are where the people are, but their supermarket bustle can reduce the sublime and the spiritual to instant packaged religion. Such churches too easily become religious filling stations, and no one is more concerned about this than the dedicated priests working in them.

The traveling American is also served by these churches; Boston, for instance, has an Our Lady of the Railways Chapel, Our Lady of Good Voyage Chapel, and Our Lady of the Airways Chapel at the appropriate land, sea, and air terminals. Other examples are the churches prominently located at the La Guardia and Kennedy airports in New York City and at International Airport in Miami. The aim of the special service church was summed up by Rev. Patrick T. Donnelly, vicar of Saint Anthony's Shrine, one of downtown Boston's busiest churches: "Our responsibility ends at the front door; we hopefully send people back to their own parishes for regular worship except for such services as we render when they are in town."[10]

By contrast, national parishes cling to a recent and persistent past of immigrant minorities who hold on to their identities. These parishes are formally constituted units, though sometimes they also emerge from the accident of neighborhood concentrations of nationalities or racial groups. Their survival is a reminder that the melting pot is still operative. For instance, in the Diocese of Gary, Indiana, where twenty-five of the forty-five urbanized parish units are drawn along ethnic lines, Slovaks, Poles, and Hungarians predominate.[11] In Chicago, one of the Midwest's oldest diocesan establishments, a 1959 study found forty-three national parishes for Poles, twenty-seven for Germans, twelve for Italians, ten for Lithuanians, eight each for Bohemians and Slovaks, seven for Greeks, five for Frenchmen, four for Croatians, three for Negroes, two each for Slovenians, Hungarians, and Mexicans, and one each for Dutchmen, Belgians, Melkites, Chaldeans, and Chinese. Thus, with 138 of 279 parishes in Chicago still tied to their congregations' origins through distinctive languages, customs, rites, and ethnic priests, half of the city's parishes remained intact in the melting pot.[12]

On a countrywide basis, about 10 percent of the parishes are still national parishes. The 1948 totals, which have changed little, show 466 parishes for Poles, 314 for Italians, 206 for Germans, 152 for Slovaks, and 114 for French (mostly French Canadians).[13] As expected, the newer immigrants predominate in the pattern of national parishes. As assimilation takes place, some national parishes lose their identity while retaining their official status. A French district carries on in a neighborhood without any French parishioners, a German parish is left without Germans, and a Polish parish finds its Sunday congregation composed mainly of Irishmen.

The typical parish with a fixed territory is often inundated by the changes taking place in American cities. Many become dying parishes in blighted areas. Churches with proud spires overlook slums and declining neighborhoods from which old parishioners have moved, leaving the parish establishment behind. No longer supported and financed by their neighborhoods, such parishes must be supported in whole or in part by the diocesan chancery office. They become missionary outposts in the heart of the city.

While some city parishes are homogeneous units in neighborhoods with similar economic, ethnic, and social groupings, most are heterogeneous pressure points caught up in urban change. Some are old parishes being transformed; others are relatively new.

Saint Philip and Saint James Parish in the Bronx, New York, surveyed by one of the authors in 1957, exemplifies the pressures facing city units. Founded in 1949 to relieve the demands of two neighboring parishes, Holy Rosary and Saint Mary's, the new parish has four distinct sections. It contains Eastchester, a recently built public housing project of 884 families who in 1957 were 43 percent Catholic, 33 percent Jewish, and 16 percent Protestant, all relative newcomers to this northeast sector of the Bronx. The parish area also has an old neighborhood, which was 100 percent Italian and 50 percent Catholic, and a newer middle-class section which was largely second-generation Italian and 55 percent Catholic but which also included upper-middle-class Jewish and Protestant families. The fourth section, Hillside Homes, contained long-standing residents; 44 percent were Jewish and 5 percent were Protestant, and the remainder were Catholic, most of them Irish who had attended Holy Rosary Church for years and who viewed the Eastchester housing project with anxiety. It brought in more Negro, Puerto Rican, Jewish, and Italian residents with lower incomes and more children. Their quiet, homogeneous, tree-lined world of private homes was being threatened.

For this single parish, "the necessary care of souls" involves a mixture of age groups, family sizes, social classes, incomes, and education levels. Differences could be seen in church attendance. Sunday mass observance was most consistent among the newer Eastchester population, where four out of every five Catholics over seven years of age heard mass every Sunday. It was poorest in the old neighborhood that contained a large number of first-generation Italians.[14] Clearly, a pastor and his assistants have to speak with many voices in many directions to serve this urban parish. It is a familiar situation in American cities.

Like other middle-class Americans, the Catholic priest usually dreams of a parish in the suburbs where the need to belong provides him with loyal, homogeneous, generous, better-educated parishioners. The suburb is clearly the comfortable new frontier that makes parish life over to fit the setting, even in the churches being built. High spires in cramped city quarters are giving way to friendly ranch-type churches with ample parking space and one-level schools with large windows.

As the suburbs go, so will the churches, and suburban

growth sets a fast pace. In the first forty years of this century, suburbs grew one and one-third times as much as the central city, from 1940 to 1950 two and a half times as much, and from 1950 to 1960 seven times as much. The trend accelerates. In the 1970s, central cities will increase by 25 percent and suburbs by 150 percent. In 1950 four Americans lived in the suburbs for every six in the city; in the 1970s six Americans will live in the suburbs for every four in the city.

In the suburbs the pastor plays a different role. He is lucky to have one assistant; often he is by himself. The active lay people in his parish become his staff assistants, and the teaching staff in his parochial school is predominantly lay. The patriarchal pastor of the city becomes a suburban joiner, turning up at Rotary meetings, interfaith dinners, and PTA meetings. He must be sociable.

For his parishioners religion has important social dimensions; the family "belongs" by having a Catholic, Protestant, or Jewish affiliation. Will Herberg's penetrating analysis of American religion applies particularly to the suburbs:

> On one level at least, the answer would seem to be that the religious revival under way in this country today—the notable increase in religious identification, affiliation, and membership —is a reflection of the social necessity of "belonging," and today the context of "belonging" is increasingly the religious community.[15]

In the suburbs "rectory" priests and "sacristy" pastors upset the much-desired harmony if they remain in their denominational strongholds and stay apart from their communities. God's ministers are expected to join hands in furthering the faith of America—"a faith in faith," as Herberg puts it.[16] Interdenominational harmony rather than competition is highly prized. In the suburbs a priest must be flexible and friendly.

Whether the setting is urban or suburban, the parish priest is confronted with a variety of roles that take him a long way from his seminary training. His functions have been enlarged beyond the traditional and strictly religious areas of preaching and teaching, moral and spiritual counseling, and providing religious services. He is involved in selecting building sites and plans, buying basketballs and furniture, directing finances, organizing and supervising clubs and organizations, shaking hands with Lions, and saying the blessing at chamber of commerce meetings. He is a community activist in the world's greatest society of joiners.

The metamorphosis has come about for various reasons. The voluntary character of religion in the United States has made the clergy highly responsive to changes in society and to the wide-ranging demands of the laity. In many ways the priest's traditional sources of religious authority no longer are enough to maintain his position of importance, and he must seek out additional areas of involvement and influence. Most of all, the American clergyman is eager to find ways to make religious faith relevant to a changing America. This makes him ready to travel far afield from a restrictive round of religious duties. The perceptive Jesuit commentator Walter J. Ong has noted that the French priest is "inner-directed" while the American priest is "other-directed."[17]

The direction being taken by American clergymen is more and more away from religiously oriented activities and toward nonreligious ones. In his illuminating study of the urban parish, Father Joseph Fichter has observed: "The priest must conform to the needs of the parish rather than insist upon doing only that for which he is best trained or in which he has the greatest talent and interest. It is a striking anomaly in an age of specialization that the parish priest (unlike trained personnel in other professions and occupations) is forced to maintain an adaptive readiness to be 'all things to all men.' "[18] The trend involves all American clergymen, whether priests, ministers, or rabbis, as noted by Professor James M. Gustafson of Yale University Divinity School.[19]

In another of his studies, Father Fichter draws a lengthy analogy between religious and industrial organizations, and stresses the importance of the managers who try to administer them: "What is true of managers in a business enterprise seems to be true also of leaders in religious organizations. Both are theoretically intent upon maintaining a group of people who are both happy and efficient."[20]

On the parish level, the manager is the pastor, graduate of an inexorable seniority system. He must hold together the human mosaic comprising his parish territory, build and maintain the physical plant containing a church, school, convent, and rectory, and create some semblance of spiritual order out of a diversity of people and problems. The external criteria of his success are thoroughly American and business-minded, as if the local chamber of commerce were the evaluating agency. His church should be in good repair and provided with the latest in the accouterments of worship. He should have his own up-to-date parish school along with a rectory and a convent fitted out in comfort, if not in style. He must meet financial quotas for the diocese as well as raise funds for parish expenses and expansion. His business is the salvation of souls, but externally it still resembles any other American business.

Saving souls and paying bills—out of this emerges a harassed hybrid, the Catholic pastor. He is described in the first person by Rev. John Hugo, pastor of the Church of Saint Germaine in Bethel Park, Pennsylvania, in the following way:

These bills are assumed in order to provide the laymen with a church and, quite commonly, a school; and modern laymen expect these to be attractive, if not beautiful, well-kept, well-heated, well-lighted, well-staffed, complete with parking lot (paved and cleared of snow when necessary). This is the pastor's problem.

In addition, on Saturday nights he should be ready, with the sureness of a John of the Cross, to guide the more devout of the laity through the vast wastes of the Dark Night. Then on Sunday morning, to prevent further articles or letters to editors, he should come up with a homily that will compare favorably with what this now educated congregation has been reading in St. Gregory or the Oxford sermons of Newman.[21]

While the American pastor can list the myriad and varied demands on his time, he has no clear answer to the simplistic question, what is a parish *supposed* to do? It is not enough to answer that the parish is a local source of sacramental means toward the end of religious salvation. A Catholic does not live by holy communion alone. He is a many-sided individual surrounded by a complex society; in his time the Catholic plays many roles, and possibly the least of the roles is that of parishioner. Even as a believer, he is a Catholic first and then only remotely a member of Saint Peter's or Saint Mary's of the Sea. And one out of five parishioners will change residences and probably parishes every year. The Catholic parish remains stationary in place while its designated population and even its physical surroundings change drastically under the dynamics of urban and suburban change.

The line drawn between one parish and another in contemporary America is an administrative decision which the pastor must imbue with a significance that is almost impossible to sustain. In fact, a parish is a community accidentally created and only temporarily stable, and a pastor is a minister of God overwhelmed by administrative duties. Yet to deprive a parish of even its paper identity is to raise a specter of confusion and threaten the physical establishment that rallies Catholics around church and school. It is much easier to pose the question than to answer it.

Bishop John King Mussio of Steubenville, Ohio, who has been outspoken on the need to find answers, states the problem bluntly: "Today's parish is hopelessly outdated. Patchwork reform is useless. The parish must be struck by the revolution that is sweeping the Church; it must be completely, radically restructured."[22] The problem of the parish also involves a shortage of clergy: while the number of Catholic priests rose 22 percent in the decade 1954–64, the Catholic population soared by 42 percent. This increases the pressure for efficient use of priestly manpower and for married deacons—even married priests.

An intriguing example of the rethinking now current relates the use of married clergy to a restructuring of the parish.[23] The territorial parish would remain the focal point for the important rites of baptisms, marriages, and funerals and for the major liturgical feasts. But the one or more celibate priests living in the rectory would be assisted by married priests and deacons who live in the parish and support themselves as professionals or white- and blue-collar workers. Their priestly activities would be among Catholics (and non-Catholics) with similar social, economic, and educational characteristics. Similarity would breed closer contact. Such a parish would expand the growing practice of celebrating mass in private homes. Mass would become a daily occurrence in the apartment building or home of the married priest, either before he leaves for work or after his evening meal.

Such innovations suggest responses to the pressures upon the parish. In general terms, the new directions are evident. Priest and pastor must be freed for priestly duties, and non-priestly roles must be turned over to laymen, whether volunteers or paid professionals. Parish organizations need to be involved in the larger pluralistic society, and not devote themselves to maintaining Catholic isolation. In the present system, only a small minority of Catholics are actively engaged in the closed circle of parish life, and neighboring parishes exist side by side as alien territories. The current conglomeration of Catholic parishes does not add up to a cohesive whole of integrated parts functioning with clearcut methods of operation. On the parish level, the pastor makes his own rules; on the diocesan level, the bishop reigns, largely by veto power.

In the past, the jumble of 18,000 parochial pieces has fallen together into a makeshift system, all patchwork and piecemeal—succeeding in spite of itself. Today the parish is an ecclesiastical unit in search of a modernized role that will make it relevant and effective in a changing America. It awaits an updating.

◇◇◇◇◇◇◇◇◇◇◇◇◇◇◇◇◇◇◇◇◇◇◇◇◇◇◇◇◇◇◇◇◇◇

CHAPTER 7

Shepherds and Their Flock: The Diocese

FOR SEVERAL MINUTES after ten A.M., stragglers in Roman collars were still arriving for the nine-forty-five meeting of the diocesan clergy. They parked their Chryslers, Fords, Buicks, and Oldsmobiles—along with an odd Volkswagen—in the schoolyard and entered through the rear doors of Regina High School auditorium. Each dropped a small white attendance card into a worn wicker basket; tallied, the cards would enable the Bishop to identify the absentees.

On stage, a veteran monsignor conversed deferentially with the Auxiliary Bishop. His Grace, the Archbishop, seldom appears for such meetings, unless a major building expansion or fund-raising drive is on the agenda. The Monsignor would chair the meeting and the Auxiliary would moderate as the representative of his Archbishop.

Finally, both rose. The Monsignor said simply, "His Excellency will open our conference with a prayer." The clerical audience stood in a body. The Bishop began: "Come, Holy Spirit, enlighten the hearts of Thy faithful. . . ." The Monsignor announced slowly, "The topic for today's conference is the question of urban renewal. His Excellency has graciously invited a guest speaker, a man much dedicated to his work with the City Planning Board, Mr. Harvey Johnson."

A typical conference of the clergy was under way, a twice-yearly formality which resembles a district sales meeting for a manufacturer, except that the guidance of the Holy Spirit is invoked. Because of the large number of diocesan clergy, the meetings are held on a deanery basis—a deanery is a district within a diocese comprising several parishes. Lasting for an average of two hours, the meetings are complete with moderator, chairman, guest speakers, discussants, question-and-answer periods, and debate from the floor. On this occasion the subject, urban renewal, was unusual, reflecting the changing problems of the American parish. More common topics would range from catechism teaching to vocation recruitment, from doctrinal questions on the resurrection to moral problems like juvenile delinquency or birth control.

At the end a clerical consensus emerges, from a combination of conviction and compliance with the episcopal cue. Through intermediaries and finally with his concluding remarks, the bishop sets "company policy" until the next meeting. The clerical audience responds with prudence, under obedience, and for the sake of the common cause.

The manifest role of the bishop as diocesan decision maker is rooted historically and theologically in his direct line of succession from the twelve apostles. He is second in power only to the chief bishop, the vicar of Rome. As management expert Peter Drucker notes, the bishop is part of the "flattest organization structure we know: there are only three levels of 'line authority,' parish priest, bishop, and Pope."[1] (However, the concept of "collegiality" which emerged from the Second Vatican Council could rearrange the structure in still unpredictable ways.)

Flat, but also wide, for the twelve of apostolic times have become the worldwide 2500 of the mid-twentieth century. In the United States some 250 members of the hierarchy act in the "fullness of authority" in 148 dioceses and archdioceses covering the fifty states like a grid. The geographical trend in the United States is clear. Dioceses are centered in large urban areas and extend outward along county lines. Archdioceses tend to develop in state capitals or metropolises and embrace all the dioceses within a state, thus reconstituting the state as an ecclesiastical province.

The tendency for ecclesiastical forms to parallel civil units is of course historical, as is the tendency for church and state to attract as well as repel each other in the City of Man.[2] As far back as the eighth century, Charlemagne, determined to restore the glories of the Roman Empire, established a model of cooperation: tribal leaders provided wealth and power and clerical leaders religious charisma to strengthen his control. Under Charlemagne's union of church and state, the governor and the bishop marched in the same procession of power. In France, Spain, and Italy—along the southern tier of Europe—the secular and the sacred cooperated, while in England and Germany—the northern tier—alienation developed. The American hierarchy has inherited both aspects of the European tradition; church and state in America have been allied and also aloof. The relationship is still ambivalent, as expressed in the current shibboleth of separation of church and state.

In the beginning American Catholics threw off the yoke of the French archbishop of Quebec with the assistance of political power: John Carroll, the Englishman who became the first American bishop, drew on his friendship with George Washington and on political influence to achieve independence from the French archbishop in the name of American values and interests. Rome acceded and made Baltimore the first diocese. In the early nineteenth century, Bishop John England, an early Irish immigrant, was so in tune with the American way that he adopted a constitution for his southern diocese and in 1823 established the first real Catholic newspaper, the *Catholic Miscellany,* in keeping with the reading of newspapers that was becoming a national habit. He was even invited to address the United States Congress.

But signs of alienation were also evident as the newer waves of Irish immigrants arrived. Theological debates took place in public, like the one in 1835 between a young priest named John Hughes (who became leader of the American Church in midcentury as archbishop of New York) and a noted Presbyterian minister. The issue was the compatibility of Catholicism with civil and religious liberty.

The elevation of Irish bishops in Boston and New York paralleled the rise of Irish politicians and established the first triangle of ecclesiastical authority in the New World. Baltimore, Washington, New York, and then Philadelphia became the collective stronghold of the American Church, a dominance which has been challenged by the focal points of power that grew up in the West with the advance of the frontier.

The westward movement of population and industry coincided with the rise of the Germans and the Poles, who were determined to place their ethnic brand on the American Church. Cincinnati, Saint Louis, and Milwaukee became a new triangle of episcopal power, soon joined by Chicago and Detroit. Within a hundred years of their founding, all five were metropolitan sees headed by archbishops, with suffragan sees (Saint Paul–Minneapolis and Indianapolis) to support their prestige and power. Midwesterners consider this the heart of American Catholicism—whose head is a core of episcopal progressivism and whose body is a laity of political conservatives.

A 1958 profile of the American bishops by John Donovan reflects the story of the American Church as it went native and cast aside dependence on Europe.[3] As late as 1897 some 66 percent of the American hierarchy were foreign-born; by 1930 the figure was 23 percent and by 1957 only 4 percent. The list of bishops' birthplaces today represents almost every state in the union. In 1957 their parents also were increasingly native-born—44 percent of their fathers and 60 percent of their mothers. Among foreign-born parents, it is not surprising that Ireland ranked first as their birthplace, followed by Germany and Poland.

In the family background of American bishops two characteristics are prominent. They generally come from large families. In 1957 six was the typical number of children in the parental home; 11 percent of the hierarchy came from families with eleven or more children, another indication that the American hierarchy is inclined toward the ideal of large families. Moreover, religious vocations run in their families. Based on the response received from three-fourths of the hierarchy, Donovan reports:

> ... 15 percent of the bishops and archbishops have a total of 24 brothers in religious life while 20 percent have 39 sisters with religious vocations. Among the children of their married brothers and sisters vocations are also relatively frequent since 25 percent of the hierarchy have a total of 48 nephews with vocations and 18 percent report 26 nieces in religious communities.

As individual success stories, the hierarchy's follow a pattern that is strikingly American. The drive to succeed was learned at home. Professor Donovan comments that "the members of the hierarchy tend to be drawn from the more upwardly mobile Catholic families in the United States." His survey revealed that "65 percent of the respondents' fathers had less than a high school education, 24 percent had either some high school or a complete high school education, 6 percent had some college and 5 percent held college or professional degrees." A notably large percentage of the fathers owned small businesses, common incubators of ambitious sons: 27 percent, in contrast with the 5 percent in the adult population of 1920.

From childhood American bishops were enclosed within a Catholic framework. In 1957, ninety-two out of 151 bishops and archbishops had attended parochial schools; 118 had attended Catholic secondary schools. Only a handful were educated entirely in public schools. The official starting point of their careers was in the seminary, for as Professor Donovan points out, "The Church, like all other large organizations, is alert to the importance of the early identification and special preparation of those who may show particular promise as future leaders." Thus, beginning in the seminary they became organization men and were earmarked for advancement.

The episcopal path is well marked: seminary training in the United States, postseminary training in Europe, an advanced degree, some parish experience, and administrative appointments, particularly those close to a bishop.

In the early 1900s there was a marked trend toward seminary training in Europe at Rome, Louvain, or Würzburg, but this has been reversed. Whereas 60 percent of the bishops earlier in the century had attended European seminaries, only 40 percent had done so at midcentury. Advanced degrees, often taken in Europe, have become important. Professor Donovan found 77 percent of the hierarchy with such degrees, mainly in ecclesiastical fields or in the allied subjects of philosophy and Church history.

At this point their upward careers veered away from the academic and toward the administrative. But with the increased number of priests and the slowdown in the establishment of new dioceses, they faced more competition and a longer apprenticeship. In the 1890s American bishops achieved consecration after nineteen years, in 1930 after twenty-one years, and in 1960 after twenty-two years. Only a small proportion—17 percent—spent the intervening years teaching; 39 percent were primarily in parishes and 44 percent primarily in administration. The choicest administrative assignments for the career-minded priest center around the bishop's headquarters, particularly as chancellor, secretary to the bishop, director of Catholic charities, school superintendent, or director of the Society for the Propagation of the Faith.

The preferability of an administrative position over a

parish assignment is particularly evident in the inter-
mediate appointment to monsignor. It reached an extreme
in the New York Archdiocese where the clergy came to exchange good-natured jibes about the "monsignor mania"
under the reward-conscious reign of Cardinal Spellman. An
analysis of New York monsignori in 1959 confirmed that a
priest with administrative duties is more likely to become
monsignor, and at an earlier age. The study reported that
the upward movement from curate to pastor to monsignor is
"the most difficult route to access to promotion and the less
specialized, yet more in the category of traditional priestly
work." Only 45 percent of the pastors in the Archdiocese
were monsignori, compared with 80 percent of those in administrative positions. The functions of specialist and gen-
eralist were identified with this conclusion:

> There is then an indication of the existence of two types of
> clergymen evolving out of the two types of functions: 1. the less
> specialized, more priestly apostle or parish priest—less con-
> ducive to promotion to monsignor or more given to the consola-
> tion type of monsignor; 2. the more specialized, less priestly
> administrator or functionary—more conducive to promotion,
> more given to recognition and to the functional requirement
> type of promotion.[4]

These career patterns have emerged more from circumstance than by design. They are the natural result of
bureaucratic reproduction; likes choose likes for promotion.
An illustrative (though unconfirmable) story concerns the
appointment of an intellectual bishop to the Midwestern
diocese he currently administers. His aging predecessor was
asked by Rome to recommend three candidates for auxiliary
bishop and heir apparent. The bishop named two senior
monsignori with excellent real estate records and a third as
an afterthought. Rome confounded and upset the bishop by
selecting the afterthought, the intellectual. Now that the
aged bishop has died, the intellectual sits behind the epis-

copal desk, confiding that he is overwhelmed by his administrative duties.

Administration is the major burden carried by American bishops, and the inevitable result is a proliferation of administrative assistants. The list is worthy of any large-scale business organization, as is illustrated by the New York Archdiocese, which assigns clerical administrators to the following: Office of Vicar and Assistant for Religious, Catholic Charities, Saint Vincent de Paul Society, Cemeteries, Catholic Youth Organizations, Radio and Television, Institutional Commodity Services, Society for the Propagation of the Faith, Holy Name Society, Archdiocesan Building Commission, War Relief Services of the National Catholic Welfare Conference, Bishop's Relief Fund of the National Catholic Welfare Conference, Near East Welfare Conference, Office of Spanish Catholic Action, Archdiocesan Committee for Vocations, Confraternity of Christian Doctrine, Family Life Bureau, Sodalities, Apostleship of Prayer, Cardinal Hayes Committee on Literature, Legion of Decency, Legion of Mary, Hospital Apostolate, New York Apostolate of the Roman Catholic Church, Catholic Deaf Center, Committee for Vigilance of Faith, Friends of Catholic Charities, and Chaplains. And there are many others.

In the Catholic diocese there is a pronounced crisis in middle management, for the bishop delegates responsibilities without authority. The bulk of the assigned administrative work is handled by conscientious and usually career-minded clerics who are subject to the whims, wishes, and sporadic attention of the bishop. In the diocese the bishop's chancellor or vicar general exercises the power of his office only as the bishop designates. The General Code of Canon Law specifies the powers and duties of only a few administrative offices, particularly in the matrimonial court.

The bishop remains as "president of the board" of every parish corporation in his diocese. In larger dioceses, he will head as many as three or four hundred local church units and will control their budgets and personnel. Legally he is board chairman of all diocesan Catholic institutions—hospitals, orphanages, educational facilities from elementary schools though universities, old people's homes. The highest executive in the diocese, he is also personally responsible for every individual Catholic unit in his territory, whether diocesan or belonging to an order.

With rare exceptions, the bishop uses only clergymen as assistants. The result is a bizarre personnel procedure which assigns the untrained to the unfamiliar. Theologians make decisions on building plans, specialists in Church history direct Catholic youth activities, priests with doctorates in philosophy administer Catholic charities. And they confront these administrative burdens without clearly defined policies or powers. Only gradually is the need for professional specialization being reflected in the training and assignment of priests, but such headway depends on the perspicacity of the individual bishop. Few qualified laymen are utilized, and these serve mainly on diocesan school boards. A rare exception is the Natchez-Jackson diocese in Mississippi (where only three out of every hundred persons are Catholic). In 1963 Bishop Richard O. Gerow appointed a woman who was an experienced administrator as diocesan secretary for lay activities, a talented organist and musician as lay consultant on music and liturgy, and a prominent architect as a member of the diocesan building commission. All three commissions were previously limited to clerics, as they normally are throughout the country.

Management surveys which assign high ratings to Catholic diocesan operations make precarious conclusions which appear to overlook the tangled lines of authority and responsibility and the ineffectual delegation of power in an administrative structure that grew like Topsy. Moreover, each bishop, as the absolute power in his diocese, makes his own rules, oblivious of his predecessor and helpless before his successor. For instance, one bishop conducted a sizable building drive in a Connecticut city in order to build a modern citywide high school; his successor turned it into a college and sent the students back to the slum-surrounded, worn-out downtown high school that had been abandoned.

On a national basis, dioceses lack coordination. Formal lines of communication exist only through the Roman Curia, episcopal meetings, and the organizational channels of the National Catholic Welfare Conference in Washington, D.C. Since its establishment in 1919 to administer the welfare activities of the Church in the wake of World War I, the NCWC has widened its scope to all areas of American life upon which the hierarchy seeks to have an impact. It is the Pentagon of the American Church. But it functions without the power and the legal instruments needed to ensure its effectiveness, and with all the red tape and paraphernalia of an official bureaucracy.

Under an administrative board that represents all bishops, archbishops, and cardinals, the NCWC maintains eight departments: Executive, Education, Press, Legal, Social Action, Immigration, Youth, and Lay Organizations. Each department has an ambitious scope, but in practice each is a paper organization whose pronouncements and policies have no binding power over the local bishop. The range of these departments is illustrated by the Social Action Department, which was established

... to serve and represent the Hierarchy in social and economic matters; to present Church teaching to government and private organizations; to promote labor-management co-operation; to assist international groups in fostering a sound world economic order; to inspire and assist clergy and laity to engage in Christian Social Action; and to encourage interracial justice.[5]

Functioning under an episcopal chairman and assistant chairman, the Social Action Department has a series of advisory posts filled by bishops: health and hospitals, charities, rural life, prisons, and family life. The full-time staff is under a director and assistant director, with specialized directors for family life and for health and hospitals. In this department as in the others, appointments are personal, turnover is rapid, and promotions are capricious. Such common administrative practices as a stable budget, long-term plans, and professional standards are either absent or applied erratically. Dedication, zeal, and the efforts of a handful of highly qualified individuals sustain an unsteady structure.

At their annual meeting in November, 1964, the American bishops announced a study of the NCWC secretariat and the by-laws and structure of the national body. In mid-1965 the committee studying the NCWC finally met, with indications that no results could be expected in less than two or three years, while the by-laws committee still had not met. Two dominant and differing camps were evident: there were the wholesale reorganizers and the cautious changers, those in favor of centralization and those in favor of continued diocesan autonomy, those who wanted to maintain episcopal authority and those who wanted to share it.

While the bureaucratic process was moving slowly, the innovators were making exciting suggestions. Nine bishops and church historians writing in the winter, 1964, issue of *Continuum* made suggestions in response to "the changing role of the American episcopate." Quoting the canon law provision that plenary (lawmaking) councils are to be held "whenever the necessity arises," Archbishop Paul J. Hallinan of Atlanta pointed out that the last one was held in 1884, and added, "It is scarcely tenable that no 'necessity' has occurred since 1884. Yet the law-making power of our national hierarchy has been held in abeyance for 80 years."[6] His proposal was a U.S. plenary council in the United States every twenty years. Other proposals included the appointment of an official representative of the American hierarchy to serve in the Vatican and the establishment of constant contacts among bishops, priests, and laity.

Another proposal, made publicly by Richard Cardinal

Cushing of Boston, is that all members of the hierarchy retire at seventy. It would revolutionize the Catholic Church in America. In mid-1965 the five cardinals in this country were aged sixty-six, sixty-nine, seventy-two, seventy-six, and seventy-nine. One-half of the more populous and important archdioceses and one-third of all dioceses and archdioceses were headed by prelates over seventy. Heads of dioceses average sixty-three and of archdioceses sixty-eight. The style of leadership is clearly more Roman than American, where senators average fifty-eight and governors fifty years of age.[7]

In the first and in the final analysis, the ongoing Catholic enterprise in America is in the hands of the local bishop. His authority is unchallengeable; his power bestrides the diocese. Nowhere is this more pronounced than in the so-called right of petition of those under him. According to canon law a priest can go over his bishop's head and appeal to the pope, but the time-honored practice has been to refer complaints back to that same bishop. It has been described as the only legal system in the world where the accused becomes the judge.

As a Los Angeles lawyer observed in calling for a bill of rights within the Church,

> We have a system where the grossest injustice can be done, and there is no right of petition. It is the general spirit of the law that first, you should have a substantive standard to apply, and second, somewhere you know you can go to apply it. The Church has neither. The most ordinary union member is better off as far as getting a grievance aired than a pastor or a curate who may have served the Church faithfully for forty years.[8]

The celebrated case of a shy, intense twenty-nine-year-old priest in Los Angeles called public attention to the system in mid-1963. Father William H. DuBay cabled the Pope and requested the removal of the Archbishop, James Francis Cardinal McIntyre, for "gross malfeasance" and "abuses of authority" in failing to exert moral leadership against racial discrimination and for conducting "a vicious program of intimidation and repression" against priests, seminarians, and laymen who showed such leadership. The charges of intimidation and of failure to support civil rights were subsequently documented in a courageous special issue of *Commonweal* on the "Church of Silence" in Los Angeles. *Commonweal* associate editor John Leo described the background of Father DuBay's public gesture:

> Along with several other priests, most of them not long out of the seminary, he had become convinced that every possible approach to Cardinal McIntyre on the racial issue had been exhausted—repeated appeals for audiences, phone calls, proddings from outside bishops, even picketing of the chancery office by laymen—and that nothing else was left but open protest, even if it meant suspension or excommunication.[9]

While the appeal for the Archbishop's removal was wildly unrealistic, the outcome dramatized episcopal authority. Father DuBay had to submit publicly in a ceremony filled with medieval melodrama. The priest was driven to the Los Angeles seminary, and before an audience of 200 priests—who were on spiritual retreat—he knelt before the Cardinal, renewed his vow of obedience, and kissed his ring. Then each of the 200 priests filed up to kiss the Cardinal's ring before filing into the dining room where they gave the Cardinal a thunderous ovation.

Aside from the nationwide indignation aroused by the Cardinal's high-handed decisions, there is a structural and moral irony. By tradition and teaching, the Church emphasizes the dignity of the individual and his inalienable rights as a creature made in the image and likeness of God. But not in the operation of its own ecclesiastical organization, particularly in the case of the army of priests serving as assistants in parishes. Out of the 2414 articles of canon law, only one is devoted to the assistant. There is no machinery safeguarding his individual rights.

In Los Angeles the diocesan statutes make lengthy statements about the obligations of assistants, and then dispose of their rights by declaring that they are entitled to one day off a week and three weeks' vacation, to be arranged at the convenience of the pastor. In Grand Rapids, Michigan, where a teen-age code imposes a midnight curfew, the curfew for junior clergy (ages twenty-five to forty) is eleven P.M. Pastors have the power to grant dispensations, though in general it is held that "no priest is doing the work of God after eleven in the evening."

In Los Angeles, where the Archbishop's reign has totalitarian dimensions, a reactionary extreme has been reached. Yet there are dioceses and archdioceses at the other end of the spectrum, like Chicago, where the late Albert Cardinal Meyer held a gentle and intelligent reign: priests could confront race and slum problems boldly; they could even picket the Illinois Club for Catholic Women for its refusal to admit Negroes. Ranging from the reactionary to the progressive, from the autocratic to the permissive, dioceses vary in administration and policy and also in their setting—from rural simplicity to urban complexity. The Dioceses of Baker City, Oregon, and Brooklyn, New York, epitomize this difference.

The Baker City Diocese, established in 1903, covers 66,000 square miles and embraces a population of 263,000 which is less than 10 percent Catholic (23,000). The rural diocese has twenty-nine parishes serving county seats and small trade centers. There are another thirty-four mission churches without resident pastors, and only two diocesan high schools and four elementary schools. The diocesan manpower consists of fifty-two priests, including five who belong to religious orders, and sixty-two nuns and five laymen who teach in the schools. The stable situation facing the diocese and the small proportion of Catholics (which is unlikely to change) require no variety of welfare services for an economy largely subsidized by the U.S. Department of Agriculture. A Catholic Rural Life Bureau runs the only social action program at the diocesan level.

By contrast the Brooklyn Diocese, dating from 1853, has one bishop with three auxiliary bishops; it covers a concentrated area of 179 square miles and embraces a population of 4.4 million which is about one-third Catholic (1.6 million). A total of 1271 priests, including 277 who belong to religious orders, serve 223 parishes with resident pastors. Another ten mission parishes have no resident pastors. There are four Catholic colleges, forty-six high schools, and 190 elementary schools, staffed by 178 priest-teachers, 486 brothers, 3363 nuns, and 2131 lay people.

As a segment of New York City, Brooklyn has a mixture of races and nationalities and a wide gamut of socioeconomic groups. Change bedevils such a diocese: neighborhoods rise and fall along with parishes; its residents are on the move economically, socially, and physically. Its problems are as fast-paced as the metropolis which surrounds it. Inevitably, social action and social welfare programs have become a central concern of the diocese, and administrative positions have multiplied. Programs like pre-Cana, Cana, and the Christian Family Movement are directed from a central office, as are activities that parallel the activities of the New York City government—radio and television programing, the Interracial Council, the extensive school department, a full-scale program of Catholic charities. Whereas 73 percent of the priests in Baker City hold more than one position in the diocese, only 15 percent of the Brooklyn priests double in brass. The larger and the more urban the diocese, the more specialization.[10]

Diocesan problems stem largely from bigness and the rapid changes in American life. The adjustments are slow. The bishop's traditional personalized role as shepherd of his flock is confronted by the modern impersonal pressures of a bureaucracy. An army of assistants stands between the urban shepherd and his flock, often obscuring rather than

clarifying his understanding of administrative problems.
Msgr. John J. Egan, director of the Office of Urban Affairs
of the Chicago Archdiocese, has remarked pointedly, "We
priests often fail to tell the truth to our bishops. We fail to
give them the unpleasant information they need to make
the right decisions."[11]

Behind the organizational façade, the operation remains
closer in spirit to a corner candy store than a corporation.
The colorful Cardinal Cushing of Boston is an example. He
is a generous and impulsive check writer for whatever cause
happens to come to his attention. These contributions follow no identifiable pattern or policy; no principle of priorities governs his generosity. No one asks whether the maximum good is being done for the maximum number. He is a
nineteenth-century philanthropist with deserved popularity, but he is a one-man show, taking in and giving out
about $20,000 a day. He has contributed $200,000 to reno-
vate the Church of the Holy Spirit in Pope John's home
town of Bergamo, $220,000 to build a cathedral for Laurian
Cardinal Rugambwa of Tanzania, and $1 million for Fu-jen
University in Formosa.

The structure of the American Church and its functioning need renovation and streamlining. In a succinct description of the situation, an anonymous writer in *Commonweal*
pointed out that the structure "is geared to a different age
and to different roles." The following points were made:

1) It [the Church] has disenfranchized the junior clergy and
laity; 2) disregarded canon law in regard to synods, deaneries,
visitation by bishops, availability of channels of communication
from the ground level up; 3) It has disregarded the basic common law, political consensus of Anglo-Saxon countries (and
even of canon law itself), in its removal of all checks and balances in the government of the Church, resulting in uncon-
trolled despotism and arbitrary rule by those possessed of authority within the Church; 4) has disregarded the notion of law
as an *ordinatio rationis,* and has instead substituted a foreign
idea, that law is an *ordinatio voluntatis,* with consequent ar-

rogance and disregard for the rights, not merely wishes, of those governed.[12]

Predictably, voices have been raised calling for a return to the "good old days." Bishop Fulton J. Sheen once thundered to a congregation of clerics, "For the love of Christ, stop being administrators and start being shepherds of Christ!" Soon after this challenging statement, Bishop Sheen himself demonstrated that he appreciated its impracticality. He left his teaching post at Catholic University and became an administrative auxiliary bishop in the chancery of the New York Archdiocese, to serve as director of the national office of the Society for the Propagation of the Faith.

The longing for a simpler past is heard more often in private conversations. For instance, one of the authors had a brunch appointment two years ago with the former secretary to a late Midwestern cardinal. The conversation with the monsignor, now pastor of a fashionable Detroit church, and a small group of clerics turned on the problem of coping with the breathtaking changes in the diocese. Finally the monsignor blurted out, "Well, when the religious all go back to emphasizing their community life, the pastors go back to dealing with their parishioners, and the teachers go back to their classrooms, the chancery offices and the bishops will be able to handle their dioceses."

However, the realistic solution appears to lie between the traditional role of the bishop as a solitary shepherd (an impossibility) and the emergence of an impersonal bureaucracy which supersedes the bishop. A complex and changing American society requires extensive Church machinery to cope with the social, political, economic, and technical as well as the spiritual. The inefficient trappings of bureaucracy can be converted into an efficient apparatus in which roles are clarified and power delegated. Specialization is inevitable, and lay professionals are necessary.

Along with a middle management in the Church which

would actually manage in the City of Man, the diocese can utilize sophisticated research methods and long-range planning. Central planning can go hand in hand with localized responsibility and leave intact the primary spiritual function of the bishop. After all, his power has a theological base which is independent of the administration of civil affairs; the bishop is a successor to the apostles in the Church as a religion, not as a bureaucracy. Rather than remove the bishop as shepherd, reforms and renovation would modernize his role as spiritual leader. He would then perhaps exercise less personal power, but he would be more effective as leader of the diocesan flock.

CHAPTER 8

◇◇◇◇◇◇◇◇◇◇◇◇◇◇◇◇◇◇◇◇◇◇◇◇◇◇◇◇◇◇◇◇◇◇◇◇◇◇◇

Islands in the Church

THE SILHOUETTE of the fortresslike monastery on the hill was visible from the low-lying exurban homes where the television sets were turned on. It was a little after nine o'clock on a December night, and one by one the lights had been going out in the monastery. But the large row of windows where Father Abbot lived were still brightly lit. Something was going on.

A summit meeting was taking place at the monastery. The Abbot, the highest spiritual authority in a monastery, had three visitors: the Prior, his chief administrative officer; the Economus, roughly the treasurer, who is in charge of temporal administration; and the Consultor, who is sometimes elected, sometimes appointed to represent the opinions of his fellow monks.

An informal night meeting was unusual, but a special problem had arisen over the new television set which had been given to the monastery by a brother of one of the monks. The problem centered around Perry Como and the Great Silence that is observed in the numerous religious communities following the Rule of Saint Benedict. Several monks wanted to watch Perry Como's pre-Christmas program, which had been filmed in the Holy City with the Sistine Choir, despite the fact that the program began at ten P.M.—one hour after compline (night prayer) and the beginning of the Great Silence.

A trivial problem? Not at all. It involved an ancient tradition which imposed the Great Silence to enable monks to concentrate on turning toward God. The aim is not a mechanical silence for its own sake, but a withdrawal for spiritual contemplation and heavenly communication. The TV problem intruded on the well-tended absorption of the monastery in its life of prayer and meditation.

In contemporary America, similar problems arise constantly in the lives of the 22,700 priests and 12,000 brothers who live out collective lives as members of religious orders and congregations. They are surrounded by a web of custom, rule, and regulation. In the monastery television case, the decision to turn on Perry Como was made after careful consideration, and carried the weight of centuries upon it. With every exception granted, the danger to the rule increases.

In each of some 125 religious orders and congregations for men in the United States, the routine and ideology are historically conditioned by a set of particular religious, historical, and social factors and by the personality of the charismatic founder. The religious orders are separate and distinct entities in the Church and technically are not under the jurisdiction of the local bishop, though they cooperate with him, of course, as highly specialized spiritual and temporal functionaries. Their line of authority runs directly to the Vatican and the pope, paralleling that of the bishop. In their multiple units spread throughout the continental United States, the religious orders and congregations are islands in the Church.

Historically, they developed as a division of labor was introduced into the early Church and as Christianity burgeoned from a self-centered sect into a world religion. A distinction arose between life in the world and life in religion, and a complex of problems and responsibilities had to be met. The religious orders arose as a series of responses to a series of historical challenges.[1] Three main historical developments have been involved, and they are still reflected in the adjustments being made by religious orders to the American situation.

In the beginning, during the first three centuries after Christ, Christians reacted to persecution by martyrdom, apostasy, or flight. The last response accounted for the emergence of the first monastic communities in the deserts of the Middle East. Flight to safety and away from the world became institutionalized in medieval communities in Europe. In the Egyptian desert, where Coptic Christians still maintain a primitive and elemental monasticism,[2] Saint Anthony, the father of monasticism, and Paul of Thebes, reputedly the first hermit, had their legendary meeting.

At this meeting, celebrated in medieval art, Paul is said to have asked Anthony, "Yet because love endureth all things, tell me, I pray thee, how fares the human race? Have new roofs risen in the ancient cities? Whose empire is it that now sways the world? And do any still survive snared in the error of the demons?" Such questions, in modern accents, might still be asked of a visitor to a Trappist monastery in Kentucky.

By the fourth century, both the Church of the East and the Church of the West were recognizing degrees of perfection in following Christ's footsteps. This gave rise to the second historical development—differing emphases on the various aspects of Christian life. Rejecting compromise with the temporal order, zealots and mystics withdrew from the City of Man to pursue perfection, or, as in the extreme case of Saint Simeon Stylites, to live atop a pillar in the city where the sinfulness of the world could be both resisted and denounced.[3]

A third development concerned emphasis on different aspects of dogma. Charismatic figures arose who felt that their fellow Christians were ignoring various biblical precepts or traditional teachings. They formed communities of men to follow their personal dogmatic orientations.

The religious orders were to the unified Church what sects were to Protestantism. They provided a safety valve for the rebel; instead of breaking away and forming his own church, he could form an order and remain within the Church. The founders of the orders were religious innovators who received recognition from Rome for their islands in the Church. Their rebellion was institutionalized.

In modern times the innovators have been replaced by administrators and organizers. No basically new religious group has appeared in Catholicism since the Jesuits were founded in 1534. In America the older forms of religious life have been transplanted and their fragments scattered across the continent, proliferating and reproducing a variety of religious bodies. No major figure has emerged in the history of religious orders and congregations in the United States, but many outstanding organizers have appeared, practical men in the American mode.

Because each religious community in America is still dominated by its roots, brief accounts of their histories will help explain their present temper, which ranges from the Jesuit "cult of obedience" to the Franciscan focus on poverty. Also, as the orders and communities cling to their origins while adapting to the contemporary, they reflect the tensions in the Church at large. Not even the silent Trappists completely turn their back on the world, particularly when America's most famous Trappist, Thomas Merton, writes best-selling books with the encouragement of his superiors.

The salient and abiding fact about religious orders and congregations is that they do not fade away.* They are both

---

* The terminology can be confusing. The all-inclusive term for orders and congregations is *religious institute.* In regular parlance all religious institutes are called *religious orders.* But according to canon law the term technically applies only to religious institutes in which members take solemn vows. Thus, properly speaking, the term *religious order* applies principally to the "old" orders of monks and friars, Canons Regular, and the Jesuits. See *A Catholic Dictionary,* ed. Donald Attwater, 3rd ed., New York, Macmillan, 1958.

self-perpetuating and self-centered, full of Balkan-like nationalism and just as fragmented. They flourish in contemporary America on a holy mixture of idealistic anachronism and practical opportunism—and also by dint of determined leadership and positive contributions to Church and country.

Their origins nonetheless hamper them, because they are rooted in a fixed point of history and yet must strive to keep up with the times. Two large divisions can be made: there are monastic and mendicant orders, each echoing a different historical period. The monastic orders, exemplifying retreat, hearken to a rural, agricultural society; indeed, some orders still help support themselves in America with agricultural income. The mendicant orders, reflecting the rise of cities, were formed to confront the world.

The two great figures of monasticism, honored both in memory and in practice, are Saint Benedict and Saint Augustine. The latter saw the sack of Rome in 410 as a sign of the new reign of Christ described in the Revelations of Saint John. He gathered priests around him and led them into a life of asceticism. The Rule of Saint Augustine has produced the constitutions of such orders as the Trinitarians, the Mercedarians, the Knights Hospitalers, and particularly the Order of Canons Regular. The last, who live a community life, undertake diocesan duties while remaining under the authority of their own superiors.

The master legislator of monasticism was Saint Benedict of Nursia, who created a basic model in the early sixth century that still dominates monastic life in the West. The Rule of Saint Benedict has been called "a monument of legislative art, remarkable alike for its completeness, its simplicity and its adaptability."[4] Moderation rather than asceticism fills the seventy-three chapters of its Rule, exemplified in Chapter 40: "We read, it is true, that wine is by no means a drink for monks; but since the monks of our day cannot be persuaded of this, let us at least agree to drink sparingly and not to satiety, because 'wine makes even the wise fall away.' "

The Rule's major characteristics, still operative, are those of the Roman *latefundia* (large estate) with its forms of extended kinship. It is literally familial, with the abbot as paterfamilias and the monks as his children. This has produced contemporary complications when administrative responsibilities are delegated. For instance, at one Benedictine college in the Midwest, the president found his authority undermined because the monks went to Father Abbot when they did not approve of his orders. The Benedictine style is still distinctly rural; at Saint John's, their college eighty miles northwest of Minneapolis, a herd of cattle roamed the campus until 1958, when it was discovered that the dairy operation was no longer profitable. The Benedictines, with 3200 members in the United States, are still locality-bound, with a basic commitment to their particular community rather than to the order.

Historically, Benedict was the first to codify and structure the evangelical counsels of poverty, chastity, and obedience into a way of life separate from the society at large. By the twelfth century, when 2000 Benedictine monasteries dotted Europe, reforms became necessary. They were first imposed by the Abbey of Cluny in France, and are reconfirmed among the Cistercians of the Stricter Observance, the well-known Trappists, who have nine abbeys in the United States. There are also two Benedictine archabbeys and twenty-eight Benedictine abbeys as well as a Cistercian and Praemonstratentian Abbey in this country—all direct descendants of the first Benedictine monastery at Monte Cassino.

The mendicant orders, which suited a changing society in the later Middle Ages, added a new dimension to monastic flight from the world. Service was added to separateness. Saint Dominic, founder of the Dominicans, and Saint Francis, founder of the Franciscans, grafted this dimension onto the rules of Augustine and Benedict. Feudal and agrarian society was giving way to the emerging bourgeoisie and city life. It was necessary to go out from the monastery walls to teach and preach.

Saint Dominic, originally a Canon Regular under the Rule of Saint Augustine, developed an elaborate, centralized organization committed to the work of conversion. It has been called the Order of Preachers, for it confronted the new learning of the thirteenth century and a restless, growing middle class. The Dominicans sought positions of prestige and influence in the new centers of learning, the universities. Dominic's most famous disciple, Saint Thomas Aquinas, rebelled against his family's intention that he become a Benedictine and eventually established the first chair of philosophy at the University of Paris. The 1500 Dominicans in the United States follow this tradition of learning, and are committed to the order as a whole rather than to an individual community. Unlike the Benedictines, their vow of obedience is to the general of the order instead of the abbot of a particular community.

The Franciscans also represent a departure from the feudalistic Benedictine approach with its economic base on the land and the fruits thereof. The Dominicans and Franciscans depend on alms or stipends given them for services rendered. Saint Francis, who personified medieval romanticism in his love affair with Lady Poverty, emphasized dependency on the generosity of others. He himself renounced his family wealth in imitation of the Gospel ideal, freeing himself to rebuild churches, preach, and lead a company of men in works of charity. The Franciscan observes "the holy Gospel of our Lord Jesus Christ by living in obedience, without goods, and in chastity."[5]

Today in the United States, the Franciscans have a highly differentiated enterprise. The Capuchins, one of several independent branches, have about 1000 priests and clerics (seminarians) in four provinces, a commissariat, and a custody, over half of them ethnically divided among German, Polish, and Italian groups. The Franciscan Fathers (the Order of Friars Minor), the largest and most complex branch, comprise six provinces, six commissariats, two custodies and two foundations, and consists of 2500 priests, 600 clerics and 700 brothers.[6] Their ethnic fragmentation includes groups of Italian, Croatian, Polish, and Spanish-Mexican extraction. Another 1,000 Franciscans in the Conventual branch bring the order's total membership to 6,000, second only to the Jesuits.

With the founding of the Jesuits, the circle was completed in the creation of religious orders. Organized as an army, mobile, flexible, and ready to carry out orders anywhere, the Jesuits were the opposite of the familial, stationary, other-worldly Benedictines. The head of the Jesuits is a commander in chief receiving policy directives from the pope and then commanding his army with full authority in the spiritual and temporal realm. As E. K. Francis has so well described them:

> The Jesuits are not so much brethren as comrades-at-arms, sometimes described as a corps of officers destined to lead the people's army of the militant church.
> It is this organizational aspect of the system which also seems to explain the great stress laid upon obedience and authority for, as the Weber school has pointed out, emphasis upon organization as against personal relations, together with the strictest disciplining and subordination under a central management are necessary correlates to individualization and a prerequisite for keeping a perfectly functioning machine, consisting of living, rational material coordinated in working conditions. Thus, simply viewed, the Jesuit Order reveals many of the characteristics commonly associated with modern, complex society which, like an army, industrial plant, or business corporation, requires rigorous conformity to rational norms of administration yet at the same time lays claim to the personalities of individual members only in so far as they serve the purpose of the institution.[7]

Distributed over eleven United States provinces, 8600

Jesuits constitute one-fourth of their order's worldwide strength. In this country, the Jesuits lead all religious orders in numbers of priests and in prestige.

The Jesuit ideology is manifestly in tune with pragmatic America. As Gustav Gundlach says, the Jesuits are ever willing "to adopt whatever appears valuable in the development of the human factor, regardless of any tradition to the contrary."[8] Their style was readily Americanized, and it is clear that all religious orders in the country are now undergoing a similar process of Americanization. The result is that the orders are becoming more alike in their activities, while obsessively clinging to their organizational independence.

Religious orders in the United States, a country that was itself missionary until the early part of the century, are engaged in missionary activities, each in its own fashion. The American bishops set up their own missionary enterprise in 1911, the Maryknoll Catholic Foreign Mission Society of America, Inc. Administered from Maryknoll at Ossining, New York, and incorporated under New York laws, Maryknoll sends missionaries to Africa, Bolivia, Formosa, Guatemala, Peru, Korea, the Philippines, Chile, Japan, Mexico, and even Italy. In founding Maryknoll the American bishops did not imitate Augustine, who gathered his clergy around him into an order; nor did they write a new rule. They modified the Dominican constitution, creating a hybrid religious order organized pragmatically for missionary activities.

Another order, the Friars Minor of the Franciscans, has traveled a long way from the simplicities of Saint Francis of Assisi with a corporate entity called Commissariats of the Holy Land. From bases in Washington, D.C., Oakland, and St. Louis, they gather money and manpower to preserve the holy places in Palestine. Others operating extensive mission undertakings include the American Redemptorists, the Society of the Divine Word, and the Oblates of Mary Immaculate.

The religious orders and congregations in America (aided by tax exemptions) have also been successful entrepreneurs. Drawing on traditional activities in printing and publishing and in education, they have built up sizable financial enterprises. Almost all colleges and universities, many high schools, and some elementary schools are owned and operated by religious orders. The Jesuits alone have twenty-eight colleges and universities and fifty-five high schools; the Franciscans have one university, twenty-four colleges, sixty-four schools of nursing, 280 high schools, and more than 1000 elementary schools. Among the orders of brothers, the Christian Brothers have eight colleges and sixty high schools, and the Xaverian Brothers twenty high schools.

The large majority of American orders is in the publishing business to some extent or other, accounting for the surfeit of more than 400 Catholic magazines. These publications, as well as pamphlets and books, either make profits in themselves or bring in revenues indirectly by attracting donations—a modern version of asking for alms.

The Paulist Order is the publishing giant of American Catholicism, with eleven different divisions. Through the Paulist Press, both distributor and publisher, the Paulists have an annual volume of 18 million pamphlets, books, and magazines. Their 54,000-square-foot plant in Glen Rock, New Jersey, maintains an inventory of more than 3.5 million books and pamphlets. A hardcover acquisition, the Newman Press, has 500 active titles and adds 50 a year. The Paulists publish three magazines: *Catholic World* (20,000 circulation), *Catholic Layman* (38,000 circulation),[9] and the *Ecumenist* (20,000 circulation).[10] Their Newman Bookshop in Maryland has built a huge mail-order business around a bimonthly catalogue mailed to 80,000 subscribers. They operate the Catholic Library Service, National Catholic Reading Distributors, and the American Library and Educational Service Company. Their media orientation is all-inclusive; they have also pioneered in religious broadcasting in both radio and television, eliciting the *Time* magazine comment, "Man for man, the 8,600 U.S. Jesuits probably have less influence than the 261 communications-minded Paulist fathers."[11] The successful American style of the Paulists reflects the spirit of their founding father, Isaac T. Hecker, a New Yorker converted from Protestantism. With their founding in 1858, the Paulists did not have to adjust to America; they were part of it.

Among the religious orders, a great deal of diversification is evident in the pursuit of economic opportunity wherever it arises. From New York to California, dozens of religious communities are mass-producing cheeses, wines, breads, jellies, and fruit cakes or selling beef on the hoof. In Washington, D.C., the Oblates of Mary even turn a profit by operating a golf course, while at Saint Benedict's Abbey near Aspen, Colorado, monks ride the range like cowboys, herding 500 cattle on a 3800-acre ranch.

Another fruitful union of religion and enterprise is the Christian Brothers' wineries, run by the order's Western Province in California's Napa Valley. Three wineries produce more than a million cases of wines and brandy a year, the virtual support of the entire province. The pride of the operation is a modern $7 million stainless steel grape-crushing machine, which was the first in the industry. In 1957 the brothers decided to pay full federal taxes, just like any other large American business.

The Trappists are another example, as described in *Time* in these terms:

As they rushed to finish a 38,000-lb. order of jelly for shipment to Chicago last week, the workers in the preserves factory outside Spencer, Mass., would have made any boss happy. They worked relentlessly, spoke not a word, took no coffee or cigarette breaks, smiled constantly. Occasionally, they glanced up at a sign that spurred them on even more: IT IS GOOD FOR US TO BE HERE. The contented workers were the Trappist monks of St. Joseph's Abbey, and their thriving jelly business (1,230,000 jars a year) is typical of a fascinating—and rapidly growing—

phenomenon: the successful business set up and run by a religious community.[12]

At Our Lady of Gethsemani Abbey near Bardstown, Kentucky, the Trappists have a flourishing mail-order business in cheeses, fruit cakes, hams, bacon, and summer sausage. And at the Abbey of the Genesee near Rochester, New York, the monks turn out a high-quality bread that is aggressively advertised in the New York subways (though the monks turned down one adman's slogan: "Baked in Silence. Too Good for Words."). The strictest of American orders, the Trappists observe perpetual silence, communicate only in sign language, abstain from meat, fish, and eggs, and have night office at two A.M. Exceptions to the rule of silence are made, however, for an abbey's selected monk-entrepreneur, a realistic relaxation arising from the worldly success of this most other-worldly of orders.

Probably more than any other factor, the demands for their religious services have blurred differences in the activities of religious orders. They are operating under a law of supply and demand, regardless of their original ideology. Several anomalies result. The liturgical lushness of the great Benedictine abbey is reduced to perfunctory service as an extra helper in a city parish. The celebrated preaching of the Dominicans appears in the routine annual mission in a city slum. The Franciscan friar pursues his Lady Poverty in an ornate gold and marble shrine where downtown shoppers tell their sins and leave their donations. The Jesuit becomes an organization man.

For many smaller orders—hybrid religious organizations founded in eighteenth- and nineteenth-century Europe—America was a land of opportunity that saved them from extinction. Their services were needed in new dioceses and among ethnic groups. The American bishops called upon them to work among the German immigrants and then the Poles and Italians, and now the newer unassimilated, the Puerto Ricans and Negroes, offer new opportunities. The

Josephites, with 235 priests, have set a laudable example of such work. A teaching order founded in Belgium in 1817, they came to America to adopt as missionary targets "the most abandoned works of God." True to this goal, they operate Negro missions in the South and in urban slums. Saint Augustine High School in New Orleans illustrates what they have accomplished without fanfare. An interracial faculty of thirty-one Josephites and 750 Negro students have developed an outstanding academic record. Only 5 percent of the students drop out, and three out of four graduates enter college; the June, 1964, graduating class won $100,000 in scholarships.

In missionary dioceses, priests from religious orders also rise to episcopacy. At present eight U.S. dioceses have members of religious orders as bishops: a Franciscan in Gallup, New Mexico; Redemptorists in Rapid City, North Dakota, and in Monterey-Fresno, California; a Jesuit in Fairbanks, Alaska; a Precious Blood missionary in Jefferson City, Missouri; a former member of the Congregation of the Holy Spirit in Covington, Kentucky; a Dominican in Des Moines, Iowa; and a Divine Word missionary in New Orleans.

Generally, a member of a religious order remains outside the hierarchical chain of command in the Catholic Church. A religious who becomes a bishop leaves a "staff" position that is in keeping with his commitment to his order and takes on a "line" position in the Church. He then steps outside the communal framework of his religious order. The conflict in style between living as a religious in community and living as a bishop in authoritarian isolation is illustrated by the case of a retired Jesuit bishop who returned to community life. In humility, he shed his red accouterments and wore the simple black cassock of his fellow Jesuits. But he soon faced a problem; he fell out with the superior of the community and constantly feuded with him. One day he quit the table in the middle of dinner after a particularly heated argument with the superior, leaving behind an embarrassed silence. Suddenly the bishop reappeared in full scarlet (which he never again discarded) and addressed the superior with hierarchical firmness: "Now, Father, what was that you were saying?"

The issue of authority and obedience is, in fact, the "iceberg" problem of religious orders. A few dramatic crises have appeared above the surface of a conforming exterior; underneath, the religious orders face their major American problem. The Roman focus on authority is confronting the American concern for personal responsibility, with the progressive and younger religious stressing the latter.

The confrontation was publicized particularly by the controversy over the exile to South America of the Jesuit poet Daniel J. Berrigan after he became prominent in the pacifist movement. It even broke the solid front normally maintained by the Jesuits. Several Jesuits in the New York area denounced their provincial's exercise of his authority over Father Berrigan by signing a protest advertisement in the Sunday *New York Times* of December 12, 1965. Among other things, the advertisement said that "the Roman Catholic manner of dealing with such a priest is not to debate him, not to offer alternative arguments, but simply to silence him and to send him to another country where his attempt to give Christian witness will not offend."

The context within which the vow of obedience operates is difficult to convey. The literature on religious life describes the religious superior as "a man who takes the place of God" and thereby gives rise to an intricate set of problems, pseudo-problems and medieval conundrums on the vow of obedience. The ramifications in the mentality of religious is well illustrated by questions which a single (September, 1963) issue of *Review for Religious* selected for authoritative answers:

We religious hold and instruct young subjects that our motive in obedience is to accept the will of the superior as the will of

God. But is this the motive of the vow of obedience, and shouldn't the vow be our motive?

It is part of the doctrine on religious obedience that the will of the superior is the will of God and that the superior represents and takes the place of God. What is the exact foundation of these statements?

May the superiors in our congregation of brothers give a precept that obliges from the vow of obedience but under venial, not mortal, sin?

If a precept in virtue of the vow of obedience is so rarely imposed, how does a religious ever obtain the merit of the vow of obedience?

Is there any system of checks and balances on the authority of a religious superior?

A religious is assigned a number of college subjects and classes that are overwhelmingly too much for him physically and emotionally, that frustrate good teaching, and make any extra reading, study, professional progress or publication impossible. I know that the religious may make the representation that he is overburdened, but can he be perfectly obedient and make a representation against the mediocre work that the assignment necessarily implies?

I have been teaching chemistry for more years than I should admit in this question. Before the advent of the leaden middle years, I acknowledged to myself that I had only average ability. But I do have that; I am neither retarded nor senile. Therefore, I know something about the efficient layout of a chemistry laboratory. A few times in my life someone in authority has indicated his preference for an arrangement in the laboratory that I was sure would be inefficient. Would it have been more perfect for me in these circumstances to have practiced blind obedience and to have omitted any representation?

Seen from within the closed circle of the religious order, these concerns are not outlandish, since the religious views every aspect of his life as an opportunity to work toward Christian perfection. Traditionally, in the lifelong imitation of Christ, unreasonable demands, harsh treatment, even nonsense have a place. They all can serve the function of providing a means of sacrifice, self-discipline, and suffering. What an outsider calls outrageous a religious may call an opportunity for sanctification. From such a supernatural reference point, a religious can focus on the other world and accept personal injustice in this one.

Meanwhile, in their pursuit of recruits, the religious orders sing a song of American salesmanship. The lyrics are written in the ecclesiastical purlieus of Madison Avenue, where the vocation's recruiter is the designated drum beater. He waits not upon the Holy Spirit to work in his mysterious ways to inspire vocations; he carries on a campaign of holy hard sell for his order. Some sample advertisements, a source of revenue to Catholic publications, are these:

FOLLOW THE LEADER, CHRIST

St. Francis did. YOU can. Be
a FRANCISCAN BROTHER and dedicate
your life to Christ in the service
of youth.[13]

BE A BROTHER

Growing New Order

Places for Writers, Typ-
ists, Cooks, Landscape,
Maintenance Men, etc.
What is your knack?
Write today!
BROTHERS OF ST. JOSEPH[14]

THERE'S NO GIMMICK!

Learn how PAULINE PRIESTS AND
BROTHERS are preaching "glad
tidings of good things"
through mass communications.
Their pulpits are editorial
desks, composing benches, drawing boards, darkroom sinks, and
presses.[15]

COLUMBAN FATHERS

. . . are exclusively foreign missionaries bringing Christ to God's most neglected children throughout the world. More Columban Fathers are needed. If you are interested in this glorious work for Christ, write for information. No obligation.[16]

DON BOSCO'S SALESIANS

Work with Boys	Boys' Schools
As a Salesian	Boys' Clubs
	Boys' Camps
Priest or Brother	Foreign Missions

Lacking in Latin?   Specially designed make-up courses in Latin available for high school graduates.   G.I. Approval.[17]

THE HOLY CROSS FATHERS

Invite and welcome alert, apostolic young men to become high school and college teachers, retreat masters, shapers of an apostolic laity, missioners in Uganda, Pakistan, Peru. VISIT OUR SEMINARY ANY WEEKEND.[18]

Some of the world's best young men will answer this ad. . . . They're in their 'teens right now, just beginning to wonder about the great big world opening up to them in the years just ahead.

They're capable, ambitious, generous and they want a really big challenge to match their generosity.

Deep inside they know that the most important job in the world is doing Christ's work . . . bigger even than space and missiles and shooting the moon.

These are the young men
who will respond to Christ's
call to serve Him as a Conventual Franciscan priest
or brother. . . .[19]

Boys—
Young Men

If you are seeking a life of complete
dedication to God—THE MOST HOLY TRINITY;
If you are attracted to both the contemplative
and active life, then write and arrange a week-end
or one day visit with us. See the life of a Trinitarian
first hand.[20]

Chal-
lenge

teacher
missionary
parish priest
hard work
long hours
no pay
Basilian Fathers[21]

In competing for recruits and for success in America, the
religious orders are sensitive to their image and relative
prestige among American Catholics. Spoofing banter and
friendly rivalries soften—but do not conceal—the sharp edge
of competition among the orders and a certain condescen-
sion toward the secular parish priest. One example of in-
group humor is the story told publicly by Rev. Vincent
Yzermans, information director for the National Catholic
Welfare Conference. He described a medieval nativity scene
with monks and friars standing around the crèche and com-
menting in the following ways: "The solicitous Franciscan
asked Mary if the Child was warm enough. The liturgi-
cally punctilious Benedictine expressed concern that He
was not facing the people. The Jesuit presented her with an
application form for the order's Georgetown University."
Father Yzermans told of repeating the story to the late Fa-

ther Gustave Weigel, the renowned Jesuit, who added a postscript: "It doesn't ring true. In the first place there would be two Jesuits—we don't work singly. And the second Jesuit would surely point out to his confrère that the family didn't look like the kind which could afford the tuition."[22]

The best clues to sources of prestige can be found in the high-prestige Jesuits. They draw on a distinguished tradition, require the longest training period (fifteen years), and set lofty intellectual goals. Each Jesuit, while trained to operate on his own, has a military *esprit de corps,* and his order has organizational strength. Moreover, the Jesuits are action-oriented and dominant in higher education; both these factors feed into the American value and status system.

The Trappists, at the opposite pole in orientation, also enjoy high prestige, for they project an undiluted image of contemplation and removal from the world. The severity of their religious lives, particularly their silence, has captured the imagination of American Catholics. For a middle-class American, the very difficulty of being a Trappist constitutes a source of admiration.

Orders which function between total action and total contemplation have less prestige. The Dominicans have an intellectual image but also a "holy aloofness" which makes it difficult for them to make an impact. The Franciscans and Capuchins, more committed to action, have less of an intellectual image. They also suffer from the fact that their great intellectual leaders have never had the political favor in the official Church that is enjoyed by Saint Thomas for the Dominicans and Suárez and Bellarmine for the Jesuits.

The religious orders of brothers are handicapped by the fact that their members are not priests and by a limited intellectual tradition. Their breathless pursuit of higher education for their members is an attempt to compensate for this deficiency. Missionary orders are limited by their service to the lower classes and ethnic groups. Religious clientele is important to the image of an order, as well as strength of numbers and financial resources.

Many in number and small in membership, the Balkanized missionary orders account for the multiplicity of some 125 religious orders for men in the United States. Examples are the Pious Society of the Missionaries of Saint Charles (eighty-one priests), the Consolata Fathers (twenty-two priests), the Xaverian Missionary Fathers (twenty-five priests), the Paris Foreign Mission Society (three priests), the Society of Bethlehem Missionaries (sixteen priests), the Sons of Mary, Dedicated to Our Lady, Health of the Sick (fifteen priests), the Mekhitarist Congregation of Vienna (four priests), the Congregation of Saint Joseph (twelve priests), and the Society of Saint Paul for the Apostolate of Communications (five priests).*

In the fall of 1965, the Second Vatican Council, in effect, put such marginal orders on notice. The Council decree, "On the Adaptation and Renewal of the Religious Life," warned that religious orders may be judged "not to possess reasonable hope for further development" and "be forbidden to receive novices in the future." They then might be "combined" with "flourishing" orders.

The Maryknoll missionaries, with over 900 priests, enjoy high prestige because they have the financial and organizational backing of the American hierarchy. They also have mastered public relations and mass media techniques, projecting a glamorized role of the missionary with the accent on action and adventure.

It's a long way from the time of Pachomius, who left a sinful world in the fourth century to live in the desert, to the time of religious entrepreneurs and promoters in the affluent society of America. It's a strange thing to see religious orders rooted in history sway like reeds in the winds of change. And it's a strenuous exercise for religious orders to

* The membership figures are those in 1964.

retain their identity and their particular ethos and also keep up with the competition as well as the times. Father Abbot pondering the threat of television to the Great Silence is a reminder that separation and service, which formed religious orders and congregations in Europe, are being redefined in America.

CHAPTER 9

◇◇◇◇◇◇◇◇◇◇◇◇◇◇◇◇◇◇◇◇◇◇◇◇◇◇◇◇◇◇◇◇

Brides of Christ

As SUSAN ENTERED George's Restaurant in the East Bronx section of New York City, she expected to have a farewell dinner with a handful of girl friends who had stayed in touch since Rosary High School days. A few diners who looked up noticed a pretty young thing of the usual garden variety that fills New York offices. Twenty-two, modestly dressed, well proportioned, as fresh as a newly cut flower, Susan was also what the boys from Manhattan and Fordham Colleges call a BIC, for Bronx Irish Catholic—outgoing but clannish, approachable but prudish, usually wearing a ribbon in her hair and a bulky knit sweater. The good sisters have placed all BICS on constant alert against the male animal.

Once inside the restaurant, Susan was ushered into a private dining room where eighty guests were waiting. It was a surprise shower. A corsage of roses was pinned on Susan, well-wishers surged around her, champagne corks popped. Waitresses frantically filled glasses in assembly-line fashion so everyone could join in a toast. The deafening girlish glee was interrupted by the only man in the room, Father Gerard, a handsome young priest who was a favorite of the parish girls. He boomed forth, in a mixture of pulpit and party tones, "To Susan. With all love and best wishes for your happiness. And may your first mission be to Daytona Beach."

Then the guests plunged into a buffet universe of baked ham, roast beef, turkey, chicken, meat balls, salad, vegetables, hot rolls, and baked Alaska. They clustered at tables, eating and chattering: Susan's young girl friends, older relatives, two sisters from Rosary High School, and Father Gerard. Only Susan's mother couldn't eat for her tears. As one of the girls played the piano, the guests switched from eating and talking to group singing, and just as abruptly to dancing. A Beatles record started off a rock-'n'-roll melee of girl couples dancing the chicken, the favorite at the time.

By eleven the older women, the two nuns, and Father Gerard had faded away, but the dancing went on until midnight. Then a few close friends walked Susan home. She was happy. She was about to fulfill a long-standing dream that had been postponed because as the oldest of six children she had had to work after graduating from high school in order to help support her family. She worked four years for an oil company, took night courses at Hunter College, and enjoyed her many girl friends but seldom dated a boy alone. Our friendly informant (who recounted the evening play-by-play) remarked that the sentimentality which everyone expected was absent. Susan was high-spirited as usual and excited about the coming days. She was about to become a bride—a bride of Christ.

Then why not a shower? In social terms it has become an inevitable American consequence of the bride-of-Christ tradition, which is institutionalized down to the wedding band worn by nuns and sisters.* While theologians may wince, modernists growl, and Freudians smile, the bride mystique permeates a woman's life in religion in America. Not surprisingly, an embarrassing literature has sentimentalized and romanticized a medieval metaphor into a literal

* We are using the terms *nun* and *sister* interchangeably as in popular usage, though there is a canonical difference. Nuns take solemn vows; sisters take simple vows. Nuns may be further divided according to whether they follow a contemplative or active life.

description of the nun's life. In one characteristic example, from a 1956 collection of nuns' autobiographies called *A Seal upon My Heart,* a Sister of Mercy of the Union in effect describes the point underlined in the book's introduction by a priest who should know better. Writing of the decision to love and serve God by becoming a bride of Christ, the priest states:

> These ideas are not mere figures of speech or poetic expressions. They are realities. For in the beautifully impressive ritual of Reception most communities dress the girl in a bridal gown. She then comes up the aisle of the convent chapel and kneels before God's representative at the altar. There she pledges her heart, mind and whole being irrevocably to Christ. Henceforth she belongs entirely to Him and wears His ring.
> The only hard part of all this is that sister does not see her Beloved face to face.[1]

As the sister describes her own "marriage," she sounds like a Catholic marriage manual:

> I think you would like to know, now, how this marriage has lasted, how it has stood up under the years. Has it held the level of high romance, or has it broken down under the strain of monotonous living? I can answer that one. Because I am a teacher and have never experienced two identical days in a row, I don't know the meaning of monotony. But to judge the durability of my romance, I ask you to look at any happily married couple in the world. What do you think has happened to their love over a period of time? Do you think anyone, even they themselves, can tell you how it has grown and deepened? When and where? Always, everywhere, silently and imperceptibly, their love has grown richer with knowledge, deeper with suffering. . . .
> So it is with the divine romance—growth in knowledge and a quiet, steady advance in love. The bride of this union must suffer too, because her Spouse has suffered. She must share with Him her joys and sorrows, her triumphs and her failures; she must become one with Him in love.
> When I started out with my tremendous Lover, I had yet to learn that love is not so much receiving as giving, not so much possessing as being possessed. . . .[2]

Meanwhile, the public image of the nun has been embellished by the ball-playing, jeep-driving, folksinging nun. (An item in the June 19, 1965, *New Yorker* magazine says, "St. Francis High School of Little Falls, Minnesota, has a choral group of ten nuns who call themselves the Hootenunnies.") From movies like *The Bells of Saint Mary's* to programs like the *Ed Sullivan Show,* the life of women religious emerges looking like a sanctified version of life with the Andy Hardy family. Behind the forbidding black-and-white paraphernalia nuns became "regular" American girls, and this almost passed for modernization.

In recent years, a ferment characterized by realism and intelligence has overtaken the lives of women religious in America. It is accompanied by considerable self-doubt, criticism, uncertainty, and in many cases emotional crisis. The ferment is particularly evident in differences between the older and younger generations of nuns, which are close to the surface within each convent. This was confirmed at first hand when one of us discussed the main points in this chapter before gatherings of three orders of nuns. Arguments between the generations are easy to provoke, as are both angry blame and enthusiastic praise.* Three of the responses to a 1965 poll of 1000 sisters among *Jubilee* magazine subscribers reflect the changing times.

Said a Benedictine nun, age fifty-nine: "I can't understand why so many religious are leaving convents. Doesn't the love of Christ satisfy them?"

Said a Visitation sister, age thirty-eight: "I am rather bothered by the vocational literature which is being put out; it is a little unrealistic. But then, a camera cannot capture the real soul-suffering that goes on within the privacy of the soul of every sister. True, Christ is her spouse, but this is a strictly spiritual relationship."

---

* The authors' article "The American Nun: Poor, Chaste, and Restive," *Harper's Magazine,* August, 1965, roused vehement comments pro and con. The article was an earlier version of the present chapter.

Said another Benedictine nun, age twenty-four: "There are many tensions in religious life today. I am well aware of these. Because I was one of the early members of the 'new breed,' my superiors were unaware of the special problems this group faces. The spirituality imposed upon me did not allow me to express in myself the wonders of God's plan. Hence conflict. Through the love and understanding of a wonderful mother superior and the professional help of a psychologist I have been led to a new appreciation of religious life which allows me to take the best of both old and new."[3]

Joseph Cardinal Ritter of Saint Louis commented on the widespread re-examination of a nun's life in America in his 1964 introduction to *Sisters for the Twenty-First Century* by Sister Bertrande Meyers. The Cardinal spoke for the enlightened segment of the Church establishment:

The criticisms which have been lodged against women religious over the past months have largely been grounded upon fact. And yet, in the context of the vast renewal programs undertaken by religious Communities, they scarcely have been just. Whatever their purpose, many Nuns and Sisters, precisely because of their own sense of fairness and humility, have come to doubt their usefulness in and to the Church. Young girls, possibly the religious of tomorrow, influenced by these criticisms, have mistrusted their own sense of vocation; many others have been advised that a more effective apostolate is open to them in the lay state.

Sister Bertrande's book will leave no doubt about the need for women religious in the Church. While it does not pretend that Christian perfection can be found only in the religious life, it does succeed in showing that the religious life is the most effective means of achieving perfection in charity and loving service toward God and the neighbor. In this respect, it is an eminent commentary on the words of Pope Pius XII: "The apostolate of the Church is almost inconceivable without the help of religious women."[4]

The significant criticisms center on the competence of nuns in their main areas of activity—teaching, nursing, and social welfare—and on the relevance of their lives to the modern world. Undoubtedly, in her day the old-fashioned nun made a major contribution to the Catholic enterprise in America. Undertrained and overworked though they were, sisters processed hundreds of thousands of Catholic school children; without them parish schools would have remained a gleam in pastors' eyes. But it became uncomfortably obvious in the postwar years that good intentions were scarcely enough.

Leading sister-educators took the initiative in evaluating the situation and prospects of women religious. Their nationwide survey in 1952 found that only thirteen of 255 orders responding had programs which enabled their members to get bachelor's degrees. And 118 orders admitted in effect that they could not educate their members if they wanted to. They had neither educational facilities of their own nor easy access to facilities in Catholic colleges.[5]

The mentality with which nuns have been imbued in the past has also been questioned, increasing the skepticism about their relevance. They have been charged with isolation from the real world of real problems. Collective self-doubt reached crucial proportions when one of the most enlightened and influential princes of the Church, Leon Joseph Cardinal Suenens of Belgium, wrote *The Nun in the World.* Running through the book, which has been taken up enthusiastically by progressive nuns in America, are criticisms better cited by a cardinal:

Religious too often seem to be living in a closed world, turned in on themselves and having but tenuous contact with the world outside.

A community of nuns often gives the impression of being a fortress whose drawbridge is only furtively and fearfully lowered. . . .

Again, physical and psychological detachment from the world leads a religious to turn in on herself and her own community. Her world shrinks, and, if she is not careful, will end up no more than a few square yards in size. From this comes a dis-torted vision, seeing everything from one angle, measuring things against a diminished scale. From this comes also the contrived and artificial nature of certain customs in religious houses—a sort of "house etiquette," a stilted, stereotyped and unnatural behaviour. It has been said of certain congregations of nuns that they are the last stronghold of the very studied manners of the middle-class woman of the nineteenth century. . . .

An observer analyzing the part played by religious today cannot help being struck by their absence from the main spheres of influence at adult levels, spheres where they have a right to be and where their talents are called for and their presence is needed. . . .

The religious of today appears to the faithful to be out of touch with the world as it is, an anachronism.[6]

An American nun, responding to the charge of irrelevance, has summed up the problem. Writing in *The National Catholic Reporter*'s influential "Sisters' Forum," Sister Charles Borromeo stated, "I would like to accept the judgment that we are increasingly irrelevant in modern America to the extent that we cling blindly to old forms and old psychological patterns." She added a recognizable description of the old-fashioned nun: "Rigidity of gesture, the extremely soft voice, the posture of cringing before authority figures imply that vigor and vitality are somehow pagan or corrupting."[7]

Women in religion have thus been called upon, by themselves and others, to confront contemporary challenges. In America particularly, this means meeting the performance standards of the American school, hospital, and charitable agency. Involved are more than 180,000 American women in no less than 480 orders of nuns and sisters, from A (for Adoratrices, with fourteen American members) to Z (for Zelatrices, with 294 American members). The proliferation —about four times as great as among men's orders—reflects a penchant for forming religious organizations with differences in style but not in substance. This has been a peculiarly feminine touch in the history of Church families and is a reminder that a discussion of women religious is all about women. The redundancy points to the problems surrounding their life in religion.

Women religious are trying to establish a modernized role in contemporary society within restrictions imposed on them by a traditional Church society where men have always dominated. It is a hazardous accommodation precisely because women are second-class citizens in the Catholic Church. (As in American society at large, the Church's two downtrodden minorities are Negroes and women.) The Vatican Council itself dramatized their secondary status by excluding them from its deliberations, thus ignoring thousands of nuns and millions of laywomen. Only belatedly a handful of voteless woman auditors, both lay and religious, were added. Moreover, the Sacred Congregation of Religious, which is responsible for the rules and regulations governing women's orders, does not even have a nun as an adviser.*

Within this context, American nuns are attempting to repeat the emancipation process undertaken by American women in the early twentieth century. They are becoming involved in social protest. (When nuns sang "We Shall Overcome" on the civil rights picket line in Selma, Alabama, their spirit belonged to Susan B. Anthony as well as Martin Luther King.) They are taking a major step by stressing education and by acquiring professional qualifications. In this sense the Sister Formation Movement, organized in 1954, is a feminist campaign designed to increase the educational training of nuns and guarantee their professional standing.

* At the annual meeting of the Conference of Major Superiors of Religious Women in Denver in August, 1965, a petition to the Vatican was unanimously adopted, "earnestly request[ing] that Sisters be asked to serve as permanent consultative or acting members" of the Sacred Congregation for Religious and other Church bodies governing the lives of nuns (see Rev. Vincent Lovett, "Nuns Ask Voice in Church Bodies," *The National Catholic Reporter,* September 1, 1965, p. 1).

The campaign is arduous, for American nuns belong to religious bodies which have institutionalized the secondary status of women. Historical origins are not easily cast aside, for women's orders were formed as subsidiaries of men's. In a spiritual analogy, religious—men and women—were joined together in God's service. Among the older orders, this was brought about through close personal ties between the founder of a male order and the foundress of the counterpart women's order, like the relationship between Saint Benedict and Saint Scholastica, between Saint Francis of Assisi and Saint Clare. Today as in the past, the work of women religious is primarily among the young, the sick, and the elderly, a historical extension of woman's traditional role.

Saint Vincent de Paul and Saint Louise de Marillac tore down the convent walls around nuns in the seventeenth century, making "their chapel the parish church, their cloister the streets of the city or wards of the hospitals." The result was the Daughters of Charity, the Church's first uncloistered community for women and now its largest order. In the United States today these nuns engage in all the activities of women religious: elementary, high school, and college teaching; nursing, and running schools of nursing; managing homes for children, working girls, and unmarried mothers; taking care of the aged; organizing day nurseries and centers for child guidance, social work, and catechetics; giving retreats; working on home and foreign missions.

But the seventeenth-century problem of the cloister, which cut the nun off physically from a needy world, has been replaced by the twentieth-century problem of enclosure, which cuts her off psychologically from the real world. The modern nun can leave the cloister to teach, nurse, do welfare work, or even shop, but she is still bound by a restricted and tightly regulated round of duties centered in the convent. She is not only wrapped in a religious costume as modern as a suit of armor; she is entangled in myriad rules, regulations, and restrictions of staggering pettiness. Like the child whose interfering parent wants to govern every part of her life, the nun must fight for maturity. Yet many nuns still defend such rules as safeguarding the spirit of the foundress, though this is as alien to the American spirit as housekeeping the way grandmother did.

In a collection of essays about convent life, one nun went so far as to call the petty differences between communities "wholesome signs, indicating a noble ideal." Yet read her account of what would happen if Mrs. X took a group of sisters from different orders on an afternoon outing, a description typifying the entangling web of regulations which women religious must follow:

> Sister A may go for the ride, but she can't get out of the car or eat an ice-cream cone on the way. Sister B may go for the ride and get out of the car, but refreshments are taboo. Sister C may go for the ride and have her ice cream, but all within the sanctuary of the car. Sister D may go for the ride, get out of the car, and eat the ice-cream cone. She may even name her own flavor if Mrs. X isn't a dictator. Sister E? She may come out to the car and wave goodbye to the others.[8]

No doubt it is natural to accept as necessary and unchangeable what has always been there, particularly after women religious have spent years in servitude to triviality. On the level of professional service, the negative results are obvious. Time-bound by an *horarium* (an all-embracing schedule of daily activities), sisters are prevented from carrying on the very life of service to which they commit themselves. Sister-teachers find it almost impossible to see parents of their pupils, much less visit homes, since the hours when parents are freest are the same hours when sisters are confined to their convents. Some nursing sisters with habits covering their ears are hardly able to take blood pressure readings or listen to the fetal heart.

Nuns are severely restricted in opportunities to enlarge their horizons, to learn, and to gain first-hand contact with the world of the laity whom they serve. When sisters do get permission nowadays to attend meetings, lectures, and conventions, it is with hampering limitations and usually within the protective Catholic environment. Moreover, the nun is cut off from friendships, contacts, and adult experiences outside her convent. As Sister Charles Borromeo points out, "Genuine friendships with other adults, as well as necessary professional involvements as an individual, are still comparatively rare."[9] Undoubtedly, the demands of enclosure within community life suffocate the typical nun.

Another pressure, obscured from the outsider, is the problem of gossip within the convent. It is the daily danger to harmony, nurtured by the close-knit and segregated communal life of many women under one roof. A nun–social scientist underlined this point in discussing convent life: "The cardinal sin of religious women is lack of charity of the tongue. It is more serious and more frequent than any other failing, causing more upsets in communities than any of the vows."

The outsider can only sense the impact of the system upon the individual religious, who is not automatically a smiling, mindless member of the stereotyped convent of Andy Hardy. Here is what a sister of thirty years' standing said of her life in religion, and it is a sobering contrast with the gushing account of the nun's "marriage" quoted previously:

We used to answer the Chapel bell at four o'clock each afternoon after school. We had a full forty-five minutes of vocal prayer, litanies and novenas, followed by a half-hour of meditation. Most of us were so dead tired after forty-five minutes of vocal prayer that we slept during meditation, or sat there dazed, unable to drum up a single reflection or affection. This was changed in 1953 to just a half-hour of mental prayer with all vocal prayer eliminated, and now it's a joy to answer the bell for Chapel—I come out feeling like a new person.

If only we'd go the whole way on *aggiornamento!* In the morning I drag myself out of bed too tired to think. I get down to the Chapel where we say Matins and Lauds, followed by a half-hour of mental prayer and twenty minutes of vocal prayers for the Church, the Community and benefactors, and then Mass starts. By Communion time I'm lost in frustration because I can feel no fervor—only fatigue. Sometimes I kneel at the Communion railing wondering if I can possibly please God feeling as I do. Then we go to breakfast and are served in rank. Since I'm near the end of my particular table, I'm served near the last, and I practically choke with smoldering resentment—and yes, let me be honest—with scruples because I'm in such a bad humor every morning. Yet, I love to pray. What a joy and peace it would be if we just had meditation as a preparation for Mass. I could sing aloud with the best of them or join in hearty dialogue at Mass in all the glory of the new liturgy.[10]

The personality consequences of such a life can be serious, as is evident in the widespread concern over mental illness among women religious. Sympathetic priests commonly encounter troubled sisters who are torn by tensions, conflicts of conscience, and doubts about the meaningfulness of their lives. Dr. John B. Wain, a Catholic physician with extensive experience treating religious, has cited his "clinical impressions" in a penetrating article for the *Review for Religious*. He presents two generalizations based on his practice and on conversations with Catholic doctors and religious nurses: "First, there is too much neurosis among religious. Second, much of it is avoidable or preventable."[11] No realistic observer close to the situation would disagree.

In a unique attempt to document the national contours of the problem, Sister Mary William Kelley, I.H.M., collected data in 1956 on the hospitalization of sisters for mental illness. In the process, she often encountered a medieval secretiveness; the main religious mental hospitals refused to cooperate, making it necessary to interpolate the statistics in order to include them. Sister found that religious had a higher incidence of both psychotic disorders (particularly schizophrenia) and psychoneurotic disorders than American women in general. Overall the religious had a lower rate of mental illness, but this finding was qualified because mental defectives are excluded in the first place and a nun's life steers her away from certain types of brain disorders, like those due to alcoholism.[12]

By comparing her 1956 study with a similar one made in 1936,[13] Sister Mary William found two disturbing trends. The rate of hospitalization of nuns for mental illness increased substantially, from 485 per 100,000 to 595, narrowing the difference between laywomen and sisters. Second, while the rate for the small minority of cloistered nuns remained greater than for active nuns, that difference had also narrowed. In fact, the rate for active nuns had increased, while it had decreased for cloistered nuns.

This led Sister Mary William to make several likely hypotheses which underscore the tension between the traditional and the modern, between the status quo and the drive to professionalize nuns within a religious context that is still hidebound and slow to change. As sources of greater stress that may be contributing to greater numbers of mental breakdowns she cites overcrowded classrooms, understaffed hospitals, accreditation demands, and various other professional pressures facing religious today. Yesterday such strains were not nearly so severe and yesterday's personal resources might have been enough to confront them. Today the figures on increasing mental illness strongly suggest that the system must be adjusted and that applicants for religious life must be better screened in the first place.[14]

Both recommendations are made by psychologists familiar with religious life in America. In the first place, as was indicated in the 1936 study particularly, many prepsychotic personalities are attracted to the religious life for what they think it will offer them. Indeed, a historical review of mysticism by Father Herbert Thurston, S.J., concludes that numbers of the Church's saints and stigmatics were neurotics.[15] The answer to this aspect of the problem is psychological examination of applicants for religious orders, a practice that fortunately is spreading.

A leading practitioner in the field, Walter J. Coville of Saint Vincent's Hospital in New York City, pointed out the importance of psychological testing before the 1964 convention of the National Catholic Educational Association.[16] He warned that the traditional criteria for identifying promising applicants can be misleading, "for what often appears to be a virtue may actually be a neurosis." He cited those candidates "who conspicuously reveal themselves as docile, self-effacing, eager to comply, pious and humble, but who actually are passive-dependent personality types." Insecure, filled with anxieties, eager to avoid responsibility, such people seek a neurotic escape into the religious life for shelter and support. Another type cited by Dr. Coville is the ambitious candidate who "needs to find status and recognition, and who may unwittingly exploit others for his own benefit." His sobering caveat raises chilling speculation on how many examples of both types have been admitted to the religious life in America. And how many have reached positions of importance because neurotic traits were interpreted as virtues?

The situation is complicated by the patterns of recruiting for the religious life. The decision to become a sister is usually made during the teen years, commonly under the influence and inspiration of teaching sisters in high school. This magnifies the danger of unrealistic and immature decisions. In a study of 2120 sisters entering the convent between 1885 and 1943, Bishop John Hagan found that the largest number (507) first thought of the convent at the age of ten, with the largest number (315) making the final decision at eighteen. The median age for entering the convent was nineteen.[17]

The sisters replying to the *Jubilee* survey underlined the point. Of 384 replying, 235 entered the convent in their teens; the largest number, ninety-six, joined at eighteen.

Another one-third joined in their twenties, and a handful after that. As noted by a twenty-eight-year-old sister who teaches high school,

> The greatest impetus to vocations is the personal witness of the individual sister. Girls are attracted or repelled by the truth they see in the lives of the sisters who teach them. High school girls are attracted to the younger religious, not simply because they are younger but because they are more alive to the currents of the age. There is a pattern in our high schools showing that vocations are forthcoming from the schools with young faculties.[18]

Once a young woman has joined an order, she is absorbed into the life of her religious community. Her training has military overtones; indeed, the famous sister formation school near Saint Louis, Marillac College, is deliberately patterned after the American military academies. The training program is designed to bring about total commitment to the religious order, with a result that has been called *depersonalization*. A more constructive and promising label is *formation* of the entire personality.

First as a postulant for one to three years, depending on the order, and then as a novice for one or more years, the young woman is under the strict control of mistresses of postulants and novices. These nuns are all-important, for they influence generations of new religious and establish lifetime patterns. They can break the spirits of postulants and novices, stifle their zeal, and fill them with negative attitudes. Or they can inspire them to heights of personal dignity and fulfillment. The selection of these mistresses, often made indifferently, is crucial to the future of religious orders in America.

After the training period, the young woman takes her vows publicly before her religious community; they are usually temporary vows, to be followed at a later date by permanent ones. At this point she has formalized her triple commitment to poverty, chastity, and obedience, the three duties around which her entire career in religion will re-volve—for better or worse.

The vows impose responsibilities in two directions, though the traditionalists think only in terms of observance by the sisters: the religious system also has the obligation of providing a framework for the healthy fulfillment of the promises. Yet, despite the admonitions of psychologists, maladjustment and neurotic behavior are commonly blamed on a poor spiritual life, and a more intense spiritual life is regarded as a panacea. When a religious superior can-not answer the objections of a sister who finds a situation, an order, or a rule opposed to both common sense and intelli-gence, the final retort is, "Pray, Sister, pray."

Unintelligent, incompetent, and wrongheaded superiors employ an ultimate tactic that cannot be coped with ra-tionally, though as administrators they confront rational, increasingly professional sisters in the ranks. They hide be-hind the Holy Spirit and make him supernatural partner to natural mistakes. As one sister has written, "In efforts to change, one encounters the 'myth' that all authority comes from God. A sort of magical interpretation has been put on this principle, back of which was a lurking dishonesty, be-cause political strategy has not been unknown in the best religious families."[19]

Of the three vows, that of poverty is the least misused in America. In Europe it is common to confuse frugality with chill penury, poverty with degrading and unhealthy living conditions. Nonetheless, the lingering presence of begging sisters and the continued risk of tuberculosis among young religious indicate that there is room for American improve-ment. Regarding the other two vows, chastity is widely dis-torted and obedience commonly misunderstood.

The difference between the older and younger genera-tions of nuns is sharply illustrated by attitudes on chastity. Memories of parochial school, where adult Catholics have had their main contact with nuns, are mingled with resentment among many educated Catholic women who remember the obsession with chastity—or rather with sex. A typical recollection, by a professional woman now working with coeds on a Catholic campus, concerns an eighth-grade nun-teacher who introduced her to "dirty thoughts" by preaching so zealously and with such detail that she in effect gave lessons on sexual fantasies. Her former pupil comments, "I didn't even know how to have dirty thoughts until Sister started to carry on about them. It's hard now to escape feeling that the poor thing didn't realize it, but she was undoubtedly enjoying it all."

Today the same woman encounters coeds arriving from Catholic high schools on the eastern seaboard bringing hangover sex advice that taxes credulity. Fortunately, with their early sophistication, the girls do not take the advice seriously, and in fact they hold "Can you top this?" gabfests in which they exchange examples of bizarre warnings about sex, invariably given by the older generation of nuns. Here are examples collected from the 1964 coed freshmen: "Don't wear patent-leather shoes, else men see your underwear reflected in them." "Beware of men who lurk by stairways in order to stare up at you." "White reminds men of bed sheets." "Put talcum powder in your bath so your body won't be reflected in the water."

Other signs of the prudery which has contaminated the vow of chastity are hidden behind convent walls. Catholic doctors have reported that gynecological complaints may be endured for years before medical aid is sought; sometimes malignant tumors have not been reported until they are inoperable. In the inhibited life of the convent, premenstrual tension among young religious and menopause among older ones cause problems unnecessarily. While the younger generation of nuns is overcoming this Victorian atmosphere, it still seems as if religious orders for women want to forget that their members are women as well as religious.

As Dr. John B. Wain points out in his careful analysis of psychological problems in religious life, such facts of life "lose some of their force if they are discussed with frankness, tact, and objectivity." He also warns that some nuns may suffer unwittingly from tensions produced by the conflict between the ideals of religious life and the natural instinct for marriage and child-bearing. Just as marriages often go through crises at the ten-year mark, so sisters face personal crises in their vocations. At such critical times, when a sister calls into question her vocation and her lifetime commitment, physical as well as psychological symptoms can develop, as in the following example:

> A typical case will find she is becoming irritable and depressed; she finds her daily work an intolerable burden and her sisters' foibles, which she previously ignored, become oppressive to her. She loses her appetite, becomes thin, sleeps badly, and has palpitations and chest pains suggestive of heart disease. She may have to accept stronger temptations against purity.[20]

The inbred community life in the convent, the suspicion of everything physical, and the inhibitions toward human relationships weaken a sister's personal resources. It becomes difficult to separate real and imaginary problems involving the vow of chastity; it is easy to feel guilty. In many convents the abhorrence of physical contact of any kind and the restrictions for the sake of modesty approach ridiculous if not morbid extremes. Some orders even forbid their members to attend a marriage ceremony (though it is a Church sacrament); most demand a shattering break with the sister's own family. And always there is the pervasive influence of Irish Catholicism with its puritanical attitude toward sex.

Left in relative ignorance in a society of women with little worldly experience, surrounded by false modesty and considerable misinformation, the typical sister is likely to suffer more from the prevailing prudery than from her vow of chastity. She is easily shaken by temptations at what she may regard as the most inopportune times, though "It is probably not uncommon for religious and lay people to experience sexual feelings at the quiet times of recollection and Communion."[21] It is not surprising, then, that chastity rather than charity seems to emerge as the greatest single virtue in the convent culture of American sisters.

While the problem of chastity is faced in silence, obedience has become the center of the growing debate about women religious in contemporary America. And it is the most important problem in terms of the modern role of women's orders within Church and community. The professionalization sought by the Sister Formation Movement is part of this problem. If training, competence, and skill are to be respected, then the professional must be free to exercise her abilities. Authority must yield to expertise in the American mode, with an accompanying danger to the authoritarian mold of the American Church.

In this regard the Sister Formation Movement has been the major development in modernization since its founding in 1954. About nine-tenths of the women's orders in this country are involved in an upgrading movement that stresses the better preparation of sisters. A juniorate program has been added to the novitiate training, with a heavy emphasis on liberal arts. Religious communities are cooperating in education programs; the more affluent orders are helping their poorer cousins. The ideal is the complete integration of a sister's preparation along "human, Christian, intellectual, professional, religious and apostolic" lines, as urged by the Vatican's Sacred Congregation for Religious.

The influence has been contagious, making it fashionable to seek both experience and education outside convent walls and also outside the Catholic ghetto. The goal of providing every sister with a bachelor's degree includes more education and training for older sisters and more advanced study for those showing promise. For graduate school, as Sister

Mary Ann Ida of Mundelein College has noted, "the best type of university is often a state or large private university, and not necessarily a Catholic one." When *Time* surveyed the Sister Formation scene, it produced a kaleidoscopic set of illustrations:

> From Columbia University last year, a Roman Catholic nun working for her M.A. in Russian flew off to the Soviet Union to do interviews on the 1917 Revolution. At the University of California in Berkeley, one of the nation's best centers for Hispanic studies, another nun, expert in Spanish, has just been offered a job as a teaching fellow. In New York, sisters attending Manhattanville College of the Sacred Heart avidly study the sometimes shocking works of Samuel Beckett, and other nuns press curiously into a Second Avenue loft to take in the blasphemous black mass of Jean Genêt's "The Blacks."[22]

Inevitably, upgrading and involvement in the contemporary world challenge the traditional concept of obedience, a sensitive point in any feminist campaign, as women's orders try to adjust their religious systems to the greater self-reliance they are seeking to inculcate and to express. This tendency is evident in the slowly changing role of the religious superior from an all-knowing, all-seeing, unchallengeable mother figure to a "first among equals." In the Catholic Church, as in any traditional society which is modernizing, the status of its women is a major criterion of change. Expressing the liberal view, Cardinal Suenens has stressed that obedience must not be confused with passivity: "The prime consideration is not the abdication of one's own will nor the submission to a person; it is loyalty to the common good as an expression of God's will."[23]

In the conservative view of Cardinal Spellman, change and modernization must be applied cautiously and kept within bounds. Addressing the Vatican Council Fathers, Cardinal Spellman used the velvet phrase "genuine religious obedience" to stress acceptance of authority. In what some of his priests called the Cardinal's "early Christmas card to religious," a text of the address was distributed in late 1964 to all religious in his archdiocese. The intricate process of reading between the lines that characterizes Church bureaucracy gave the message the interpretation: don't get carried away by all this talk of modernization and step out of line. Cardinal Spellman, like other conservative members of the American hierarchy, runs a tight ship, particularly for women religious.

In technical terms, the debate over obedience is complicated, but the issue is clear. The traditional status of the second sex is being challenged within the Catholic Church, and the drive toward more education and training for sisters gives the feminist campaign motive power. At this point, the authors can cite the many intelligent, independent-minded sisters whom they have met as university students and professors throughout the country. In fact, some of the best Catholic colleges are run by sisters, just as are the worst ones.

By establishing their qualifications as professionals, the sisters are bringing the American feminist movement into the heart of the Roman Church. In the final analysis, however, they cannot manage emancipation alone, but must await full acceptance of their new role by the male-dominated establishment. For the time being, ability is an important stride forward on the road to equality.

PART III

In Many Roles

CHAPTER 10

◇◇◇◇◇◇◇◇◇◇◇◇◇◇◇◇◇◇◇◇◇◇◇◇◇◇◇◇◇◇◇◇◇◇◇◇◇◇

The Press

IN FEBRUARY, 1963, a story that appeared first in a college newspaper threw an embarrassing spotlight on the policies and practices of the American Catholic press. *The Tower,* the student newspaper at Catholic University, broke the news that four distinguished Catholic theologians had been banned from participating in a student lecture series. The theologians were known to non-Catholics as well as to Catholics, indeed to any intelligent reader of the daily press: Father Gustave Weigel, Father John Courtney Murray (who had even been on the cover of *Time*), Father Godfrey Diekmann, and Father Hans Küng (one of the most influential and the most glamorous of Catholic theologians).

The story was news by any standard. Four famous Catholic theologians who had played a prominent role in the epochal Vatican Council were prevented from speaking at the citadel of Catholic higher education in America. After the story was lifted out of collegiate obscurity onto the front page of the February 14 issue of the *Catholic Messenger* of Davenport, Iowa, it moved coast to coast on the wire services and into the pages of daily newspapers and news magazines. The Washington, D.C., papers covered it like a congressional investigation; the *Washington Post* headlined it on Sunday, February 17, "Catholic U. Accused of Censorship for Banning 4 in Lecture Series."

Yet the story was ignored by a majority of Catholic papers. Publisher Dan Herr of *The Critic,* who qualifies as the A. J. Liebling of the Catholic press, confirmed this in an examination of ninety-one out of 115 weekly diocesan papers.[1] Two-thirds of the papers printed nothing about the incident in their February 22 issues, despite the attention it had received during the previous week. On March 1 thirty-nine papers belatedly joined the twenty-eight which had printed the story during the first week with varying degrees of enthusiasm, giving the story a treatment which ranged from front-page headlines to a small insert at the bottom of the last page.

Meanwhile, the NCWC News Service, the official Catholic news agency in America, tiptoed toward the story. Its first report, sent out on February 16, was not a story but rather "editorial information." In this background report, the service assured its subscribers in spite of the facts: "A spokesman for the Catholic University of America has denied reports that four prominent theologians were barred from speaking on the university campus." When the story refused to fade away, the NCWC News Service began to cover it, though it never caught up with the superior coverage provided by the interdenominational Religious News Service.

Most Catholics turned to the secular press to learn what was happening at the Catholic university to which they donate money annually in a special nationwide church collection. It was the same "hungry interest" cited by the associate editor of the San Francisco *Monitor,* John O'Connor, when he commented that Catholics were also turning to secular publications for news of the Vatican Council, the most important Catholic story of the postwar period. He pointed out that the interest "is not only an expression of confidence in the professional competence of these publications but is also a bald indictment of the irrelevancy of diocesan weeklies and a stinging rebuke of their editorial timidity and institutional complacency."[2]

The history of Catholic journalism has thereby gone full cycle in America. The Catholic press was developed to fill a vacuum in Catholic news in secular publications and to counter any anti-Catholic bias in their reporting. Today the best and most reliable coverage of major Catholic news often appears in non-Catholic publications. The Catholic University story exemplifies the sins of omission in the Catholic press, while the timid, routine coverage of the Council exemplifies its sins of commission.

The opinion of knowledgeable Catholics on Council coverage was summed up by John G. Deedy, Jr., editor of the *Pittsburgh Catholic,* after the first session, which ended December 8, 1962:

Many spokesmen congratulated the Catholic press on its coverage; however, it was embarrassingly obvious that the Catholic press's cautious coverage was second-best to that by large sections of the Protestant and secular presses. More specifically, apart from the Gregory Baum articles in the *Commonweal* and the Claud Nelson–Robert Graham reporting for Religious News Service, there was very little in the Catholic press during those months that compared with "Xavier Rynne's" reports from Vatican City in *The New Yorker* (surprisingly enough), or with Harold E. Fey's coverage in *The Christian Century,* an undenominational but Protestant weekly.[3]

With magnanimity, the Catholic Press Association confirmed this opinion by presenting a special citation at its 1963 Miami convention to *The New Yorker* for its Council coverage, despite hierarchical pressure to quash the citation. The same convention closed with an episcopal warning to the assembled Catholic journalists about embarrassing the Church, for the handling of the Catholic University affair was still a sore point.

As with so many other Catholic institutions which have been taken for granted, the Catholic press in America is undergoing soul-searching and re-examination at a time when it has reached enormous dimensions. It is by far the country's largest enterprise in denominational journalism, and it surpasses European efforts as well. A comparison with seven European countries has found only one with higher per capita coverage of Catholics by its religious newspapers. Indeed, the Catholic propensity for founding newspapers and magazines is second only to the propensity for building schools. The 1964–65 edition of the *Catholic Press Directory* listed 559 Catholic newspapers and magazines with a total circulation of 28 million. Of the total, 151 Catholic newspapers sold 6 million copies, more than double the number sold twenty-five years ago, while no less than 408 Catholic magazines sold 22 million copies.

This enterprise has developed in three phases, beginning with the immigrant period of the nineteenth century, when the Catholic press was so oriented to the old country "that there was frequently cause to wonder whether a given publication was first Catholic or first Irish, German, French, and so on."[4] The Catholic press mirrored the melting pot of American Catholicism and also the intense intramural controversies which enlivened its nineteenth-century development. Then, from 1900 through World War II, the Catholic press became housebroken and docile, reflecting the warning by Pope Leo XIII about the contentions disturbing the American Church. In this period, as Catholic newspapers came under tight diocesan controls, Deedy points out that "the loudest voices of the Catholic press were conservative and reactionary, and this fact no doubt explains at least partially the subsequent unblushing romance of so many Catholics with McCarthyism, and the furtive later flirtation of many with Birchism."[5] In the postwar period a transfusion of competent and committed laymen upgraded the professional quality of many Catholic publications, creating in the process uneasy partnerships between lay journalists and ecclesiastical publishers.

The Vatican Council appears to have ushered in a new period of rejuvenation for the Catholic press, bringing a heightened awareness that it was trailing behind the laity rather than leading it. This was evident with the healthy sign that critics emerged within the field of Catholic journalism. It is their criticisms appearing in Catholic publications that we are citing, not those of outsiders. Their case has been building up since the end of World War II in a reaction against the parochialism, the house-organ mentality, the supineness, and the remoteness from current issues that undermine the impact of the Catholic press.

In a 1957 symposium on religious journalism, Donald McDonald, then editor of the *Catholic Messenger* of Davenport, Iowa, wrote "that the Catholic Press, particularly the diocesan newspaper, has little or no sustained, constructive interest in matters which do not directly concern Catholics." After allowing for "very few" exceptions, he added:

I see more than forty-five diocesan newspapers every week and more than fifty Catholic magazines. The matter and form of the great majority of these publications are best typified by the now-familiar headline from one of them last year: "No Catholics Slain in Oklahoma Storm." Or by one equally as telling: "Suicide Was Not a Catholic." Or by a recent headline which, by its size and position on the front page, proclaimed the most important news story of the week: "Cardinal Will Fly Across North Pole."[6]

On the eve of the Vatican Council, one diocesan paper carried this parochialism to a ludicrous extreme. It spread an eight-column display of pictures across the front page showing what the bishop was going to wear in Rome on various occasions. The big news for that week was the bishop's wardrobe!

In his critique, John O'Connor of the San Francisco diocesan paper complained, "For the most part, it [the Catholic press] has remained at the level of the American newspapers of General Washington's time: a government press and a party press. It is time we grew up."[7] He cited three reasons for upgrading the Catholic press, each pinpointing an area of prevailing weaknesses.

First, the level of the readers is rising, and they are "not attracted by a clericalistic medium, stuffed with organizational trivia, column after column of mediocre writing, picture parades of religious and the 'saved' laity."[8] The high ecclesiastical visibility in these papers—published for the laity—was evident in a 1964 survey of the pictures in eighty diocesan papers. The majority (55 percent) of the pictures had monsignori, priests, brothers, or sisters in them and only thirty-two of the papers went to press without a picture of the local bishop. Forty-eight had at least one picture of the bishop, including thirteen which had two, four which had four or five pictures, and one which had six pictures.[9]

Second, editorial improvements strengthen the financial structure of the Catholic press, since advertising follows readership: "Too often the diocesan press boasts about circulation—when readership is the true test."[10] Knowledgeable observers have long advocated readership studies so that the Catholic press will learn whether anyone is listening and to what.

The Catholic press tends to have the characteristics of a kept press because it is subsidized, depending on quota systems, school subscription crusades, and complete parish coverage plans. For instance, *The Long Island Catholic,* which incidentally turned out to be a respectable product, had an automatic circulation of 208,000 when it was launched on May 3, 1962. The bishop not only provides financial support; he mobilizes his pastors in support of buying or selling a quota. But a paper's presence in homes is no guarantee of its being read, and certainly the circulation of the diocesan press would collapse if left to the vicissitudes of the marketplace.

Finally, said O'Connor,

There is still another reason to improve the diocesan press: the health of the church as an organism. As it generally looks now, the diocesan paper overdoes its work as an administrative bulletin. In these new and demanding times, it holds the pink mirror up to personalities, and to organizations of questionable viability. The result is a type of organization narcissism—the parochial mind admiring itself, the parochial voice talking, the parochial ear listening and the parochial head nodding in birettaed approval.[11]

The insensitivity of the Catholic diocesan press to social issues is disappointing. It has been slow to respond to the race issue in particular. Given the fact that so few Negroes are Catholics, parochialism helped the Catholic press wear blinders, though here, too, change is evident. A revealing content analysis of the October 5, 1963, issues of ninety out of 118 diocesan papers underlined this failure. The editorials in almost two-thirds of the papers ignored the rioting which accompanied integration during the previous week at the University of Mississippi—"a crisis that would seem to demand commitment by Catholic editors, a crisis that would call for blunt editorial denunciation of the evil forces of racism."[12] This silence stems from the "habitual disinclination of the Catholic press to fret about injustices other than those imperiling Catholics or specifically Catholic interests," Deedy has noted.[13]

The diocesan press was also a disappointment when a study was made of its coverage of congressional foreign aid hearings on President Eisenhower's request for budget appropriations. The findings covered forty-four representative diocesan newspapers having more than three-fourths of the total weekly circulation of such publications: "A broader survey of 6 full weeks (two in May, four in June), covering 264 issues while the mutual-security struggle was in its crucial stage showed that 222 of these issues carried nothing on the economic-aid legislation in either their news, editorial or feature columns." The study concluded by pointing out that diocesan newspapers opposing foreign aid were in a minority, but the coverage left much to be desired:

While a larger number of papers gave a few inches to news reports of Catholic individuals or organizations who favored foreign aid and felt that it was basically a moral question, only four papers in six weeks "exhorted" their readers editorially to look at the merits of the U.S. program for helping needier nations.

The small number of papers in which each individual story appeared, plus the small size of many stories, plus the fact that one-third of these papers carried nothing at all over six critical weeks—all these seem to indicate that there was very little interest in the pros and cons of the 1957 Mutual Security program in the American Catholic diocesan weekly press.[14]

Yet any account of the Catholic press must be balanced by the observation that the criticisms resemble those made about the American press in general, as Father Albert J. Nevins, the highly respected editor of *Maryknoll*, has pointed out.[15] The press, particularly in the American grass roots, is notoriously mediocre and parochial and subject to the whims of publishers. For the Catholic press, it is often the bishop and his overly cautious clerical representative; for the daily press, it is the indifferent owner and his profit-obsessed, conservative managers. Unfortunately the Catholic press does not take advantage of its freedom from commercial pressures to aim at higher standards and to be bold and daring. It hesitates to offend. Its approach has been closer to *L'Osservatore Romano*'s than to *The New York Times*'s.

Nonetheless, enough outstanding Catholic papers have emerged in the postwar years to set good performance criteria. These include *The Oklahoma Courier,* the Davenport *Catholic Messenger,* the Kansas City, Missouri, *Catholic Reporter,* the Indianapolis *Criterion,* the Boston *Pilot,* and the *Pittsburgh Catholic.* Just as American dailies accept the leadership of the excellent few, the Catholic press is increasingly influenced by the best examples of its weekly journalism.

Undoubtedly the outstanding Catholic newspaper in the country is *The National Catholic Reporter,* founded in the fall of 1964. The venture was launched with episcopal encouragement but not control; under its talented editor, Robert G. Hoyt, it serves as a news medium whose "client is simply the reader, and [whose] product is accurate information, made intelligible by competent analysis, made relevant by candid comment."[16]

The *Reporter*'s success has been both journalistic and commercial. Beginning with a modest $15,000 investment and a press run of 11,238, the Kansas City, Missouri, weekly attracted more than 1000 new subscribers a week until it announced, fourteen issues later on Feburary 3, 1965, a total of 27,932 subscribers. By October 27, 1965, the date of its first-anniversary issue, the circulation had passed 50,000. Its subscribers, about half of whom are priests and religious, are spread from coast to coast, with Illinois, New York, California, Michigan, and Minnesota the leading states. As the *Reporter* confirmed in a readership survey,* a spontaneous word-of-mouth campaign was a major factor in the escalation.

The *Reporter* has won its readers with a product that is literate, aggressive, and enterprising. It is even relieved by adult humor, which is almost totally absent from Catholic newspapers and magazines in America. Inevitably, it has been criticized, for it has probed such matters as clerical celibacy, birth control, secret communiqués from the apostolic delegate, and diocesan fund-raising troubles. More than anything else, the *Reporter* has been guilty of not respecting sacred cows.[17]

Its lay readership is a profile of the rising generation of articulate, educated, and influential Catholics. Of its lay subscribers, seven out of ten are college graduates, half of them with master's degrees. Half of those who head households earn more than $10,000 a year, and six out of ten are

* The *Reporter* found in a mail readership survey conducted in May, 1965, that 56 percent of its readers first heard about the newspaper through a personal contact and 70 percent pass a copy along to a friend ("Reader Survey Results," *The National Catholic Reporter,* October 27, 1965, p. 16).

thirty to forty-nine years old; four out of ten are self-employed in business or the professions.

The diocesan press, as John Cogley pointed out in a *New York Times* column, can be divided into liberal and conservative papers.[18] The latter, which are defensive in tone, have the bulk of the circulation, but the former have the influence. Among the liberal papers, *The National Catholic Reporter* is the most searching and the best informed in its critical approach.

The influence of the liberal papers and their editors is evident in the Catholic Press Association. Founded in 1911 "to assist members in publishing effective periodicals according to the demands of technical standards, and the truths of human reason and the Catholic Faith," the CPA has gradually become a force for improving the Catholic press; particularly with its annual awards to magazines and newspapers. The laymen who have given Catholic journalism its postwar transfusion have become leaders in the CPA, and its annual convention has developed into a vehicle for comparing notes and for setting individual standards of courage and performance.

Meanwhile, Catholic editors are increasing their demands upon the NCWC News Service, which is criticized for timidity in handling controversial Catholic news. A growing number of Catholic newspapers in recent years have subscribed to the Religious News Service, an affiliated but independently managed agency of the National Conference of Christians and Jews. This provides another source of news and a healthy competitive stimulus for the NCWC service, which has become the world's largest dispenser of Catholic news and information since its founding in 1920 by the American bishops. The agency has 150 foreign and 120 domestic correspondents and serves more than 550 publications and radio stations in sixty-five countries. Like any news enterprise with a wide variety of clients and a demanding board of directors—the American hierarchy—it straddles the editorial fence.

In their journalistic role, Catholic newspapers concentrate on an auxiliary function, making no attempt to duplicate the non-Catholic press and steering clear of political partisanship. As the critics complain, their definition of news is too parochial; they take a narrow view of what involves Catholics as Catholics and avoid local applications of social doctrine. From time to time the suggestion of establishing a Catholic daily has reappeared, but it hardly seems practicable. The 1884 Baltimore Council even decreed, "It is greatly to be desired that in some of our large cities a Catholic daily newspaper be maintained fully equal to the secular daily newspapers in financial strength and sagacity, vigor and authority of its writers." The decree cited a need to defend the Church from the "assaults and calumnies of its enemies," but a daily defense in print is hardly necessary in the present American climate. The Kansas City, Missouri, *Sun-Herald,* the last attempt at a Catholic daily, failed in the 1950s after only 142 issues. The audience was not there, and the competition of the daily press was too much for it. (The dream of a counterpart to the *Christian Science Monitor* has haunted American Jews as well as Catholics, but the two major ingredients are missing—an enormous subsidy and a substantial, responsive readership.)

Of the Catholic press in general, Dan Herr has irreverently commented, "There is nothing basically wrong with the Catholic press in America that an acute paper shortage would not cure."[19] But even that solution would probably not work, answers editor Deedy: "The trouble is that since Catholic reading habits are what they are, a paper shortage would likely mow down the good publications and leave the mediocre to continue their commonplace service."[20] Both quips, of course, ignore the realities of media consumption in a mass society: general reader tastes do not agree with those of highbrow critics and professional pundits. It seems unrealistic to expect more of Catholics than of other American readers; this expectation is a flaw in much criticism of the Catholic press.

While it is reasonable for each diocese to establish a direct line of communication with its Catholic membership, the failures of most Catholic diocesan newspapers are that they do not hold the attention of their audience and do not stay "alert" to the issues of the day, despite the claim of the Catholic press' slogan. Hardly any knowledgeable observer will disagree with this general criticism, and even apologists for the state of the Catholic press end by urging improvements—after pointing out how much worse things were twenty years ago.

When *The Critic* magazine polled various authorities with the question, "Are too many Catholic newspapers and magazines being published in the United States today?", the most critical answers came from the Catholic experts. Philip Scharper, a former editor on *The Commonweal* staff and now executive editor of the prestige Catholic publishing firm Sheed & Ward, replied:

> In short, the arguments used for proliferating Catholic periodicals to fill doubtful needs with dubious distinction are similar to those which have led to the proliferation of small Catholic colleges. In both cases, the concomitants, too, are the same —duplication of facilities and personnel, erosive incompetence, substandard wages and conditions for lay employees, and a mindless competition the ultimate victim of which is the Church.
>
> There is not, however, any strong indication that the trend to more and more publications will be reversed or even stabilized. Cubs are being fed with eye-droppers at this very moment, and they will grow to siphon off in ever thinner streams the available supply of talent and subscription funds.

George N. Shuster, another former *Commonweal* editor and former president of Hunter College, commented: "Are there too many flowers in the Catholic journalism garden?

There are. Can somebody do a little weeding out? I very much doubt it."

Journalism Professor Edward A. Walsh of Fordham University, who has supervised the annual judging of magazines for the CPA, answered:

If the question means are there too many dull, vapid and indifferent Catholic newspapers and magazines being published in the United States, the answer is "Yes." If the question means are there too many Catholic newspapers and magazines with dynamic editorial leadership, enterprising reporting, sparkling writing and appealing typography and layout, the answer is "No." The heart of the matter is not quantitative output, but qualitative production. We have far too few Catholic publications of distinction; we have far too many that are, or ought to be, candidates for extinction.[21]

The range and variety of the 408 Catholic magazines are reflected in the categories of judging for CPA awards: general interest magazines, magazines of criticism and culture, journals of opinion and public affairs, professional and other specialized publications, mission magazines, youth magazines, devotional magazines, and trade publications.

The Cinderella of this assortment is *Catholic Digest,* similar in content and success to *Reader's Digest.* Father Louis A. Gales, a priest in Saint Paul, started the monthly in 1936 with $1000, a modest charter subscription list, and a stack of mailing labels; by 1954 the magazine reached almost a million in circulation.[22] Today it has a circulation of more than 700,000, foreign editions, and substantial advertising revenues, and it attracts one-seventh of its readership from among non-Catholics. Its gross in 1961 was reported as $5 million, and it has succeeded in the perilous magazine market without subsidies.

Catholic Digest's unpretentious and successful formula, which evokes criticisms similar to those leveled at *Reader's Digest* because of its popularization and conservatism, is summed up by its publisher, Father Paul Bussard: "We are not particularly interested in controversy as such. We steer clear of the negative and report accomplishments rather than spelling out action or describing plans."[23]

Whereas *Catholic Digest* is popular and professional, succeeding in its admitted aim of providing a magazine so that "girls working in a five-and-dime would have no difficulty with either the words or the content,"[24] the Catholic field is overrun with magazines which only exist because religious orders are dazzled by the magic of print and want a vehicle for collecting money.

At the other extreme, the serious Catholic magazines set high standards comparable to those of secular journals of opinion. The list is headed by *The Commonweal* and *The Critic,* both in the hands of laymen, and *America,* operated by the Jesuits.* In recent years *America* has achieved the ideal of any journal of opinion—making money and influencing people. Combining professional standards with aggressive promotion, *America* pushed its circulation to over 99,000 in 1965, a remarkable achievement for a weekly magazine of its kind.

Whereas *America* is responsible and moderate, *The Commonweal* is a model of courageous journalism which also suffers from the economic perils of such a role. However, many American Catholics, in the spirit of *aggiornamento,* are catching up with *Commonweal* (though it is still forbidden fruit in some Catholic seminaries). Deedy's verdict on *Commonweal* is now generally accepted: it is "a weekly review which since 1924 has faced squarely the religious, political, social and cultural issues confronting the American Catholic, and has done so with an intelligence and conviction that have gained for it a prestige few others in the Catholic press have ever known even briefly."[25]

Commonweal's forty-year weekly performance provides a demonstration of the part to be played by an emerging

---

* In March 1964, *America* hired Paul K. Cuneo as assistant managing editor, the first lay editor since its founding in 1909.

Catholic press and of the contribution to be made by laymen. Its editors personally as well as its editorial pages are
influential far beyond the magazine's 1965 circulation of
45,000. They have been singled out as a lesson "in the witness which can be carried into the temporal order by a publication making no claim to be official or to speak for the
Church, and whose editors possess competence, direct responsibility, and the inspiration of Catholic conscience."[26]

Commonweal succeeds editorially by recognizing the
crucial distinction between the Church as an infallible
teaching authority in faith and morals and as a fallible
human organization. Most news about Catholics and their
Church concerns the latter, information on a society of
clergy and laity which is coping with ambiguous reality and
many-sided problems. Legitimate differences of opinion as
well as mistakes are inevitable. Writing about such a society, with all its contradictions, differences, and deficiencies,
does not involve conflicts with required beliefs. The small
nucleus of dogmatic infallibility is surrounded by a welter
of fallibility.

Basically, the failure to separate a commitment to the
supernatural Catholic faith from its human and social aspects and a hesitation to stand independent of the Church
establishment account for the mishandling of the Catholic
University story. The offending editors did not want to
embarrass the Church as an organization because they regard themselves as its instrument. Similarly, most Catholic
publications approached the Vatican Council like a trade
publication covering an annual convention. But journalists
on house organs are primarily technicians and not professionals, the role which leading Catholic journalists want to
establish for themselves. In an essay written for the *1965
Catholic Press Annual,* one of the authors made this point
with the opening statement: "If there is a single undermining theme in the Catholic press in America, it is the attitude
that the press is mainly an instrument of the Catholic

Church. This journalistic misconception shackles the many Catholic newspapers and magazines that are semi-professional, timid, uninteresting, and worst of all, ineffectual."[27]

As professionals, many lay Catholic journalists are in conflict with the understandable commitment of ecclesiastical superiors to the Church as an organization. It is not only that the priest-supervisor of a diocesan weekly wants to become a monsignor. Naturally, he defends the Church system to which he belongs; for him, the system serves the larger truths to which he has committed his life. On the other hand, the lay journalist regards his profession as having its own ideals and standards, which indeed will also serve the larger truths and the goals of the Catholic Church. He gives witness to his faith in his work as a professional, and the ecclesiastical veto often stands in his way. In fact, the Catholic journalist has been advised to be ready "to defend and help defend truth, justice, honesty, even before religion and the Gospel." The advice was given in 1961 by Pope John XXIII to the Catholic Union of the Italian Press.

Msgr. S. J. Adamo of the Camden, New Jersey, *Catholic Star-Herald* has questioned the "psychological fitness" of priest-reporters. His remarks, published in a column for his newspaper and reprinted in the *Catholic Journalist* of March, 1964, were occasioned by the controversial reporting of the Vietnam troubles by Father Patrick O'Connor, NCWC correspondent. Msgr. Adamo charged that Father O'Connor was guilty of special pleading in favor of the Catholic position in Vietnam. His criticisms reflect the uninhibited self-examination taking place on the lay-clerical relationship in the Catholic press:

It must also be said that there are some laymen who can out-priest any priest in this field. But here I am concerned solely with priest reporters because I feel that their very mission and vocation militate against their being good reporters and because I feel their poor example has led many lay newsmen astray. I am not saying priests can't be good commentators on the news, but gathering the news should be left entirely in the hands of professional laymen and their hands must be free.

A priest is a preacher, a persuader, a prophet. He is a man dedicated to helping people live better lives. His whole mental frame of reference is turned toward that goal. Instinctively, as it were, he tries to make the news serve the task of salvation as everything should. Consequently he finds it nearly impossible to admit that bad news won't drive people to be bad also. So he behaves like a good mother who tries to shield her children from harsh reality. For the priest the people are his children, his little ones, his flock to be tended and guarded, nourished and guided. Tell them that a Church official did something stupid or dishonest or unfair? Heavens, no! This will make the flock distrust all its shepherds. Tell them that a group of Catholics did something brutal or shameful or inhuman? God forbid! This will make other Catholics wonder about the holiness of the Church and keep converts from crossing the threshold.

Such fears are based on a simplistic view of the Church and its work in the world, but it is the dominant view in the Catholic press in America today. It is the reason why so much bad reporting by priests and near-priests in the laity is done in the name of defending the Church.[28]

Robert Hoyt of *The National Catholic Reporter* has commented on improper attitudes that afflict the Catholic press and the proper aims it should set before itself. He cites among the purposes of the Catholic press "to investigate the quality of Catholic life, measure the performance of Catholic institutions, report the actual content and trend of Catholic thinking, or stimulate discussion about Church policies and problems."[29] By contrast, he notes that Catholic publications approach Catholic subjects and personalities with a public relations rather than a journalistic mentality and an attitude of compliant collaborator rather than independent reporter.

Hoyt argues persuasively for a free Catholic press:

A free press is not to be defined as a press without values or commitments; a free Catholic press is not a press which is neutral toward the Church as the ark of salvation, the guardian of revelation, the source of sacramental life. We who operate this press do not set ourselves over or apart from the authority of the Church. But as journalists we have a function which also has a certain sacredness: to report what we see, what is actually going on; and, secondarily, to evaluate what we see and to contribute to the clarification of thought.[30]

Those who stress the importance of public opinion within the Church cite the address made by Pope Pius XII in 1950 to the international convention of the Catholic press. He said that the Church is "a living body, and there would be something missing from her life if there were no public opinion within her, a defect for which pastors as well as the faithful would be responsible."

The demand for an independent Catholic press in America stresses the role of newspapers and magazines in the opinion-making process. In reporting the operations of the Church as a temporal organization and the activities of its members, a journalist would express rather than reject his commitment to a religious witness in the world. He would serve it. He would provide information as the personal right of his readers. He would risk passing embarrassment for the long-run benefits of the truth, and choose full revelation instead of partial concealment.

The more the Catholic Church in America sheds its parochialism and defensiveness, the readier it will be to encourage free, responsible, and even critical journalism. And the more the laity demands, the more it will receive. Thus, the Catholic press will be Americanized in the best sense of the term, confronting the American situation and relating it realistically to the lives of Catholics in America. The Catholic press can then become an influential reflection of what is happening within American Catholicism.

CHAPTER 11

<><><><><><><><><><><><><><><><><><><><><><><><>

The Voter

DURING John F. Kennedy's campaign for the presidency, a Catholic college alumnus ran across his old ethics professor, an elderly, stiff-necked Jesuit slightly to the right of McKinley in his politics. Curious about the professor's choice between his religious and political preferences when a presidential candidate was both liberal and Catholic, the former student asked the old professor whether he would vote for Kennedy.

"Of course," he snapped. "How else are we going to answer the anti-Catholic bigots? This is the biggest chance we'll ever have to put a Catholic in the White House."

That in essence is the religious vote which registers automatic election day support for Catholic candidates. It is the same primitive religious appeal which influences Protestants and Jews as well as Catholics. It is also accompanied with backlash, by Protestants voting against a candidate because he is a Catholic, and counterbacklash, by Catholics voting for Catholic candidates because they feel Protestants will vote against them.

When Barry Goldwater, partly Jewish in origin and Episcopalian in affiliation, picked Representative William E. Miller as a 1964 running mate, the latter's Catholic faith was universally noted. With characteristic flippancy Miller said, "Barry's a Protestant and a Jew, and I'm a Catholic. Anyone who's against *that* ticket is a damn bigot."[1] When

Senators Eugene J. McCarthy of Minnesota, Mike Mansfield of Montana, and Edmund S. Muskie of Maine were mentioned as choices for President Johnson's running mate, the label *Catholic* was inevitably underlined. What everyone had in mind was obvious: Catholic voters, who constitute more than one-fourth of the nation's electorate.

A study of the "religious factor" in Detroit pointed up the political aspect of the Catholic vote—its built-in Democratic loyalty. Said a Catholic stock handler in a large department store, "I am a Democrat because I am a workingman and history shows us the Democratic Party has always helped the workingman." Said the Catholic wife of a machinist, "It seems like the Republicans are too much for the big capitalist."[2] From the percentages of the Gallup poll to the statistical coefficients used in sociological studies of voting, the fact is clear: Catholics are largely Democrats. A Gallup poll found that nearly six out of ten Catholic voters consider themselves Democrats, and less than two in ten consider themselves Republicans. The rest are independents.[3]

The Catholic-Democratic alliance has been formalized in party politics. National committee chairmen are usually Catholics. (In 1964 so was the Republican.) A comparison of federal judgeship appointments made under Harding, Coolidge, and Hoover with those made under Roosevelt and Truman shows that Catholics accounted for one out of every four judges appointed by the Democrats but only one out of every twenty-five appointed by the Republicans.[4] In 1960, just before Kennedy's election, over 80 percent of the Catholics in Congress were Democrats. Among all Democratic congressmen, one-quarter were Catholics; only 7 percent of the Republican congressmen were Catholics.

Thus, when Kennedy ran in 1960, he attracted Catholic voters as a coreligionist and as a fellow Democrat. It had the expected results among Catholics, with predictable backlash reactions among non-Catholics. George Belknap, former consultant on polling to the Democratic National Committee, summed up the Kennedy victory this way: "Kennedy's religion elected him and it also very nearly defeated him."[5] This is reflected in the fact that Kennedy received just over 50 percent of the popular vote, while Democratic candidates for the House of Representatives received 55 percent of the vote.

A close look at Kennedy's performance in 1960 is the best synopsis of the Catholic vote in America. In his victory, as noted, he epitomized the twin pillars of that vote: favoritism for a fellow Catholic and political commitment to the Democratic Party. Catholics were won back from the Republicans in dramatic numbers; a Gallup poll reported that 62 percent of the Catholics who said they had voted for Eisenhower were switching to Kennedy. The change in the Catholic vote from 1952 and 1956 was startling, rising from 56 percent Democratic in 1952 and 51 percent in 1956 to 78 percent Democratic in 1960. Whereas 44 percent of the Catholics voted Republican in 1952 and 49 percent in 1956, the figure was only 22 percent in 1960. Meanwhile, the Protestant vote remained consistent, at 63 percent Republican for 1952 and 1956 and 62 percent for 1960. Moreover, an overwhelming majority of independent Catholic voters went to Kennedy. His support was equally strong among Catholic men and women. For Catholics who were already Democrats, the vote was 95 percent for Kennedy![6]

Kennedy's areas of strength matched the concentrations of Catholic population, which is mainly urban and heaviest in the Northeast. A 1958 report showed that 44 percent of American Catholics are in the Northeast, 30 percent in the North Central states, and the remaining 26 percent evenly divided between the South and the West. Kennedy carried ten of the fourteen most Catholic states, losing only Ohio, Wisconsin, Montana, and California. In many Catholic neighborhoods the Republican vote dropped by 20 to 25 percent. In an analysis of 171 counties with Catholic populations of 40 percent or more, the research staff of the Republican National Committee found that the Republicans had a loss of 20 percent or more in fifty-four of the counties. Ninety-seven others had Republican losses ranging between 8 and 20 percent, while seventeen counties had losses below the national average. Only three showed a Republican gain.

A sophisticated political strategy based on the affinity between Catholics and Democrats was worked out in 1956 by Kennedy's brain-truster Theodore Sorensen when the Boston senator was seeking the vice-presidential nomination. The strategy argued that a Catholic could win back the populous industrial states which have heavy Catholic votes and predominant weight in the Electoral College. The Sorensen memorandum listed the fourteen most Catholic states with 261 electoral votes, five short of a majority: Rhode Island (60 percent Catholic in population), Massachusetts (50 percent), Connecticut (49 percent), New Jersey (39 percent), New York (32 percent), Wisconsin (32 percent), Illinois (30 percent), Pennsylvania (29 percent), Michigan (24 percent), Minnesota (24 percent), California (22 percent), Montana (22 percent), Maryland (21 percent), and Ohio (22 percent).

The memorandum argued that the Democrats carried thirteen of these fourteen states in 1940, twelve in 1944, and eight in 1948, but in 1952 all of these states had gone to Eisenhower. In 1960, as noted, Kennedy took ten of these fourteen states, bearing out the argument. But William V. Shannon has properly pointed out that the strategy applies to the head of the ticket and not to the vice-presidential candidate.[7]

A green streak runs through the close ties between Catholics and the Democratic Party, and it was painted by the rambunctious Irish immigrants of the nineteenth century. They have left their stamp on politics as on religion; they have stood out on Sunday morning and on election day, but of course most on Saint Patrick's Day. And if anything signals a decline in Irish hegemony, it was Mayor Wagner's decision in 1963 to bar colored stripes on New York's Fifth Avenue for any parade, even an Irish one. However, he acted after having overruled his traffic commissioner, who had refused permission for the Italians to have a purple stripe for their Columbus Day parade. So, of all things, the mayor of New York City let the Italians have the last stripe.

Political analyst Samuel Lubell has pointed out that the political coming of age of Italian Americans has coincided with the career of Senator John Orlando Pastore in Rhode Island, a Catholic stronghold.[8] In 1946 Pastore became the country's first elected governor of Italian origin, and in 1950 the first to sit in the United States Senate. And in 1964 he gave the keynote address at the Democratic National Convention. That same year the Republican and Democratic candidates for governor in the traditional Yankee and Irish stronghold of Massachusetts were both Italian Americans. Former Governor John A. Volpe ran against Francis Xavier Bellotti, father of twelve. It was the first such all-Italian contest in the state's history.

For the Democratic Party, the predominantly Catholic Irish and Italians have been particularly loyal supporters among all ethnic groups, a loyalty exemplified by their participation in party organizations. For instance, an extensive study by the University of Michigan of the 1952 presidential elections found only Jews and Negroes more loyal than Irish Catholics to the Democratic ticket. From a national survey it was found that 55 percent of the Irish Catholics voted for Stevenson and 38 percent for Eisenhower. The Italians were not far behind, voting 49 percent for Stevenson and 38 percent for Eisenhower. The Poles were almost equally divided in their vote, while 58 percent of the Germans voted for Eisenhower and the remainder were equally divided between voters for Stevenson and abstainers.[9]

The Catholic-Democratic alliance has developed as a matter of predictable course ever since the immigrant waves began in the 1800s. During his two terms, 1829–37, President Andrew Jackson, the son of poor Irish immigrants, had marked the Democratic Party as the party of the people, governing for the benefit of the small man, whether backwoodsman or farmer on the frontier or laborer and mechanic in the Eastern cities. The Democratic Party became a hospitable reception center for the immigrants. After the party was crippled by the Civil War, its strength resided in the big-city political machine, which took care of the common man and processed immigrants into Democratic voters. Meanwhile, the Republicans were the established interests and the white Anglo-Saxon Protestants who were the "old" Americans and the "enemy" to the immigrants.

The Irish made a distinctive contribution to the big-city political machine, which was a humanizer and softener of the cold, cumbersome processes of government. Lincoln Steffens, in his memorable muckraking, reported the essence of the system in the words of two outstanding practitioners. In New York Richard Crocker, who had followed Honest John Kelly as Tammany boss, gave a blunt answer to Steffens' question of why a city needed a political boss when it had a mayor, a council, and all the formal apparatus of government.

It's because there's a mayor and a council and judges and—a hundred other men to deal with. A government is nothing but a business, and you can't do business with a lot of officials, who check and cross one another, and who come and go, there this year, out the next. A business man wants to do business with one man, and one who is always there to remember and carry out the business.[10]

In Boston Boss Martin Lomasny explained what the machine meant to the little man: "I think there's got to be in every ward somebody that any bloke can come to—no matter what he's done—and get help. Help, you understand; none of your law and your justice, but help."[11]

The political machine was characteristically "a merger of rural Irish custom with urban American politics," as Glazer and Moynihan have noted in describing the Irish affinity for big-city politics.[12] Besides an indifference to the proprieties of the Yankees, the Irish had the attitude that government should be conducted on a personal basis. Favoritism was fine. Moreover, formal government had always been against the Irishman in his homeland; it had been the agent of oppression which deprived him of power over his political and religious lot. America was a different story and presented uninhibited opportunities. The Irish thereupon transferred the traditional power structure of the rural village to the big-city machine. It was a significant contribution to the complexities of American politics:

> Instead of letting politics transform them, the Irish transformed politics, establishing a political system in New York City that, from a distance, seems like the social system of an Irish village writ large.
> The Irish village was a place of stable, predictable social relations in which almost everyone had a role to play, under the surveillance of a stern oligarchy of elders, and in which, on the whole, a person's position was likely to improve with time. Transferred to Manhattan, these were the essentials of Tammany Hall.[13]

Out of the Irish propensity for Democratic politics emerged the sterotyped image of the beer-drinking, back-slapping papist politician. The stereotype also provoked one of the most indiscreet remarks in American political history. A Protestant minister, Rev. Samuel D. Burchard, visited the Republican presidential candidate, James G. Blaine, a week before the 1884 election, and assured him in a meeting with a delegation of New York ministers, "We are Republicans and don't propose to leave our party, and identify ourselves with the party whose antecedents have been rum, Romanism, and rebellion."[14] Any support Blaine was gathering among the Irish was wiped out by their reaction; he lost New York by 1077 votes and the election as well.

The "Happy Warrior," as Franklin D. Roosevelt called Alfred E. Smith the second time he nominated him for President, was the natural culmination of this political tradition. He was a big-city Irishman who emerged from the political machine. In style, background, and experience, he was the opposite of the Catholic who would be elected President three decades later, the epitome of the unassimilated Irish by contrast with the acme of Irish assimilation. An altar boy and then organ pumper, a child of the Irish stronghold of the Fourth Ward and Saint James Parish, Al Smith was educated on the streets of New York in a string of jobs familiar to the immigrant: newsboy, laborer, trucker's helper, Fulton Fish Market employee, and finally real estate man and politician. In characteristic Irish fashion, he revered his mother, who reared him and his sister following the early death of his father. Even after Al Smith grew up and married, he spent every Sunday with his mother. In 1916, when he was inaugurated sheriff, she said of him, "Alfred has been a good boy."[15]

Al Smith didn't lose his bid for the presidency in 1928 primarily because he was a Catholic, but the memory of the flagrant bigotry lingered on when Kennedy stood for election, undoubtedly contributing to Catholic solidarity in 1960. Actually, prosperity and the wet issue defeated Smith more than bigotry. In that prepollster era, the most persuasive evidence was a 1929 analysis of 173 randomly selected counties in eight key states by Professor William F. Ogburn of the University of Chicago. He found the actual vote still slightly in Hoover's favor after statistically removing the issues of prohibition, religion, and immigration from the urban areas.[16]

The Smith campaign severed the Democratic South, but it also demonstrated the political power of the nationality groups in the big cities: Smith split the Republican North as well. In the country's twelve largest cities, the Republicans had a plurality of 1.6 million in 1920 and 1.3 million in 1924, but in 1928 Smith won a plurality of 38,000 in these cities. Moreover, Smith swung the French Canadians in New England and the Midwestern German Catholics solidly into the Democratic column.

An element of sophistication enveloped the religious issue when it was Kennedy's turn. Protestant skepticism about a Catholic in the White House was expressed in intellectual and theoretical terms, while in 1928 the Democratic platform openly condemned the "political crusade . . . against Catholics." When General Motors industrialist John J. Raskob, a Catholic, was named Smith's national chairman, a "Catholic plot" was charged and a resurgent Ku Klux Klan openly sowed seeds of bigotry. Smith's reaction to an attack on his dual loyalty to Church and U.S. Constitution was characteristic. He called a meeting of his advisers and burst into the room asking, "Will someone tell me what the hell a papal encyclical is?"[17] Kennedy's response, as illustrated by his celebrated Houston appearance before a meeting of Protestant ministers, was considerably more elegant.

The Catholic vote has also become considerably more complicated. For one thing, the religious issue has been deflated by the fact that a Catholic has been elected President and accepted by the American public. By August, 1965, Gallup reported that 87 percent of Americans were ready to vote for a Catholic for President, compared with 68 percent in 1958. As a parallel development, Catholic spokesmen rebelled against a suggestion that Lyndon B. Johnson make a point of selecting a Catholic to run for Vice President. A group of Catholic editors and Rev. Robert F. Drinan, influential dean of the Boston College Law School, wrote Democratic National Chairman John M. Bailey (a Catholic, incidentally) about the speculation that the Democrats should match the Republican vice-presidential candidate with a Catholic of their own. They argued for competence as the sole qualification and warned about "exploiting a religious issue for partisan purposes."[18]

Archbishop Paul J. Hallinan agreed in a public statement, arguing that many Protestants, Jews, and Catholics voted for Kennedy as a stand against allowing any religion to bar a man from office. Now, he urged, "the issue should be put to rest," adding that "Most Catholics resent the assumption that they should vote for a Catholic because they are Catholics."[19] *America* stated it best of all: "If the old 'religious issue' [you *can't* pick a Catholic] was shameful, its new version [you *must* have a Catholic] is ridiculous."[20] The attitude was reflected in the general Catholic opinion on the choice of a vice-presidential candidate: only one in ten Catholics felt it was important that Johnson select a Catholic running mate.[21]

Other factors have been at work in the Catholic vote, reinforcing the ethnic and religious affinity for the Democratic Party. A large proportion of Catholics have been members of the lower and working classes. An analysis of four surveys taken in 1945 and 1946 showed that 66 percent of the Catholics were lower class, 25 percent middle class, and only 9 percent upper class. The totals for all religious groups showed 13 percent upper class, 31 percent middle class, and 56 percent lower class. The Catholics lagged particularly behind the Jews (who had 22 percent in the upper class and 46 percent in the lower) and such established Protestant groups as the Episcopalians (24 percent upper, 42 percent lower), the Presbyterians (22 percent upper, 38 percent lower), and the Congregationalists (24 percent upper, 33 percent lower). Catholics also had the highest percentage of urban blue-collar workers (55 percent) and the largest number of union members (28 percent).[22] This, of course, is the stuff of which Democratic voters are made.

Since voting is linked to social position, the Catholic vote must be seen in terms of where Catholics are located in the American scene. Liston Pope writes:

All told, information from public opinion polls indicates that Protestant and Jewish adherents come more largely from the middle and upper classes than do Catholics, with significant differences between the major Protestant denominations in this respect. At the same time, Protestants are more largely represented in the lower class than has been commonly supposed; a significant change in this respect may have occurred during World War II. Protestants, and Jews even more largely, come typically from business, professional, white collar and service occupations; Catholics are more typically workers; Catholics, Jews, and Episcopalians have comparatively few farmers. Each major religious body has a sizable percentage of trade unionists in its membership. In the overall picture, Protestants and Jews have had more education than Catholics.[23]

However, these economic and social factors are losing their impact among the increasingly Americanized, assimilated, and socially mobile Catholic community. Catholics are going middle class, suburban, and even to some extent Republican. For the past thirty years, the automatic trinity of Irish, Catholic, and Democratic has been facing increasing pressure. Between 1940 and 1946, Irish Catholic Republicans were elected as United States representatives from New York, Pennsylvania, Michigan, Wisconsin, Minnesota, and California. And in 1938 Connecticut sent its first Republican Irish Catholic Senator, John Danaher, to Washington. Such a possibility had once seemed so unlikely that when Danaher's father switched family allegiance to the GOP, one old Irish lady is said to have remarked to her friend, "Have you heard the news? John Danaher has become a Republican!" The other replied, "It can't be true. I saw him at mass just last Sunday."[24]

The general impression that Catholics are on the move socially, economically, and geographically is reflected in the available data. In the late 1950s the rising position of Catho-

lics was evident when three national surveys collected information on education, occupation, and income—the three
main indicators of social class. Catholics compared favorably
with Protestants particularly. In the sample, 32 percent of
the Catholics had four years of high school compared with
27 percent of the Protestants, whereas 9 percent of the Protestants had four or more years of college compared with 5
percent of the Catholics. Managerial or professional positions were held by 19 percent of the Catholics, compared
with 21 percent of the Protestants. In skilled and semi-
skilled jobs, the Catholic figures were 22 and 20 percent
respectively and the Protestant 17 and 15 percent. More
Catholics earned over $5000 (52 percent), and more Prot-
estants under (55 percent).[25]

These figures are excessively favorable to Catholics because of the large number of Baptists—particularly from the
South—in the groups studied, for they are invariably the
lowest on any measures of education, income, and occupation. If further adjustments were made for rural and urban
residence, the Catholic profile would not be so favorable.
Nonetheless, these summaries, taken from three national
surveys conducted by the University of Michigan Survey
Research Center in 1957 and 1958, do indicate the upward
trend of American Catholics on the socioeconomic ladder.

This mobility translates into Republican votes, particularly among younger Catholics. In a celebrated 1948 voting
study made of Elmira, New York, the social scientists found
that the younger generation of Catholics voted less by religion than did their elders, with those over fifty-five the most
steadfastly Democratic.[26] By contrast, there were more
Democrats among the younger Protestants than among their
elders, indicating that the religious vote should diminish in
the coming years. Younger Catholics and Protestants were
likely to vote in terms more of class than of religion.

A Republican drift was even discernible in Kennedy's

dominance of the Catholic vote. His slim New Jersey plurality reflected a failure to win the vote of well-to-do Irish suburbanites, while in Illinois he needed the Negro vote to counteract the falling away of the wealthier Irish in Chicago's suburbs. In Philadelphia the Republican National Committee found that Nixon made greater inroads among the Irish than among the Jews, Negroes, and Poles. In private polls the Kennedy team found that some Irish voters decided in favor of Nixon simply to prove there is no Irish Catholic bloc. Moreover, the percentage of Catholic businessmen and professionals who voted for Nixon (about one in three) was approximately twice the percentage supporting him among lower-income Catholics.

The archconservative wing of Catholic voters also drains off Democratic votes, particularly when its members focus their hysteria on the soft-on-communism charge that has hurt the Democrats. For them, Barry Goldwater in 1964 was a knight in shining armor. Though this was a negligible factor in the election outcome, the appeal was evident in surveys of Catholic voters. A Gallup poll released August 4, 1963, found that Goldwater had more support among Catholic voters than did either of two other Republican contenders for the presidential nomination, Romney and Rockefeller. Just before the 1964 election, the Gallup organization compared Goldwater's popularity against Johnson with his popularity against Kennedy. The results, announced a week before the election, showed that Goldwater had lost ground in his campaign in every age, occupational, regional, urban, educational, racial, political, and religious category—except among Catholics. In November, 1963, 19 percent of the Catholics polled were in favor of Goldwater; a year later, in late September, 1964, the total was 20 percent.

For twice-defeated presidential candidate Adlai Stevenson, the soft-on-communism charge was undoubtedly a political handicap that cost him Catholic votes. No less a Catholic Democrat than Jim Farley told the Rotary Club of Los Angeles in 1960, "To send Governor Stevenson to negotiate with Mr. Khrushchev is to send the cabbage to the goat."[27] For Republican Senator Joe McCarthy, anticommunism by any demagogic means was a highly negotiable issue among American Catholics. Early in 1954 the Gallup Poll reported that nearly 60 percent of American Catholics approved of McCarthy. Catholic organizations and the Catholic press provided his most enthusiastic support, and he was for the most part the darling of the Catholic hierarchy. In some Catholic circles McCarthy's political canonization is still being pursued, as shown by the continuing panegyrics to be found in the panting pages of the Brooklyn *Tablet*. Glazer and Moynihan evoked the mood of the McCarthy era with a flash of insight when they commented, "In the era of security clearances, to be an Irish Catholic became prima facie evidence of loyalty. Harvard men were to be checked; Fordham men would do the checking. The disadvantage of this is that it put the Irish back on the force. It encouraged the tendency to be regular rather than creative."[28]

The McCarthy era encouraged core attitudes evident in American Catholicism—defensiveness and inflexibility. In historical perspective, it provided another chance to strike back, particularly for the Irish. It also glorified an oversimplified response to the challenge of communism, negative in tone and indiscriminate in application. The McCarthy association became a natural prelude to the John Birch Society, whose founder, Robert H. Welch, Jr., once claimed that 40 percent of its membership was Catholic. Catholic spokesmen and publications did little to dispel the unfavorable image. In Boston the archdiocesan publication called the aims of the Birch Society "good," though it said the Society was "unbalanced," and Cardinal Cushing contributed two public letters of support for Welch, "a fellow fighter against communism." In Los Angeles Cardinal McIntyre became known as "the Archbishop of the John Birch Society."

Despite various inroads, the overall Catholic trend has continued in the direction of increased support for Democratic presidential candidates. Political analyst Lubell notes that a drop in Democratic strength among Jews after World War II was counteracted by a stronger Democratic allegiance among Catholics particularly the Irish, Germans, and Italians. He attributes this "new Catholic voting solidarity" to the end of the war and Roosevelt's death, and says it was strengthened by the removal of any overtones of communist influence in the Democratic Party and by Henry Wallace's bolt to lead the Progressive Party. Truman, Lubell notes, received a record Catholic vote, even exceeding Al Smith's in some areas: "This heavy Catholic turnout—perhaps the most astonishing single aspect of Truman's surprising victory—resulted largely from the return to the Democratic Party of supporters of Father Coughlin."[29]

As already noted, the Democratic strength among Catholics in 1952 was 56 percent; it dipped to a bare 51 percent majority in 1956, and then rose to a peak with Kennedy's victory and remained there: Johnson received 76 percent of the Catholic vote, approximating Kennedy's 78 percent. While Johnson's election success among Catholics was undoubtedly helped by Goldwater's unpopularity,[30] Johnson as President has had overwhelming Catholic support. In Gallup polls reported on May 2 and October 3, 1965, about eight out of ten Catholics approved of the way Johnson was handling the presidency, while his popularity among Americans in general did not go higher than seven out of ten.

Clearly, the Catholic vote transcends the single dimension of religion. The same combination of social, economic, political, and ideological factors that is affecting Catholics as

Americans affects them as voters. This is all the more evident now that the Catholic voter has had a Catholic president. In 1964 the race issue replaced the religious issue, which is not likely to predominate again among American Catholics.

CHAPTER 12

✧✧✧✧✧✧✧✧✧✧✧✧✧✧✧✧✧✧✧✧✧✧✧✧✧

The Joiner

SHORTLY after eight o'clock on a blustery evening in
November, several young men entered a dark doorway
leading to a church basement on New York's Lower East
Side. Talking loudly in Spanish, they were exuberant and
sometimes boisterous; one of them, jostled good-naturedly,
fell down the short flight of steps.

Once inside they headed for the Coke machine, which was
open and needed no coins. The juke box was out of order so
they broke into song, singing in Spanish of their island in
the sun. Arms around each other, they jumped from song to
song, laughed, shouted, and displayed the *machismo* or cult
of masculinity which the Puerto Rican immigrant has
brought with him.

A young priest in a soiled cassock strode through a rear
door, shouted *"Hoy!"* above the din of the singing, and then
quickly made the sign of the cross: *"In nomine Patris. . . ."*
The group then switched to the recitation of the *Ave Maria*.
The Spanish Catholic action group of Saint Patrick's Parish
was ready for a meeting to discuss plans for a Cursillo de
Cristiandad, or Short Course in Christianity. This new
movement of religious revivalism conducts intensive three-
day programs of prayer, study, and discussion aimed at
transforming the believing into the zealous. (The Cursillo's
critics say it sets out to transform the fervent into the
fanatical.)

In Fort Wayne, Indiana, just before Labor Day, another kind of meeting was held by a group of young Catholic laymen planning their fall campaign. These were white-collar Catholics in action: an insurance salesman, a young lawyer, a real estate man, a few junior executives. They drove up the tree-lined street of $20,500 homes with attached garages, parked their late-model cars, and rang the chimes. The lady of the house being out, the husband answered, remarking, "We sure are getting Indian summer this year."

The evening began with polite inquiries about the state of the family's health, how much Henry liked his new convertible, the news in the ponderously Republican local paper, and a few comments on the afternoon picketing of downtown real estate offices by the wife of a local doctor. The doctor and his wife were Negroes protesting segregation in Fort Wayne.* But this meeting was not about civil rights. It was about dirty magazines, of the kind that were scattered on the coffee table—as incongruous in that house with a large picture of the Sacred Heart over the mantel as a low-cut dress at a Rosary Society meeting.

A touch of Irish Jansenism in Fort Wayne, Indiana, and a flavoring of Spanish fanaticism on New York's East Side, something traditional, something borrowed from the American setting, something reassuring, something religious, and most of all something to join. The Catholic in America is no less a joiner because he is Catholic or American. As an American, he belongs to a nation of joiners; as a Catholic, he belongs to a Church which once embraced all aspects of human life, an embrace which has contemporary expression in the myriad Catholic organizations. It is clearly a case where a Catholic penchant is reinforced by an American tendency. The result is the Catholic joiner.

---

* One of the authors was there gathering material on a "typical American community" for a two-part series in *The Sign*, November and December, 1962. See note 5 for this chapter and note 13 for Chapter 15.

There are American Catholic organizations for intellectuals, teachers, bandmasters, audiovisual educators, accountants, druggists, shut-in sodalists, Jewish converts, Slovaks, Thomists, and wearers of brown scapulars. Here is an alphabetical sampling to illustrate the organizing frenzy:

Albertus Magnus Guild—to promote scientific activities and scholarship among Catholics.

American Catholic Correctional Chaplains Association—for the spiritual rehabilitation of prisoners.

American Christmas Crib Society—to promote the use of Christmas cribs.

Blue Army of Our Lady of Fatima—to pray for the conversion of Russia and world peace.

Catholic Council on Civil Liberties—to promote Catholic participation in civil rights actions.

Catholic Evidence Guild—to spread Catholicism by outdoor speaking.

Catholic Institute of the Food Industry, Inc.—to promote high standards of morality in dealing with others.

Catholic Petroleum Guild—for workers in the petroleum industry.

Catholic Total Abstinence Union of America—"to promote the moral virtue of total abstinence." It has a youth section.

Church Music Association of America—founded as recently as 1964 in response to the decree of the Second Vatican Council, with the aim of fostering music in the liturgy.

Convert Makers of America—to foster convert-making by the laity under clerical guidance.

Czech Catholic Union of Texas—to provide religious and social activities and fraternal insurance.

Edith Stein Guild—to assist Jewish converts.

Guild of Saint Apollonia—to provide dental care for parochial school children.

League of Saint Dymphna—to care for the spiritual needs of those with mental and nervous disorders.

National Association of Priest-Pilots—to promote private aircraft in priestly work.

National Catholic Bandmasters Association—to coordinate Catholic band activities nationally.

Pious Union of Saint Joseph for Dying Sinners—to offer prayers and masses regularly for dying sinners.

Saint Gabriel's League—to promote Catholic action and companionship among Catholic postal and other federal employees.

Scapular Apostolate—to spread devotion to Our Lady of Mount Carmel and to promote wearing of the brown scapular.

Women's Catholic Order of Foresters—a fraternal insurance society headed by a lady "high chief ranger." It also has religious, social, and charitable programs.[1]

The American roots of Catholic organizations are exemplified by the best-known agglomeration, the Knights of Columbus. So are their major failings: negativism, defensiveness, muscle-flexing group activities, and empty pomp. When twenty-nine-year-old Father Michael McGivney founded the K of C and obtained a Connecticut charter in 1882, he was supplying a need for Catholic men—a lodge to call their own. America then had about 300 secret societies; in the beginning of this century, 6 million men in a population of 85 million belonged to lodges. In that distant preautomobile, pretelevision era, such societies and their lodges offered safety from women, enjoyable male company, the appealing hocus-pocus of secrecy and ritual, elegant uniforms, and a promise of help in time of need.

The K of C rigmarole imitated—in the most natural of processes—that of the hated enemy, Freemasonry. However, it was a clumsy imitation, according to William Whalen:

I happen to be familiar with both the K of C and the

Masonic initiation rituals. The latter was composed during the early decades of the 18th century and has served as a model for the rituals of most other secret societies. Considered strictly as a literary and dramatic composition, the Masonic ritual far surpasses that of the K of C. The first two K of C degrees are quite undistinguished and the elements of sadism and buffoonery in the third degree find no parallels in the Masonic rites.[2]

Today the K of C has long outlived the usefulness of its original service as a lodge. Its current membership of more than 1.1 million men rests shakily on a small minority of active members; a typical local council of 500 members depends on a handful of forty regulars who attend meetings. By contrast, its residual function of insuring members rests on a very solid financial foundation of a quarter-billion dollars in assets.

With its organizational magazine, *Columbia,* which is billed as "the largest Catholic magazine in the world" owing to a circulation over one million, the K of C holds a mirror to itself. Besides a general editorial diet that is regarded among professional editors as "corny Catholicism," the magazine presents a lengthy roundup of organizational news. What emerges is a thoroughly American variety of activities—charity donations, banquets, and athletic projects. The Catholic accent comes from communion breakfasts, Church-oriented gifts, and a surfeit of clerical guest speakers.

The K of C is no better and no worse than any other amorphous, somewhat moribund society of joiners. It does its share of good. But it takes its cues from its environment rather than from Catholicism: well-meaning, middle-class, mediocre, conformist. On two issues in particular, the K of C has demonstrated isolation from Catholic ideals. Local councils have practiced segregation, in keeping more with community patterns than with Catholic ideals, and K of C labor policies toward its employees have shown an indifference to the social teachings of the Church. When office workers at the New Haven national headquarters struck in 1955, the archbishop of Hartford personally intervened, calling the strike "a matter of serious embarrassment." And then there was the time an Eastern bishop had to berate a K of C council for raising funds through a benefit performance by fan dancer Sally Rand.

The most visible K of C activity is a standard American advertising campaign in secular publications. An institutional pro-Catholic series begun in 1947, it had drawn over 5 million inquiries by 1964. Over half a million responded by enrolling for religious instruction. In trying to win converts, the K of C ads have a persistent quality of defensiveness, unmitigated by the changing times and the fact that a Catholic can be President. The May, 1965, issue of *Columbia* contained a full-page advertisement divided between testimonials from converts who had responded to the K of C campaign and the offering of a pamphlet, "The Catholic Religion and America." The copywriter's mixture of drumbeating and straw-snatching in the answers to self-posed criticisms of Catholicism epitomizes the posture of defensiveness that distorts so much of Catholic organizational life. The copywriter speaks for the K of C, and the K of C speaks for itself in the advertisement:

Certain self-appointed critics have called the Catholic Church alien, undemocratic and out of step with American tradition.

They argue that the traditions and ideals of the United States are largely of non-Catholic origin. And they are especially vehement in their criticism of Catholics on such issues as the separation of church and state.

Catholics ask their non-Catholic neighbors to remember these historical facts:

America was discovered by a Catholic. Most of those who explored its vast wilderness and charted its oceans, rivers, lakes and mountains were Catholics. Catholic missionaries were preaching Christ's Gospel and saying Mass from Canada to the Philippines nearly a hundred years before the Pilgrim Fathers landed at Plymouth Rock.

And as far as religious freedom and separation of church are concerned, the only one of the 13 original colonies that granted religious liberty from the beginning was Maryland, settled largely by Catholics and ruled by the Catholic Lord Baltimore. In the other 12, Catholics and non-Catholics of certain sects were victims of religious oppression.

These self-styled critics like to claim that American liberty was won by a non-Catholic colonial army and sealed by a non-Catholic colonial congress. And Catholics do not challenge the magnificent contributions of our non-Catholic forefathers.

But neither should these historical facts be overlooked:

Fully one-third of the troops of the Colonial Army were Irish-Catholic volunteers. The largest single contributor to the support of the colonial troops was a Philadelphia Catholic, Robert Fitz-Simmons, and one of the most ardent champions of the cause of liberty was the great Catholic patriot Charles Carroll, wealthiest man in all the colonies and a signer of the Declaration of Independence.

Catholic John Barry, "Father of the U.S. Navy," was the only officer given the title of Commodore by the Continental Congress, in which role he outranked the great John Paul Jones. And no distortion of history can erase the fact that the only nations which came to aid our fight for freedom were Catholic —France, Spain and Poland . . . that the foreign heroes of our revolution were Lafayette, Rochambeau, De Grasse, Kosciusko and Pulaski—all Catholics.

If you would like to read the exciting tale of Catholics and America—write today for our new pamphlet KC-67 which will be sent free. Nobody will call on you.

Catholic fraternal organizations like the K of C and such competitors as the Catholic Knights of America, Catholic Knights of Saint George, and Knights of Saint John incorporate religious trappings and observances in their activities. By contrast, devotional organizations emphasize religious participation and solidarity and offer fraternizing as an auxiliary attraction. Here, too, the sexes are commonly separated: the Holy Name Society, for instance, is for men, the Rosary Altar Society for women. Each claims 5 million members. Each also demonstrates the ability of American Catholicism to get its members, even male members, **to** church, a source of amazement to European Catholics. The Holy Name Society, founded in 1909, "promotes reverence for and devotion to the Holy Name of Jesus." The Rosary Altar Society was established in the United States in 1891 "to help parishes and schools establish the Rosary Confraternity, and to foster the Rosary devotion." The two societies are constants in Catholic parish life in America, the third element in a pastoral trinity of church, school, and society. No pastor hopeful of becoming a monsignor would be without them.

Holy Name Societies have popularized the communion breakfast and Holy Name parade. Besides the laudable purposes of encouraging the reception of the eucharist and creating a sense of community, the Holy Name communion breakfast has become a stronghold of political conservatism, reflecting the attitudes of the older generation of clergy. In the McCarthy period the breakfast had a fixed menu of soggy rolls, tepid coffee, and a Communist-turned-Catholic as guest speaker. Today the echo of McCarthyism and the voice of the extreme right wing are still heard at Holy Name communion breakfasts.*

For its part, the Holy Name parade has been a demonstration of group muscle. However, the increasing liturgical sophistication among Catholics has created a demand for a demonstration of group piety instead. The cancellation of the 1965 Paterson, New Jersey, Holy Name parade in the face of declining turnouts is an example. A parish Holy Name president made the significant comment, "I think the people are just not interested in a show of strength any more. Something of a spiritual nature, like a holy hour, might draw just as many men." Another Holy Name presi-

---

* In addition to parish Holy Name Societies, there are specialized groups, particularly in city government. One example is the Holy Name Society of the New York City Police Department, which created headlines in 1954 by inviting Senator Joseph McCarthy to address its annual communion breakfast and in 1965 by inviting the articulate conservative spokesman William F. Buckley, Jr.

dent sounded this realistic note: "The parade had become too expensive for the small parish societies, and frankly, there was too much competition from the World Series. You would even see men marching with transistors [to] their ears."[3]

Between the devotional and the fraternal, other types of Catholic organizations can be identified: the professional, the occupational, the ethnic, the specialized, the missionary. Some are officially recognized by the Church and are granted special spiritual benefits for their members; others provide insurance benefits only. It is easy to become entangled in a maze of specifics, but one generalization is secure: most Catholic organizations are experiencing social lag. They have not kept pace with changes within the Church and the world at large; this is particularly true of the fraternal and devotional organizations.

The defensiveness of many Catholic societies is an example. Anti-Catholicism as the enemy was a useful, though negative, reason for existing and the source of a simplified ideological purpose. But the battle is no longer against environment. It goes on in men's souls, as is reflected in Father Gustave Weigel's remark: "The American Catholic's attempt at adaptation to his milieu has been successful, perhaps too successful."[4] Not only is the mainstream Catholic indistinguishable from his American counterparts, but he wants to be, even though he is often out of step with Catholic ideals.

When Catholic organizations pursue active campaigns, the aims are often negative and the goals safely within the American consensus. Indeed, the McCarthy era enabled adherents to the immigrant religion to dress as superpatriots. As for putting Christ back into Christmas, the goal is applauded by the Protestant majority. But it is in the fight against pornography that the organization-minded Catholic has found a natural stance. The campaigns can be laudatory, but they can also be viewed as an avoidance of more

controversial and more pressing social problems. For instance, a New Jersey attack was mounted against pornography in the spring of 1965, and the K of C and the Holy
Name Society immediately climbed the ramparts; yet this is
a state where Catholic civil rights activists have been ignored, rebuffed, and frustrated on both the parish and the
diocesan level.

In Fort Wayne, the original home of the National Office
for Decent Literature before it moved to Chicago in 1955,
the young men meeting to combat dirty magazines could
feel righteous and also ignore pressing social issues. As reported by one of the authors:

> But Fort Wayne is not an island unto itself, nor is it Dream-
> ville, U.S.A. Its teenagers are rebellious and causing considera-
> ble concern. Its young adults are infected with over-spending.
> The city's pattern of housing segregation is as unyielding as any
> in the country, and its Negroes have four times the rate of
> unemployment as its whites. Its downtown area is hardly be-
> ginning to emerge from the Dark Ages of urban blight.[5]

In that pleasant Fort Wayne living room, the cause of the
Catholic young men was undoubtedly just and of some
merit, but it was also safe and on the sidelines.

As with anticommunism, the antipornography campaigns
of Catholic organizations have been taken to extremes by
local zealots.[6] Consequently, organized Catholic activity in
recent years has earned the two tarnishing labels of witch-
hunting and censorship. While neither is the intent or the
logical outcome of Catholic ideology, the climate surrounding much of American Catholicism has provided a basis for
the charges. For reasons that have nothing to do with Catholicism as a religion but everything to do with the American
Catholic situation (as outlined in Chapters 1 and 2), the
organization Catholic often goes overboard when he takes
action.

In the 1960s, the "emerging layman"[7] has raised hopes
for a rejuvenation of Catholic organizational life. Except for

the episode involving lay trustee control in the early American Church and a brief flowering of lay activity during the 1880s and 1890s, the Catholic layman has followed rather than led. In this passive characteristic possibly more than any other, he has been out of tune with his American environment. In the late-nineteenth-century emergence, an upper-class intellectual convert, Orestes Brownson, played a major role with challenging criticisms that parallel the contemporary indictment made by restive Catholic laymen. His anticipatory targets were the Irish, the clergy, seminary education, Catholic higher education, and Catholic insensitivity to the slavery question. But the lay activism which Brownson epitomized and which culminated in lay congresses in Baltimore and Chicago was a limited phenomenon and short-lived.

A consistent theme in American Catholicism has been the subservience of the laity and therefore of Catholic organizations. As Father Weigel has noted, "The loyal solidarity of the faithful is inspiring, but it entails a lack of sense of responsibility in the formation of programs of activity. The inauguration of projects and their direction are largely left to the clergy."[8]

At the end of the nineteenth century, the lay-organized Federation of Catholic Societies "amounted mostly to a device for an annual convention at which papers were delivered and resolutions passed."[9] To mobilize the Catholic effort in World War I, the National Catholic War Council was formed and eventually became the National Catholic Welfare Conference, the bishops' centralized agency in the United States. The bishops' Conference displaced the lay Federation and added formality to fact. In setting up the NCWC, the bishops' pastoral letter of 1919 addressed the laity as "beloved children" and commended them for two things: their financial support and "your correspondence with the intent of your pastors."

Daniel Callahan, in his excellent analysis of the layman's

current role, has summarized the favorable conditions that
are needed for a lay emergence:

> As previously indicated, a number of conditions appear nec-
> essary for a genuine lay movement: the support of the hier-
> archy; a general Church renaissance; a confident Church; lay
> leaders who have come to terms with the society in which they
> live; an educated body of lay leaders; the existence of a tension
> between the values of the Church and the values of society; and
> a desire on the part of the layman to achieve some of the same
> privileges within the Church that he enjoys in society. All of
> these conditions were present, for a small minority at least, dur-
> ing the late 1880s and early 1890s. They are now present again
> —yet this time on a scale which far surpasses anything known to
> the American Church in the past.[10]

Certainly in the 1960s more lay activity, more initiative,
even more independence from clerical control are evident
among the estimated five million Catholics in lay organizations.* But outmoded structures, inhibited values, and rigid
orientations in the organizations still leave the inertia of
the many unchanged. In American Catholicism, the sound
of a vocal few is often taken as the voice of great prophecy.

Whereas Catholic organizations have made few demands
upon their members and have not come into conflict with
church or society, Catholic movements constitute a distinctly different phenomenon. As outlets for the Catholic
joiner, they are characterized by an excess of idealism and a
shortage of realism. Whether political, as in the case of Father Coughlin's, or revivalist, as in the case of the Cursillo,
Catholic movements have had their greatest appeal outside
the conventional middle class. A full-fledged and durable
Catholic movement which is in the American mainstream
and produces social changes has never materialized. It probably cannot. Catholics resist going against the American
grain and would resist movements separating or possibly
alienating them from the conventional American setting.

---

* Excluding devotional and fraternal organizations.

The Cursillo movement, which arose in the 1960s, is a typical American Catholic example. The characteristics are familiar: idealistic, individualistic, unrealistic, dependent on personal charisma, having limited though dramatic impact. Although the first Cursillo in English took place in the United States only in 1961, the intensive three-day programs had spread to more than thirty dioceses by 1964. When the movement held its annual conference in 1965, 800 delegates from thirty-six states attended, including four bishops.*

Unlike parish retreats, in which the remote voice of doom explodes from the pulpit, the Cursillo involves a group of thirty to forty interacting and reinforcing each other in fifteen highly personalized sessions. Cursillos have been called three-day Pentecosts which transform the participants for life. The graduates, called cursillistas, are supposed to be inspired to live God-centered lives and to be active in apostolic works. It is the nearest thing to revivalism that has developed in American Catholicism.

As described by a Steubenville, Ohio, priest-participant, his Cursillo "consisted of five meditations on Christ, 15 talks on grace, piety, study, the sacraments, Catholic action, leadership, laymen in the Church, the Mystical Body, obstacles to holiness." It also included "spiritual exercises, stations of the Cross, rosary, Holy Hours, full liturgical participation in the Sacrifice of the Mass and visits to the Blessed Sacrament."[11]

A penetrating and persuasive description of the Cursillo as "brainwashing . . . for God's Sake?" has been made by columnist Garry Willis in *The National Catholic Reporter.* He cites the use of planted guides to stimulate activity and discussion, disorientation through fatigue and an unpredicta-

* Cursillos, at first given only in Spanish, originated in a Spanish monastery in 1949 and were imported to the United States in 1957 by two Spanish air cadets in Texas.

ble schedule, silence on the first night to create an appetite for togetherness, and the use of nonsense songs and highly emotional, precisely paced talks.[12] As the Cursillo has moved from lower- to middle-class settings, the psychological gadgetry has been modified, but the basic aim persists: an emotional release and a psychological transformation, induced by and manipulated in a group experience. Because it does not blend into the middle-class American concept of religiosity, the Cursillo has no potential as a broadly based movement; its appeal is limited to the fringes of society in the lower class and to some in the middle class.

In May, 1965, when Bishop Stephen S. Woznicki of Saginaw, Michigan, denounced the Cursillo's "fanatical" wing before a graduating class of cursillistas, he exemplified the inevitable cleavage between the Church's organizational life and movements that threaten to get out of hand. Bishops smile encouragingly at organizations because they can be controlled; movements threaten the status quo, particularly when—like the Cursillo—they are operated by laymen. Bishops, who want to conserve rather than overturn, were not appointed to preside over the dissolution of their authority. Bishops are realists, weighted down with the baggage of power and responsibility; idealists in the Church travel light and can afford to be unrealistic.

Said Bishop Woznicki, in an argument that illuminates the difference between the Catholic organization and the Catholic movement, "If Christ came to earth today, he would use the means of spreading the Gospel that we have today. You cannot fit our conditions into circumstances they had in the world at the time when Christ was on earth. The Church administers the Gospel of Christ in accordance with the necessities of the changing world." Here is the voice of realistic adaptation which a reformer hears as compromise, while a bishop hears the retort of reform as the sound of irresponsibility.

But it is not the business of a bishop to be impartial and

to see merit in the other side's argument. He is an organization man. Bishop Woznicki, for instance, particularly criticized those Cursillo "fanatics" who felt that the clergy should have little to do with temporal matters and who even regarded his new diocesan seminary as "a terrible mistake." The Bishop also complained that they thought he should resign because of his age and "should sell his big house and give the difference to the poor—he should live in a small cottage, the smaller and more dilapidated the better."[13]

Woven into the Bishop's remarks is the tension between environment, culture, and temporal realities and the idealism of a religion which is supposed to comfort the afflicted and afflict the comfortable. All organized religions experience the inevitable conflict between conforming to the contemporary ways of men and risking rejection by demanding revolutionary changes. The latter is the gamble of epoch-making religious leaders, of saints, of martyrs, but it is no way to run a diocese.

Insofar as Catholic movements involve innovation and change, they represent potential threats to the stability of the Church as institution, and they therefore risk official denunciation. But since their idealism runs to impracticality, the threat has not materialized. Thus, the pattern of Catholic movements consists in short-lived controversy followed by dissolution, marginal existence, or readjustment by Church and movement to the American consensus.

Labor policy is an example. In the late nineteenth century, James Cardinal Gibbons of Baltimore established a friendly alliance between the Church and unionism—but just barely. He had to journey to Rome to have the Vatican ban lifted on the Knights of Labor in the United States; otherwise its Catholic leader, Terence Powderly, and its large Catholic membership might have been excommunicated. Despite a prolabor tradition which the Cardinal solidified in a Church of immigrants and workingmen, a discordant note has persisted. The American hierarchy, despite its largely working-class background, is imbued with a laissez-faire mentality and has only belatedly applied the ideals and goals of unionism to Catholic institutions, which are among America's most backward employers.

In 1949, for example, Cardinal Spellman created a lasting bad impression by using seminarians to break a strike of gravediggers at Calvary Cemetery, which is run by Saint Patrick's Cathedral. After leading the seminarians past the picket line, the Cardinal said bluntly, "I admit to the accusation of strikebreaker, and I am proud of it. If stopping a strike like this isn't a thing of honor, then I don't know what honor is."[14]

A Catholic columnist, Msgr. J. D. Conway, openly admitted in his January 31, 1964, "Question Box" in the Davenport *Catholic Messenger,* "We do much preaching about the duty of an employer to pay a living wage, but very often we do not practice what we preach." He added, which is also true, that "the majority of Catholic institutions are now paying a just and living wage." But this is a reflection more of pressures from the American marketplace than of Catholic ideology.

In fact, the American labor movement—so heavily populated with Catholic members and leaders like Philip Murray and George Meany—is hardly influenced by Catholic social teaching. Discussing this situation, Edward Marciniak, a leading Catholic labor expert and activist, cites a 1954 study in a Midwestern city where a Benedictine monk found that the inspiration for Catholic prounion attitudes was exclusively secular.[15] In other words, the survey showed that the Catholics in the labor movement are so thoroughly Americanized that they have no distinguishable impetus that is Catholic.

The promulgation of the liberal social encyclical *Quadragesimo anno* in 1931 did set in motion an idealistic Catholic labor movement in favor of innovations along the lines of medieval guilds. It was called the Industrial Council Plan and it even gained approval from Philip Murray,[16] but it turned out to be "little more than an expanded form of union-management cooperation."[17]

In the field of politics, the most controversial movement has been the Charles Coughlin adventure, which began with a bang and ended in silence. Actually, Father Coughlin's movement had an idealistic base in the progressive social encyclicals and originally had the backing of liberal Catholic circles. But it soon turned irrationally right in the face of Coughlin's two devils: world communism and international banking. His scapegoat was the American Jew; his policy of isolationism was paranoiac; his America was haunted by Roosevelt. Coughlin first had supported F.D.R., using the slogan "Roosevelt or Ruin," which he changed to "Roosevelt and Ruin." In 1936 he started a third party—with disastrous results. After a humiliating defeat at the polls, Coughlin left his famous Sunday afternoon radio broadcast. But his rabid followers conducted a successful campaign to get him back on the air. The disoriented, the discontented, the fanatical—the fringe of a society experiencing social unrest—still rallied to his siren call and to his rabble-rousing weekly, *Social Justice*.

But by 1942 an America at war would no longer tolerate such a divisive and radical force. Coughlin's conspiratorial mentality was epitomized in this charge printed in the February 23, 1942, issue of *Social Justice*: "Unbelievable as it is, there appears to be a plot hatched in Moscow, blessed in Berlin, grinned at in Tokyo, and executed in Washington to defeat the United States of America from within." The twin stabilizing forces of the government and the archdiocese of Detroit intervened with the twin threat of defrocking and a trial for sedition. Father Coughlin retired to the quiet life as a pastor in Royal Oak, Michigan, where he lived on into his seventies as a memento of a brief, passionate, misguided, ill-fated movement.[18]

While World War II and American public opinion

swamped the Catholic wing of the country's isolationists, a know-nothing reactionary image of American Catholics was reinforced. The image lingers on, not because the isolationists won over the majority of Catholics but because they were the most audible. The Brooklyn *Tablet,* an heirloom of the 1930s which continues to distort the virtue of consistency, still looks suspiciously on a world permeated with conspiracy, communism, and anti-Catholicism. The *Tablet's* intractable editor, Pat Scanlon, deserves the major credit for his paper's consistency—still recognizable even in its newly designed typographical clothes. On the other hand, the *Catholic World,* published by the Paulist Fathers, has deserted the editorial wasteland of its former leader and intellectual mastermind of Catholic isolationism, Father James Gillis. Under its present editor, Father John B. Sheerin, the *Catholic World* has become ecumenical and internationalist, a reputable highbrow journal.

In retrospect it is clear that the United States, unlike Europe, has not produced Catholic political parties or labor groups, but only amorphous movements generated by charismatic idealists who manage to seize the platform and rally a noisy crowd of Catholics. They pass rather quickly from view, the noteworthy exception being the Catholic Worker Movement. Founded in 1933 by Peter Maurin and Dorothy Day, the movement has demonstrated remarkable powers of survival under the vigorous leadership of Miss Day, aided by flexibility in action and simplicity in form. Its size is slight—a hard core of workers surrounded by sympathizers, particularly intellectuals—but it acquired new prestige in the 1960s after America's belated rediscovery of its poor.

The country's new awareness pointed up the fact that Dorothy Day had been minding the store for the poor while the affluent society was preoccupied with installment buying. Indeed, the most influential book in the rediscovery of "the other America" carried this acknowledgment from author Michael Harrington: "It was through Dorothy Day and the Catholic Worker Movement that I first came into contact with the terrible reality of involuntary poverty and the magnificent ideal of voluntary poverty."[19] In action closest to the Salvation Army, in spirit pacifist, the Catholic Worker Movement is imbued with Christian ideals and is at odds with the bureaucratic processes of American welfare. It also has neither sought nor received the blessings of the American hierarchy.

Both the ineffectuality of Catholic movements and the weaknesses of Catholic organizations are expressed in two attempts to revitalize Catholic family life—the Cana Conference and the Christian Family Movement. They have issued from an arranged marriage of Catholic movement and official Catholic organization. In the genetics of American Catholic life, the offspring carry the weaknesses of both parents.

As movements, their origin is found in the wartime Family Renewal Days given in New York City in 1943; as organizations, they are allied with the Family Life Bureau of the National Catholic Welfare Conference and are under parish and diocesan supervision. Cana, which takes its name from the marriage feast of Cana (John 2:1—11), holds conferences focusing on four areas of family relationships: husband-wife, parent-child, God-family, society-family. The Christian Family Movement emerged in 1947 as a reaction against the overorganization of the Cana movement and sought to take a communitywide view. CFM's policy of Catholic action—observe, judge, act—aims at small group discussions and involvement in specific projects. It is concerned with changing the environment which affects family life; Cana limits itself to the family.

Taken together, Cana and CFM have a limited impact. Even their numbers are small. Cana attracts about 150,000 persons annually to conferences held in about 125 dioceses, and CFM has 40,000 couples as members. As a movement,

CFM has idealistic overtones in its goals of active participation in the liturgy and in the community; Cana's strength is in organization and official support. But Catholic family life in America has hardly been affected by either, though there are highly committed couples who constitute inspiring exceptions in both movements.

Whereas Cana tends to present official Church views and advice on family life and to remain more aloof, CFM has blended into middle-class settings. Its ideals often become homogenized standard American ideals; its small group discussions follow the path of togetherness, summer vacations, in-law problems, décor, women's rights—all subjects treated in more interesting and more authoritative ways in secular women's magazines. Close questioning and observation of CFM couples have revealed reactions on such issues as civil rights, poverty, the United Nations, Southeast Asia, and so on, which are indistinguishable from the responses of others in the same socioeconomic group. This was borne out, for instance, in a study of selected CFM couples in the New York–New Jersey metropolitan area.[20]

Actually, one issue has come to preoccupy both Cana and CFM couples obsessively, and that is birth control. Though not the automatic topic for meetings, it dominates the informal conversations as Catholic couples worry it, trying to comfort and reassure each other. Cana and CFM leaders in turn feed back information at the diocesan level and offer their opinions on the problem. While Cana and CFM have created a more liberal atmosphere on family planning, their approach has lacked both depth and influence.

The comment can be extended to the American Catholic joiner in general. He has not been a significant force either in Catholic or in American life. Catholic movements have had a negligible influence on American society, generating sound and fury but signifying little. Catholic organizations have had limited success in enriching appreciation of Catholic ideals and in elevating personal involvement. They have strengthened not Catholic ideology but Catholic identity. And in this they perpetuate a function prevalent in a pluralistic society filled with ethnic, religious, social, economic, political, and professional organizations. In America, labeling is the main result of joining.

But there is a negative side to Catholic organizations, as there is to ethnic and religious organizations of any kind. They tend to cut Catholics off from the main activities of American society. Catholic schools, for example, have been accused of encouraging a ghetto mentality among their graduates. A bold statement of the charge was made in *The Critic* by Father John M. Joyce, editor of the Oklahoma City–Tulsa diocesan paper. He noted, for instance, that in any sizable city the Notre Dame Club includes men in prominent business and professional posts—"men capable of community leadership, but, for the most part, they are not community leaders." He contends that graduates of Catholic schools "tend to involve themselves almost exclusively with church groups and in church activities."[21]

The problem is double-edged. The Church needs and encourages such participation to maintain its myriad organizations, but insofar as such participation siphons off Catholic energies, it limits direct Catholic involvement in and impact on the larger society. Moreover, as Catholics increase their activity in the larger community, ecclesiastical influence over them will diminish. In selecting Catholic organizations, the Catholic stresses a significant part of his identity, but because those groupings conform to American patterns, he also expresses the other part of his identity. The American Catholic compromise is thereby epitomized in the role of joiner.

◇◇

CHAPTER 13

The Negro

FROM the rear of the Church of the Resurrection on West 151st Street in Harlem, a solitary white intruder can watch the Negro Catholic at Sunday worship. Between intruder and white priest at the altar, there is a subdued black congregation, white-collar in appearance. It is a Catholic island within a ghetto, where the universal sacrifice of the mass unfolds with the same drab diocesanwide sermon, where the same solemn mystery is celebrated in the company of the same mechanical exhortation for the special collection, where the same sacred communion is offered to the congregation along with the same rack of pietistic pamphlets and lifeless magazines. But it is a world apart from white parishes in the Archdiocese of New York.

In the Catholic Church, the Negro is an outsider, an equal from afar; mostly he has been the target of missionary activity, as in Africa. An annual collection is taken up for this work in America under the Commission for the Catholic Missions Among the Colored People and the Indians, an organization established by the American bishops in 1886. By the early 1900s the missionary effort became concerted; by the 1920s there were some signs of success; by the post–World War II period, there was an upturn in the results, though hardly a widespread response. In 1928 the United States had some 200,000 Negro Catholics and in 1940 some 300,000, approximately 2 percent of the Negro population.

By 1965 about 4 percent of the country's Negro population was Catholic.

Catholicism and the Negro have been kept apart by historical, social, and psychological factors. When the Negroes arrived as slaves, they followed the religion of their owners, who were mainly Protestant. The Catholic population was small, and except for a handful of well-to-do families in Maryland and Louisiana, it consisted of frontier farmers too poor to own slaves.[1] (However, the American Catholic slavery record is by no means blameless; among other things, the Jesuits once owned slaves on their Maryland estates.) In the eighteenth and nineteenth centuries, the Negroes were located largely in rural areas while Catholicism was concentrated in the cities, and there the Church was overwhelmed by the problem of caring for the waves of Catholic immigrants.

When Negroes came into contact with Catholic immigrants, particularly the Irish, it was in the desperate competition for unskilled jobs. The competition created antagonisms that erupted into race riots by the mid-nineteenth century. Because Catholic immigrants were so prominent in these disturbances, Negroes were repelled by their Church as well. Father John Gillard notes, "Irish and Catholic were one to the Negro, and he hated both, thoughtlessly blaming the mother for the sins of her sons."[2] The problem is still acute. On the eve of the 1965 Saint Patrick's Day parade, Father Philip Hurley, a Jesuit prominent in civil rights, told a Fordham University rally that there would be units in the parade which were unwilling to march side by side with Negroes. His very public remarks were recorded by television news cameras.

A choice example of the residual attitudes in the Catholic establishment was furnished by the American Catholic Historical Association from its headquarters at Catholic University. A memorandum came to light in early 1965 which advised heads of history departments in Catholic colleges and universities about job-seeking teachers. The memo carried the assurance: "All the registrants listed below are of the Catholic religion and of the white race."[3]

The persistent missionary approach, while declining, has maintained a safe social distance between Negro and white Catholics. The mentality of "them" and "us" has been typified by Cardinal McIntyre of Los Angeles, who invariably is cited as the most embarrassing example of Catholic indifference to the civil rights struggle. In discussing grievances with a Negro leader in his archdiocese, the Cardinal once pointed out that he had recently discussed race relations at the Vatican Council with "your Cardinal." He was referring to the African Cardinal, Laurian Rugambwa.

The attitude permeates individual contacts between Negroes and the Church: every Catholic Negro has his own bitter examples. For instance, a devoted Negro parishioner recalls what happened when, as a teen-ager, she considered becoming a nun. When she approached the white nuns who had taught her in a Harlem parochial school, it was suggested that she would be happier in an order where "you would be among your own kind."

A Negro priest in Chicago cites two similar examples. A Negro girl applying to an order desperate for vocations was advised by a religious superior that the order would no doubt pray to the Holy Spirit to guide her somewhere else. And there's a parish school in Chicago where the nuns avoid talking of religious vocations out of fear that a Negro girl might ask to join their order.[4]

The consequences of this mentality are evident in the paucity of vocations among Negroes and in the relative isolation of Negro religious and priests in the United States. Of 983 Negro sisters in 109 religious communities, most belong to three Negro congregations; the remainder represent token integration. Of the 115 Negro Catholic priests, only thirty-four are parish priests. When these priests were surveyed in 1964, eighty-one replied to a questionnaire on their work and experiences. Only three were in all-white parishes.

In a summary of the survey, Father Rollins E. Lambert, a Negro priest assigned as Newman chaplain at the University of Chicago, began:

I am a Negro priest.
This simple statement disconcerts many Americans. To many
    Negroes, I have become the minister of what really seems to
    them to be a white man's religion.
To many Catholics, I am a problem.
I really don't think I'm a problem.
Just what kind of problem am I supposed to be?
In cooperation with *The Sign,* I sent out a questionnaire to the
    115 Negro Catholic priests in the United States asking them
    about their experiences, their work, their attitudes, their
    problems, their "acceptance"—a word they have reason to
    hate.
Eighty-one thought it problem enough to reply with candor.
None seem bitter. I'm surprised.[5]

Father Lambert reported that "many priests are outspoken in their embarrassment" at the gap between Catholic principles and practices, particularly "because they ache for the conversion of Negro America." The limited response of Negro Americans to Catholicism reflects the consequences of this gap as well as its historical prelude. Today the Negro Catholic remains a minority surrounded by a minority and wrapped in isolation. He is three times removed—by his color from white America and from white Catholicism, by his religion from black America. As noted in *Black Religion,* Americans recognize five major faiths: Protestantism, Judaism, Roman Catholicism, secularism, and the religion of the Negro.[6] The clustering of Negroes in religious isolation is underlined by a March, 1957, religious accounting of all U.S. nonwhites over the age of fourteen: 61 percent were Baptist, 17 percent Methodist, 10 percent in other Protestant denominations, and 7 percent Catholic.

At the same time, a gradual but perceptible closing of the gap between Catholic preaching and practice has paralleled the increase in the number of mobile Negroes in large cities. In the postwar period, this has been reflected in the steady, though limited, increase in the number of Negro converts. Between 1945 and 1955 about 75,000 Negroes became Catholics, 8 percent of all Catholic converts; between 1950 and 1960 the number increased to 225,000. Negro conversions now run to about 10 percent of the total. As of January 1, 1964, there were 722,609 Negro Catholics in 65 archdioceses and dioceses.[7]

While Catholicism does not have mass appeal among American Negroes, it does attract the aspiring middle class. As Negroes turn from their traditional Baptist and Methodist congregations, Catholics, as well as Episcopalians, Presbyterians, and Congregationalists, gain recruits. The urban style of Catholicism has social and educational benefits for Negroes, as it once had for immigrants. In *Black Metropolis,* St. Clair Drake and Horace R. Cayton summarize the many-sided appeal of Catholic parishes in Chicago's Black Belt of the 1940s:

> Interviews with Negro Catholics, and with non-Catholics whose children go to parochial schools, seem to indicate that one of the primary attractions of the Catholic Church is its educational institutions. With the public school running on double shifts during those years, many parents felt that the parochial school offered a more thorough education in a quieter atmosphere with adequate discipline and personal attention for all students. The Catholic approach to the Negroes has been aided by the establishment of a small community house, by the extensive athletic program of the Catholic Youth Organization, and by the forthright stand against race prejudice taken by an auxiliary bishop of the Chicago diocese. In 1944, the Catholics purchased the most imposing piece of church property in Bronzeville—Sinai Temple, a wealthy Jewish synagogue—and converted it into a school and community center.[8]

In effect, parochial schools are doing for Negro children

what they once did for immigrant children. They are training them for the American middle class, particularly in the
white-collar traits of neatness, punctuality, and politeness,
and aspiring Negro parents place a high value on their well-
disciplined classrooms. For instance, in Harlem, at the
height of agitation over school segregation in December,
1963, a *New York Times* survey found non-Catholic as well
as Catholic Negroes eager to send their children to the eight
Harlem parochial schools, which are predominantly Negro
and which charge tuition.[9] The appeal of the Harlem parochial schools is so great that Msgr. Paul Haverty, archdiocesan superintendent of schools, said enrollment could easily
be doubled if teachers and facilities were available.

But a major handicap facing Catholicism has been a lack
of Negro priests—a mere 115 today, only thirty-five in 1949,
and twenty-three in 1941, with six of them on foreign missions. And in this century, an American-born Negro did not
become a bishop until the fall of 1965, when forty-eight-
year-old Harold R. Perry was named auxiliary bishop of
New Orleans.*

Generally speaking, crusading white priests have had
more impact on convinced white liberals than on Negroes
or unconvinced Catholics. They have improved the
Church's image more than its performance. Bishop Bernard
J. Sheil spoke out courageously for civil rights in the 1940s
and 1950s in Chicago, a city where three Black Belt Catholic
churches had been set aside as "Negro" and where the archdiocese did not ordain its first Negro priest until 1949. A
survey in 1949 revealed that Catholic Negroes in Chicago
were forced to hold membership in three Jim Crow

---

* The first and only other Negro bishop was James A. Healy, born in
slavery to a Negro woman and a white planter and named bishop of Port-
land, Maine, in 1875. In 1965, when Bishop Perry was named, he reported
that there were 164 Negro priests in the United States (*The National Catholic Reporter*, October 13, 1965, p. 2); this conflicts with the total of 115
cited by *The Sign* in its survey of Negro priests in November, 1964 (see
note 4 for this chapter), and reflects the lack of reliable statistics.

churches and to be married and buried from them, no
matter where they lived in the city. Also, there were several
cases of Negro children who were refused admission to the
nearest parochial school, in violation of canon law.[10]
Though the segregated pattern was broken in the mid-
1940s, it was the reality which drowned out the voice of
the crusader. In New York the country's most celebrated
Catholic civil rights advocate, Father John LaFarge, died
in the fall of 1963 a beloved and much-honored figure
—the same Jesuit who had been "exiled" early in his career
for progressive views, the influential liberal who had cru-
saded in an archdiocese which held steadfastly to a do-
nothing policy on civil rights.

The significance of Catholic Negroes far exceeds their
numbers because the Negro, as a Catholic and as a human
being, challenges white Catholics, as a community of believers and as a hierarchical institution, to honor and obey
their Catholicism, to practice what is preached. Beyond this,
the civil rights problem tests the relevance of American
Catholicism and its capacity to be engaged in contemporary
issues.

The conflict in the dual identity of American and Catholic is nowhere more striking than in the area of civil rights.
Catholic ideals and formal ideology pull in the direction of
equality; community pressures and attitudes have pushed
backward toward discrimination and prejudice. As individuals, Catholics have been slow to respond to the civil rights
struggle; their institution, the Church, has also lagged behind. The Catholic hierarchy has shared the reluctance of
the so-called American power structure to confront the
Negro problem. Big business, big government, and big
Church have only recently begun to foster Negro equality.
As Professor Gordon Allport has said of the Christian
Church in general, "the criticism seems justified that
through most of America's history the Church has been a

preserver of the status quo in race relations rather than a crusader for improvement."[11]

If anything demonstrates the evolution of Catholicism from ethnic religion to respectable middle-class entity, it has been the position of the Catholic Church on the race issue. By the time the Church became committed in significant terms, the civil rights struggle had been baptized with every sign of respectability, from the sanction of a Southern President to the commitment of middle-class whites. By the time nuns as well as priests were permitted to join in demonstrations, only extremists opposed the civil rights movement. To support it was not revolutionary but in step with the American mainstream. Individually, the nuns and priests were imbued with idealism; institutionally, their Church let them express their ideals very late in the day.

Officially the stand of the American bishops has been impeccable. Their position was summarized by their August 23, 1963, statement:

Nearly five years ago, we, the Catholic Bishops of the United States, proclaimed with one voice our moral judgment on racial discrimination and segregation. This judgment of November, 1958, simply reaffirmed the Catholic position already made explicit in a much earlier statement in 1943.

In the present crisis, we wish to repeat these moral principles and to offer some pastoral suggestions for a Catholic approach to racial harmony.

We insist that:

"The heart of the race question is moral and religious. It concerns the rights of man and our attitude toward our fellow man. . . . Discrimination based on the accidental fact of race or color, and as such injurious to human rights, regardless of personal qualities or achievements, cannot be reconciled with the truth that God has created all men with equal rights and equal dignity."

We reaffirm that segregation implies that people of one race are not fit to associate with another "by sole fact of race and regardless of individual qualities. . . ." We cannot reconcile such a judgment with the Christian view of man's nature and rights.

These principles apply to all forms of discrimination and segregation based on prejudice. . . .[12]

The most notable Catholic response followed the historic 1954 Supreme Court ruling on school desegregation. By the fall of 1962, there were integrated Catholic elementary and high schools in Arkansas, the District of Columbia, Florida, Georgia, Kentucky, Louisiana, Maryland, Missouri, North and South Carolina, Oklahoma, Tennessee, Texas, Virginia, and West Virginia. Generally the timetable was ahead of that of the public schools.

Otherwise, the Catholic position on civil rights was hardly translated into meaningful action, as Matthew Ahmann, executive director of the National Catholic Conference for Interracial Justice, has pointed out. He observes that "by and large the Church is not deeply and practically committed to the solution of this national issue. There are still few bishops who have energetically involved their vast material and administrative resources in the battle for racial justice. Few of them really understand what the current direct-action battle is all about. There are some exceptions, of course."[13]

The exceptions include Chicago, Saint Louis, Detroit, San Antonio, Oklahoma City—Tulsa, and Tucson, where Church leadership and actions are dynamic and meaningful. In most other dioceses a pattern of evasion is evident, expressive of what might be called the principle of remoteness that emerges in the face of so many public problems. The Church establishment takes its moral, universalistic stand, and then the bishops wrap their scarlet robes around the hierarchical presence and remove themselves. Sober, steadfast, and prudent, they have done their duty and left the scene of action.

However, on the civil rights issue, as on other issues in this time of modernization and challenge from the laity, remoteness no longer silences the critics. It becomes evasion and is labeled as such. Even the moderate Catholic magazine

Ave Maria pointed this out after a 1964 survey of Catholic archdioceses and dioceses regarding what was being done about civil rights. The magazine's report began by noting that "forming commissions and committees is often a way to avoid action, rather than a way of promoting it." And indeed, even on this formal count, the evidence was limited, since only fifty-two out of 136 archdioceses and dioceses replied to the survey. Presumably, those with the most to report were the most likely to reply. The survey concluded:

> A high percentage of dioceses and archdioceses have done a thorough job of publicly backing civil rights through pastoral letters, endorsement of civil rights legislation and actual integration of their own institutions. However, the more we move toward action apart from teaching and establishing of institutional policies, the more the number of "yes" answers dips.
> ... [The survey] has shown us two things rather plainly. The first is that where the Church in the United States has taken an active interest in racial injustice, there are many examples of Christianity at its finest. The second is that, as in so many things, we talk more than we act.[14]

The *Ave Maria* survey, despite its limitations, dramatized the chasm between talk and action. Thirty-seven out of forty-six dioceses reported that pastoral letters on race had been read from the pulpits. But only eight out of forty reported that diocesan funds had been used to aid minority groups when discrimination had barred their obtaining funds, particularly for mortgages.

The first significant move by the Catholic hierarchy in the civil rights struggle did not come until mid-1965. At that point, the Detroit and Saint Louis archdioceses adopted a policy of granting preferential treatment to suppliers who gave equal opportunity to minority group members, with the intention of extending the policy to contractors. The consequences can be extensive, for a typical archdiocese spends more than $100 million a year running its manifold operations.[15] It has been predicted that by 1968 at least forty dioceses will have adopted the policy.[16]

In California on election day, 1964, Catholic leaders learned a lesson that applies nationally. The Catholic hierarchy and clergy had waited so long to provide leadership in the civil rights struggle that the laity was not ready to follow. In fact, some of the California laity openly resisted clerical attempts to rally support for the concept of fair housing legislation.

The issue was embodied in Proposition 14, a proposed amendment to the California state constitution which would nullify all fair housing laws and prevent the state and local governments from outlawing discrimination in housing. The proposition passed by 2 million votes—4.1 to 2.1 million—and not all the strong denunciations by major civic and religious groups had succeeded in stemming the California backlash. The California hierarchy had tried vainly to marshal massive Catholic opposition to Proposition 14. In August, 1964, all eight of the state's bishops had issued a joint letter condemning racial discrimination; five bishops at one point or another had specifically condemned the proposition. Yet when sermons had been preached on the moral issue involved, some Catholics had stood up and walked out of church. (Meanwhile, the consistent Cardinal McIntyre, clinging unerringly to the principle of remoteness, had refused to take a stand, on the ground that the issue was political, not moral.)

Various Catholic clergymen faced the failure realistically. It was a matter of too little too late. After so much silence, it was overoptimistic to expect a change overnight. Father Ralph Brennan, a leader of the Oakland Conference on Religion and Race, said, "I think it was a revelation to many priests, as it was to me, to suddenly realize that the general Catholic population was very unaware of what social justice and charity meant. I can't blame the people because their feelings may well go back to how they have been educated by our clergy and our hierarchy."[17] Father Eugene Boyle, chairman of the San Francisco Archdiocesan

Commission for Social Justice, cited the "failure of Catholic people to have any real knowledge of the Catholic teaching on the state, on the whole notion of the right and duty of civil government to enact legislation in areas of this kind."[18]

A Jesuit, Father Niels J. Andersen of Alma College, Los Gatos, California, summed up the situation in *America:*

Many today find it difficult to accept the statement that seg-regation is immoral. For years, hundreds of years, the clergy not only overlooked the moral implications of segregation and racial prejudice; in a sense, they encouraged it by allowing separate schooling facilities, segregated churches, lily-white reli-gious groups and priestly congregations. When suddenly the "Church" followed the lead set by others in doing something concrete about the racial problem, many found it difficult to understand how the morally white had turned morally black.[19]

Nonetheless, the California reaction did point up one change that reached its climax in the 1960s: the Catholic conspiracy of silence on civil rights had ended. Catholics said *nostra culpa* publicly, and, in the analogy of the confes-sional, that was the beginning of reform. Even the Catholic press began to publish public admissions of guilt about the "skeletons in the closet," as a Jesuit professor of law at Boston College, Father William J. Kenealy, put it in de-scribing "our failure as Catholics to practice in our daily lives the teachings of Christianity" in racial matters.[20]

The founding in 1960 of the National Catholic Confer-ence for Interracial Justice was a landmark in this growing sense of responsibility. When the Conference was founded, there were thirty-five local Catholic interracial councils; by early 1965 there were 112, with fifty-four more being organ-ized. Twenty-four councils were formed in the South be-tween 1961 and March, 1965, when the National Confer-ence sponsored the first meeting of Southern Catholics on race problems. While the Conference works closely with official Church organizations, it is semiofficial and lay-dominated. Its dynamic thirty-three-year-old executive director, Matthew Ahmann, is the outstanding Catholic layman in the civil rights struggle.

Another militant Catholic layman, Dennis Clark, demonstrated the new outspoken style in April, 1963, when as head of New York City's Catholic Interracial Council he addressed the annual convention of the National Council of Catholic Men. He accused the Catholic lay leadership of "failing to appreciate the significance of the racial problem" and of "still failing to have a significant impact upon community practices, even where Catholics are present in overwhelming numbers."[21]

By Easter Week, 1965, the crescendo of self-criticism had reached the normally staid convention of the National Catholic Educational Association, with its attendance of 20,000. Father Louis J. Twomey, director of the Institute of Human Relations at Loyola University of New Orleans, said bluntly that racism was "characteristic of a significantly large number" of Catholics. He added that there are inactive nonracists "who want no part of the heresy of white supremacy, but who recognize no personal obligation to participate in the struggle to eliminate racial discrimination." Then, said this Catholic priest at the sixty-second annual meeting of Catholic educators, "If we were to total the racists and the inactive nonracists in the Church, we would probably come to a figure that would cover the large majority of clergy and laity in the United States."[22]

The Knights of Columbus have likewise undertaken some soul-searching. With its membership of over a million Catholic men, the organization has exemplified the disappointing Catholic record in civil rights. For years racial discrimination within local K of C councils was ignored as they operated under a rule which enabled five bigoted members to bar any Negro applicant. Finally, several bishops criticized the K of C, and members began to resign in protest against the practice of bias. Then came the refusal of Chicago's Loop Council to admit an All-American basketball player from Notre Dame, a Negro. The changing mood was immediately evident: the council's top officers resigned, and the acting head of the Chicago Archdiocese condemned the barring.

After Supreme Knight Luke E. Hart said he favored a new look at membership procedures, the K of C adopted a regulation in August, 1964, requiring a one-third disapproving vote for an applicant to be rejected. Progress, but hardly a commitment to the civil rights struggle. The following winter five applicants were presented to an important K of C council in the New York area. Four were voted in; the fifth, a Negro, was not. In the summer of 1965, the grand knight who had resigned after the Chicago council rejected a Negro told *Newsweek,* "The downtown council is as segregated as ever."[23]

Public censures of the American Church's inaction were heard even in the Los Angeles Archdiocese, which many Catholics have regarded as their Mississippi. Two priests put the intransigence of Cardinal McIntyre in the national spotlight in blunt confrontations. The first challenge, a sensational one, was Father William DuBay's cable to the Pope in June, 1964, asking for the Cardinal's removal from office. Six months later, Father John V. Coffield left his downtown Los Angeles parish for a "self-imposed exile" in Chicago; his exit, covered by network TV cameras and in national news magazines, made the reason clear. Father Coffield could no longer tolerate "the continuing evil of silence" on civil rights in the Los Angeles Archdiocese.

In March, 1965, the *nostra culpa*s took the shape of a dramatic public involvement in Negro demonstrations by priests and nuns. It was the time of the Selma, Alabama, demonstrations for voter registration. The symbol of the commitment was the nun on the picket line, a contrast to the ball-playing and folksinging sister. According to a number of priests and nuns, the reaction among civil rights workers to their arrival was, "It's about time—we've been waiting for you." The reaction was understandable. Previously, the only noteworthy civil rights demonstration by religious had been in the summer of 1963 in the picketing of the Illinois Club for Catholic Women in Chicago for barring Negro members. And of the 210,000 participating in the march on Washington of August 28, 1963, only an estimated 10,000 were Catholics.[24]

This time hundreds of nuns and priests from sixty dioceses played a prominent part in the Selma demonstrations, and thousands joined sympathy marches at home. Saint Louis, Chicago, Oklahoma City–Tulsa, and San Antonio sent priests and nuns; so did Washington, Boston, Baltimore, Brooklyn, and New York. Cardinal Spellman, so often criticized for ignoring the civil rights struggle, provided funds for sending nuns and priests and permitted more than 200 nuns to march in Harlem as well.

However late in the day, the religious gave strong witness that a large part of the Catholic establishment had joined the civil rights struggle. The pictures of the nuns in the demonstrations had an incalculable effect, particularly on Catholic public opinion, in both the North and the South. To an angry Alabaman who shouted, "What are you doing to the white race?", Sister Mary Peter of Chicago said, "Educating it." A memorable sight one rainy night in Alabama was that of nuns linking arms with tall young Negroes, swaying and stamping their feet as they sang, "We Shall Overcome."

The outside Catholic participation was counterpointed by the order of Archbishop Thomas J. Toolen of Mobile-Birmingham forbidding local priests and nuns to participate in the demonstrations. It was the familiar voice of conservative Catholicism: a bishop who had led his flock of 125,000 Catholics since 1927 said that "certainly the sisters are out of place in these demonstrations. Their place is at home doing God's work. I would say that the same is true of priests." He called them "eager-beavers who feel this is a holy cause," and his audience of 400 men at the annual banquet of the Friendly Sons of Saint Patrick applauded.[25]

In Selma new dimensions were added to the confrontation between the American Negro and American Catholicism. There was a dramatic challenge not only to the gap between preaching and practice among Catholics but also to traditional lines of authority, as an unfamiliar spark of individualism was touched off for nuns, priests, and laymen too. Clerics and sisters came to Selma without obtaining the customary permission from the local bishop, a requirement rooted in canon law. The New York Archdiocese issued the remarkable statement that explicit permission is not required for religious to participate in demonstrations—clearly an expedient explanation, and one setting a precedent, moreover, which can only threaten the authoritarian power of the hierarchy. In San Antonio Archbishop Robert E. Lucey used a biblical allusion to endorse participation by nuns and priests; he noted that Christ "demonstrated vigorously" in driving the money changers out of the temple.[26]

Catholic leadership in Selma was in the hands of the National Catholic Conference for Interracial Justice, independent of direct episcopal control. The rush of nuns and priests to Alabama bypassed the National Catholic Welfare Conference. Said one Catholic civil rights leader, "The NCWC is an outmoded bureaucratic machine. No one from the NCWC was seen officially in Selma. They are totally irrelevant and totally ignorant of racial matters." Said a priest, "Whatever Martin [Luther King] wants, I will do."[27]

The Selma events showed equally that priests and nuns could act independently and with unprecedented freedom of movement. For women's orders, the nun demonstrating in Selma was more than a civil rights crusader; she was an individual asserting herself in following her conscience, engaged and committed to a cause. In June, 1965, nuns were even arrested in Chicago in a demonstration against school segregation, a development that startled Catholic civil rights supporters.

In Milwaukee in the fall of 1965, the fallout from the rights struggle affected the authority position of the Bishop himself. Auxiliary Bishop Roman R. Atkielski prohibited five pastors from making their parish facilities available as "freedom schools" during a civil rights boycott against the public schools. As a result, Catholic laymen picketed the archdiocesan chancery, four priests placed a newspaper advertisement announcing their disagreement with the Bishop's order, and four of the five freedom school pastors issued a statement that set forth the wider dimensions of the civil rights issue for the American Church: "We thought that the Church in Milwaukee was being given the historic distinction of being the first place in our country where a church authority would apply in a specific case the declaration of freedom of conscience as enunciated just a few weeks ago in Rome by the Second Vatican Ecumenical Council. It seemed that we overestimated the situation."[28]

In these terms, civil rights constitute an issue with implications for the entire body of American Catholicism. The nuns, priests, and laymen fighting for Negro rights are also fighting for their own rights within the Church. Moreover, the bishops inadvertently cooperated in the struggle by permitting their nuns and priests to go to Selma, in violation of the traditional prerogative of the local bishop. They sowed a seed of freedom upon the wind, and a stirring challenge to authority has taken root.

For Catholics in general, the final stage of confronting the race issue has not yet been reached. First came the self-criticisms, and then the public demonstrations. The ultimate *engagement* must proceed from Catholics as individuals. Even after Selma, Catholics did not wholeheartedly support clerical participation in civil rights marches. A Gallup poll released April 11, 1965, reported that 44 percent of the Catholics disapproved of the participation, slightly more than the 40 percent who approved. Still, this was a more favorable response than that of the Protestants (60 percent disapproved).

A positive straw in the wind was the finding of the Gallup poll released March 10, 1965, that a majority of Catholics disapproved of laws banning interracial marriage and that a majority of Protestants approved of such laws. And on August 6, 1965, Gallup reported that more Catholics (17 percent) felt the pace of integration was "not fast enough" than Protestants (11 percent) and Jews (12 percent). Forty-five percent of the Protestants felt integration was progressing "too fast," compared with 30 percent of the Catholics. However, comparison with Protestants must carry the qualification that they include many more Southerners than do Catholics.

While the data on prejudice do not yield reliable conclusions on differences between Protestants and Catholics, there is no evidence that religious affiliation produces more tolerance. In fact, there is evidence that churchgoers and religious believers express more intolerance toward racial and ethnic groups than do nonbelievers. Professor Allport, whose book *The Nature of Prejudice* is a standard work in its field, has reported that "on the average, churchgoers and professedly religious people have considerably more prejudice than do non-churchgoers and non-believers."[29] Professor Milton Rokeach of Michigan State University reports similar findings, with the qualification that while non-believers are more tolerant toward racial and ethnic groups, they are not necessarily more tolerant in other respects.[30]

Whereas studies generally show that Jews are more tolerant than other religious groups, the differences between Catholics and Protestants vary from one study to another and are probably more the result of geographic, social, economic, and educational factors than of religious denomination.* Targets of prejudice may also vary by religious group. One study of 900 incoming freshmen in an Eastern college found that Catholic students "stood highest" in rejecting Chinese, Hindus, Japanese, Negroes, and Filipinos—a distinctive nonwhite pattern. For the Protestant students, the main targets of prejudice were Armenians, Greeks, Italians, Jews, Mexicans, Poles, and Syrians—all of them members of the newer immigration waves.[31]

Similarly negative attitudes toward Negroes were found among Catholics in a Detroit study. Catholics were more likely to be "unhappy" if Negroes moved into their neighborhood than were Protestants or Jews. The concern was most pronounced among middle-class Catholics, 67 percent of whom said they would be disturbed about having Negroes on their block, compared with 56 percent of the Protestants and only 16 percent of the Jews. Taking all social classes into account, the difference between Catholics and Protestants was less marked: 58 percent of the Catholics would be "unhappy," compared with 53 percent of the Protestants. The survey also found that two-fifths of the white Catholics and Protestants in Detroit "gave answers which clearly indicated a negative image of the Negro group." By contrast, only one-eighth of the Jews did.[32]

But no simple statistical relationship has been established between a particular religious denomination and prejudice. The issue is wrapped in all the variables of ethnic and family background, socioeconomic status, and educational level. In citing the two-way pull of religion—toward prejudice and away from it—Professor Allport makes a persuasive distinction between the believer who has a deep,

* Professor Allport has written: "Where differences have been found it seems likely that the variation is not due to religious affiliation directly. Thus in regions where Catholics are less educated and of lower socioeconomic status, they may show the slightly higher degree of prejudice appropriate to these nonreligious variables. In communities where Protestants are less educated and of lower status, they seem more prejudiced." (Gordon W. Allport, *The Nature of Prejudice*, Garden City, Doubleday Anchor Books, 1958, p. 419.)

personal, "interiorized" grasp of his religious faith and the one who has a mechanical, "institutionalized" outlook.[33] Various analyses of prejudice by social scientists indicate that the believer deeply involved in his religion is motivated toward supporting human equality—an irreplaceable foundation stone of the Judeo-Christian heritage.

The point is expressed in liturgical terms by Father Andersen, who relates the race problem to liturgical renewal in the Catholic Church. It is a suggestive juxtaposition. He stresses the impact of the mass when it "awakens true interior sentiments," and says that "rightly carried out, the liturgy will form in individual Catholics an attitude of mind and heart reflecting Christ's admonition" to be reconciled with one's brother.[34]

Ideally, the religious impact of Catholicism should reinforce the social thrust of American principles of equality. But both American and Catholic principles have been ignored. Bias has characterized the American social setting from which Catholics have unerringly taken their cues.

The civil rights issue revolves not around the few Negroes in the Church but around the many white adherents, including members of the hierarchy, who have ignored Catholic teaching on the brotherhood of man. It has summoned forth a variety of American Catholic tensions—between authority and freedom, between parochialism and social responsibility. It has created a crisis of conscience for Catholics and raised a challenge to authority when Catholics have demonstrated militancy. The issue stands out as one of the crucial tests that loom large in times of great social change. Catholics and their Church are too thoroughly enveloped by America to escape the revolutionary impact of the civil rights struggle.

◇◇◇◇◇◇◇◇◇◇◇◇◇◇◇◇◇◇◇◇◇◇◇◇◇◇◇◇◇◇◇◇◇◇◇◇◇◇

CHAPTER 14

The Intellectual

THREE assorted pronunciamentos demonstrate the strain of the Catholic effort to gain intellectual recognition in America, like the second-generation immigrant child raising his hand frantically in the back of the room to get the teacher's attention.

Example 1: "This is an intellectual age. It worships intellect. It tries all things by the touchstone of intellect. By intellect, public opinion, the ruling power of the age, is formed. The Church herself will be judged by the standard of intellect. Catholics must excel in religious knowledge; they must be ready to give reasons for the faith that is in them, meeting objections from whatever source, abreast of the times in their method of argument. They must be in the foreground of intellectual movements of all kinds."

Example 2: "Our need of Catholic leadership places a mighty responsibility upon our Catholic colleges. . . . We must learn a lesson from secular education and teach our boys how to stand upon their feet intellectually. Hitherto, we have coddled them; we have done too much for them; we have spoon-fed them too long. The land is full of new difficulties, novel situations to which the old answers will not fit. Graduates of Catholic colleges will never attain true leadership unless they have been taught to think for themselves."

Example 3: "Admittedly, the weakest aspect of the

Church in this country lies in its failure to produce national leaders and to exercise commanding influence in intellectual circles. ..."

These three statements on American Catholicism and the intellectual life, similar in their defensive tone and clerical origins, are as current as the latest Catholic newspaper quote, magazine article, or speech before Catholic educators. However, their vintage varies: 1889 (a sermon by Archbishop John Ireland), 1936 (a speech by Rev. Thomas J. Higgins, S.J.), and 1955 (a discourse by Msgr. John Tracy Ellis).[1]

Msgr. Ellis's discourse became a manifesto nailed on the library door, particularly at Catholic institutions. His preeminence as an American Church historian and the compelling analysis he offered created a stir among Catholic influentials as well as intellectuals, inaugurating a decade of discussion and debate (and sometimes diatribe) which received new momentum from the Vatican Council.

A summary of what has become the point of departure for any discussion on Catholics and the intellectual life runs like this: an immigrant Church arrived on a hostile Protestant shore and consumed its energies in assimilating, providing for, and protecting the religious faith of uneducated newcomers; a harassed hierarchy, primarily concerned with administrative burdens, and a poorly educated clergy served a defensive, anti-intellectual laity.

In the final segment of his discourse, Msgr. Ellis applied the *coup de grâce:*

The chief blame, I firmly believe, lies with Catholics themselves. It lies in their frequently self-imposed ghetto mentality which prevents them from mingling as they should with their non-Catholic colleagues, and in their lack of industry and the habits of work, to which [Robert] Hutchins alluded in 1937. It lies in their failure to have measured up to their responsibilities to the incomparable tradition of Catholic learning of which they are the direct heirs, a failure which Peter Viereck noted, and which suggested to him the caustic question, "Is the honorable adjective 'Roman Catholic' truly merited by America's middleclass-Jansenist Catholicism, puritanized, Calvinized, and dehydrated ... ?"[2]

Msgr. Ellis thereby defined another dimension in the indictment of Catholic intellectual life: he placed blame on Catholics themselves. In the immediate reactions, Catholic influentials took sides; there were defenders and there were attackers. Father Gustave Weigel was blunt: "The general Catholic community in America does not know what scholarship is."[3] The president of the University of Notre Dame, Father John J. Cavanaugh, asked rhetorically, "Where are the Catholic Salks, Oppenheimers, Einsteins?"[4] Msgr. Joseph Fenton, a colleague of Msgr. Ellis's at Catholic University, and Father Robert I. Gannon, president of Fordham University, criticized the critics. The latter, a celebrated speaker, reassured the Manhattan College alumni at a January 8, 1958, banquet with a talk entitled "Enough Breast-Beating!"

Sociological analysis (in Harvard tones) was added to historical perspective when Professor Thomas F. O'Dea probed the characteristics which inhibit mature intellectual activity among Catholics: formalism, which replaces experience with abstractions and sees the world as "finished"; authoritarianism, where those in authority take over all intellectual functions, "which, in the nature of the case, they are incapable of exercising"; clericalism, a parochial, priestly view that ignores secular realities; moralism, which views the world exclusively as a place of moral danger; defensiveness, the strongly felt need to repel attacks, even when they do not exist. O'Dea makes it clear that he is not proving the Ellis indictment—"it is almost too self-evident to need further documentation"—but is looking for causes.[5]

While arguments on the issues run the risk of boring outsiders and inflaming insiders, the controversy itself illuminates the evolution of Catholicism in America.* The participants in the discussion, their qualifications, and the subjects are determined by American criteria. Lay rather than clerical voices predominate, and their credentials are more likely to come from training and associations outside the Catholic establishment. And the argument is conducted by judging Catholics according to accepted American standards of achievement. In 1955 Msgr. Ellis applied the American criteria of listings in *Who's Who* and *American Men of Science* and pursuit of graduate degrees. Ten years later a young sociologist, Father Andrew M. Greeley, used similar measuring rods, citing the number of Catholics in graduate school, their academic performance, and their career goals.

In the 1960s the discussion on Catholic intellectuals has been dominated by a newly emerging generation of Ivy League commentators, mainly Ph.D.s from non-Catholic universities. The trend was illustrated by the group of "younger intellectuals" whom Daniel Callahan gathered for his provocative book of self-portraits, *Generation of the Third Eye*.[6] The twenty-three contributors included only four priests and one nun. One writer was a convert. Of the remaining seventeen, nine had Ivy League graduate degrees, practically all doctorates. Only one had a graduate degree from a Catholic university, a master's from Saint Louis University.

Youthful Andrew M. Greeley combines the old and the new look in Catholic intellectuals. He has a doctorate (Chicago, 1962), has written four books and well over a hundred magazine articles, and is now a weekly pundit in the diocesan press. He might be called the Catholic Church's company sociologist. He is also a senior project director at the National Opinion Research Center at the University of

* Daniel Callahan has commented that "the discussion about Catholics and the intellectual life turned out to be only a useful point of departure for a discussion about the nature and direction of contemporary American Catholicism" (*The Mind of the Catholic Layman*, New York, Scribner, 1963, p. 99).

Chicago, where he might likewise be designated the company priest. His own revealing testimony describes the secular-religious traffic in the new generation of Catholics in the intellectual mainstream of America. They gravitate to non-Catholic environments and are welcomed when they arrive. Father Greeley reports:

> The tone of my years of graduate work was set after a conference with Philip Hauser, the chairman of the sociology department. He took me into his outer office where a group of faculty members had gathered for a thesis hearing. "The Cardinal has sent Father Greeley to study with us," quoth he. "We must see that he does well." (It is nice to be around when new eras begin.) I was prepared for the department to be reasonably friendly, but hardly prepared for it to be as overwhelmingly friendly as it was.[7]

The experience is particularly revealing when it is noted that "overwhelming" friendliness is no longer the standard response to clerics at Catholic graduate schools. They are treated the same as other students in reputable Catholic graduate schools and flunked with impartiality (to their occasional surprise).

By the mid-1960s Father Greeley had emerged as chief defender, just as Msgr. Ellis had been chief critic a decade earlier. In the process Father Greeley had turned a thoroughly American tool into a defensive weapon: he had used a computer to analyze a national survey of college seniors and found that Catholics were as intellectual as the rest of America.* He spoke glowingly in the accents of empirical sociology about what he had wrought: "Make fun of statistics if you will, but there is no surer way of cutting through the accumulated nonsense of the conventional wisdom than a modern statistical table."[8]

However, in subsequent discussions Father Greeley was caught with his tables down. His competently presented

---

* According to Father Greeley, "The Catholic parity with the average American in inclination to the intellectual life holds up under a vast variety of controls" (*Religion and Career*, New York, Sheed & Ward, 1963, p. 137).

findings were not directly germane to the intellectuality of Catholics: he reported on educational aspirations rather than intellectual attitudes. He found that "occupational values and career plans of the Catholic graduate are not such that one could argue that Catholicism inhibits his interest in economic activity nor his intellectual curiosity."[9] In other words, Catholics are as ambitious as other Americans, but this is a misreading of *intellectuality* that an anti-intellectual would make. But Father Greeley's mentor, Peter H. Rossi, expressly avoids this pitfall in a foreword to the Greeley study: "It is important for the reader to understand that this book is not a study of American intellectuals. Rather, it is a study of a typical group of recent college graduates from among whom some of our intellectual leaders will be drawn."[10]

The state of the debate was synthesized in the special *Commonweal* issue of October 2, 1964, on "Catholic Intellectual Life—The New Debate." Father Greeley of the University of Chicago emerged as defender and Dr. James W. Trent of the University of California as critic, with Boston College Professor John Donovan as a judicious middleman clearly inclined toward the critic. Though they had not seen each other's articles, the three were obviously familiar with each other's views.*

Dr. Trent cites data from both regional and national surveys indicating "a disproportionate lack of intellectual interests and attitudes among Catholic graduate students. Significantly more than non-Catholics, these students exhibit a tendency toward closed-mindedness and authoritarianism, traits marked by provincial, stereotyped, uncritical, and un-

---

* Professor Donovan remarks that "Father Greeley's empiricist concern with the hard facts of computer sociology barely conceals his own modest anti-intellectualism." He could have added that Father Greeley had learned his American sociology too well. Similar anti-intellectual charges were made by the late C. Wright Mills against his Columbia University colleagues in *The Sociological Imagination* (New York, Oxford University Press, 1959).

creative thinking."[11] He adds that these characteristics are even more pronounced among Catholic undergraduates.

At this point, the debate resembles the disputes of the two washerwomen who were always shouting at each other from neighboring tenements; they could never agree because they were arguing from different premises. It bears repeating that the confusion over the definition of an intellectual reflects an anti-intellectual spirit on the part of the defenders. Both Donovan and Trent differentiate *intelligent* from *intellectual*.* Professionals and technicians can demonstrate penetrating intelligence without having "the free-wheeling, critical, creative, and speculative bent of mind that marks the intellectual."[12]

While the debate on intellectuality among Catholics is far from resolved (the facts are lacking), emulation of the style of American intellectuals has presented a disturbing challenge to the Catholic Church in the 1960s. Regardless of number or strength, the younger intellectuals are audible. They cannot be ignored because they publish in both Catholic and non-Catholic magazines and newspapers and are invited to lecture before Catholic and non-Catholic groups. They even have a name—the New Breed. They are bold, demanding, analytical, critical, impatient, and irreverent. In *Generation of the Third Eye,* Daniel Callahan describes their self-appointed function and posture: "In the past, it was the non-Catholic who cast a critical eye on the Church. Now it should be the Catholic himself who does so—not for the sake of the status quo, or for the sake of reform, but simply in order to insure that the truth is being sought without fear."[13]

The New Breed's style is a departure from the familiar genuflection of the Catholic intellectual, which is illustrated by Rev. William L. Doty's typical volume on trends and

---

* In his *Commonweal* article, Professor Donovan stresses the "critical distinction between 'intelligence' and 'intellect,' " citing Richard Hofstadter's book, *Anti-intellectualism in American Life.*

countertrends among American Catholics. One particular
passage captures all the standard ingredients. First Father
Doty fends off non-Catholic critics: "Clearly, within the
Church there is room for all sorts of temperaments and for
many shades of opinion on a multitude of subjects." Next
he reassures the Church establishment: "Fortunately, however, all Catholics worthy of the name are united in their
obedience to the teaching authority of the Church and in
their reverence for the bishops and the supreme pontiffs."
Then he advises the intellectual: "The first effort on the
part of any true son of the Church in formulating a position
on any subject involving religious values, will be to discover
the mind of the Church, realizing that this does not imply
an intellectual subservience, but rather an intellectual enrichment, since the mind of the Church is the mind of the
divine Christ who is at once the way, the truth and the life."
Finally comes a concession to freedom of decision—"in matters where there is room for disagreement or development"
—mixed with a reminder to be "the enemy of hardened
opinions and subjective patterns of thought."[14] Leaving
aside questions about the practical value of the advice—or
even its theological validity—the statement illustrates perfectly the tense ambiguity between freedom and obedience
that plagues Catholic intellectuals.

The troublesome difference in style between the new
generation and the previous two generations of Catholic intellectuals hinges on reverence, a lubricant which can help
the establishment to accept the intellectual and the intellectual to accept the establishment. By being irreverent the
younger generation has drawn attack from the establishment, particularly in the kept Catholic press. John Leo, in
his often penetrating, acerbic column for the exceptionally
independent *National Catholic Reporter*, speaks out for the
Americanized Catholic intellectual. He says that the latter
now resembles his non-Catholic counterpart: "The careful
and closed Catholic rhetoric is giving way before the more

open irreverent criticism that dominates so much of American writing and expression. Catholics are simply joining the mainstream."[15]

Actually, the critical Catholic intellectuals are adding a third response to the two cited by Professor O'Dea: leaving the Church or leaving intellectual activity.[16] They are staying inside the Church and criticizing—with typical American lese majesty.

In the past, the Catholic intellectual in his native habitat of Catholic campus or professional organization had an aura of emasculation about him. Of course, there were many exceptions (just as many young Catholic careerists still conform to the older model), but the characteristics of timidity, prudence, and excessive politeness among the majority evoked visions of prepuberty choirboys. They were so reverent, even funereal in manner, those establishment Catholic intellectuals. That is why the abrupt change to outspoken criticism and irreverence has been a shock, though this more characteristic American style is no guarantee of greater competence or more profound content.

A nostalgic piece of patriarchal advice on how intellectuals should behave was offered by Bishop George J. Rehring of Toledo, Ohio, in a spring, 1965, dedication of a men's residence at Bowling Green State University. Betraying the uncomfortable adjustment of the hierarchy, the Bishop recommended that the lay critic "modify his style of writing, that he drop flippancy, cynicism, brashness, sarcasm, fault-finding, castigation, vitriolic and acrimonious language, and adopt the attitude of Cardinal Newman's gentlemen—the attitude of courtesy, consideration, docility, respectfulness and open-mindedness, without, however, any thought of sacrificing sincerity, forthrightness and outspokenness."[17] A noteworthy invocation: the echo is from another century and another country.

But the strain between intellectuals and the Church establishment also springs from profound sources, which are evident in the repeated pleas for an "intellectual aposto-late." This is a contradiction in terms, and the plea threatens to subvert the intellectual and turn him into a holy panderer for the Catholic Church.* The problem arises from the primary commitment of the intellectual to ideas—free of prejudgment insofar as is possible. The primary commitment of the apostle is to dogma—bound to the monumental prejudgment that the Catholic Church is the unique teaching authority on faith and morals. Intellectuals *can* be apostles—and vice versa—but the two roles are merged at the risk of intellectual honesty. The roles are intrinsically separate, as the late Father Weigel tried to point out: "The intellectual life is neither committed to Christianity nor does it antecedently reject it."[18]

When placed in this perspective, the constant concern about the intellectual life is seen for what it is: primarily a devotion to the Church, not a love of intellectuality for its own sake. This order of priorities means that the Church regards intellectuals as valuable instruments, who not only can write persuasive apologetics and apologetic persuasion but who also stand as Christian witnesses in a secularized environment. Without Catholics who are intellectuals, the Church's influence and relevance is considerably weakened. For the apostolic camp, the maximum joy is produced by the conversion of an intellectual—whether he comes from Anglicanism or communism.

Even Msgr. Ellis raises the apostolic cry in his critical essay by bemoaning "the absence of a sense of dedication to

* One of the most significant instances of the strain between the intellectual and the Church establishment in recent times occurred when four outstanding Catholic scholars were officially refused an academic forum at Catholic University, as mentioned in Chapter 10. The grounds, as Msgr. William J. McDonald explained at the time, were that "The Catholic University is under the jurisdiction of all the bishops of the United States. Because of this unique status it takes no official position on those issues and policies still unresolved by the [Vatican] Council." The four scholars "were known to hold a similar definite point of view on pivotal ecclesiastical issues being debated in the Council." (Quoted in John Victor, "Restraints on American Catholic Freedom," *Harper's Magazine,* December, 1963, p. 34.)

an intellectual apostolate,"[19] while Bishop John J. Wright of Pittsburgh, reputedly the "intellectuals' bishop," seconds the motion in a prefatory note: "The problem of the apostolic role of the Catholic intellectual cannot be too often emphasized."[20] This shotgun marriage of the intellectual and the apostle runs through both the praise and the blame of the past eighty years—an obvious reason why the intellectual honesty of Catholics has been suspect in America.

The risk involved in joining the "intellectual apostolate," at least from the viewpoint of American intellectuals, is demonstrated by reactions to Jacques Maritain. He has become a chief philosophical spokesman for the Catholic Church, but because his profundity has been put to work on behalf of dogma, his philosophical writings are viewed suspiciously, as subtle apologetics. In a penetrating review of Maritain's *Moral Philosophy* (1964), Harvard philosopher Morton White comments that the book is "not a history of moral philosophy so much as an apologetically motivated polemic." He adds that the philosopher who provides ground rules for all men while staying within the confines of a specific religious institution "moves from the level of mere technique to the level of dogma, and not to the heights of free and unobstructed vision."[21] Thus, the apostolic dominates the intellectual.*

A young Catholic philosopher has appropriately labeled the American philosophic viewpoint as "the American angle of vision,"[22] and it creates an atmosphere opposite to the inhibiting Catholic milieu summarized by Professor O'Dea. From the American angle, the world is unfinished and filled with uncertainty; experience, experiment, and the existential predominate, and meaning is not so much found in the world as made by man. Such an approach is the

* Obviously, we are purposely avoiding a discussion of philosophical content and validity, and are only citing the contradiction inherent in the role of "intellectual apostle," judged from the American viewpoint.

American expression of an Anglo-Saxon challenge. It is at odds with the closed universe of the Roman, the Scholastic, and the traditionalist.

Psychologically, both the intellectual and the Church suffer from what Karen Horney would call the typical American anxiety about failure,[23] though they define failure differently. The Church fears that the intellectual may fail as a Catholic by rejecting its authority and creed. The intellectual fears he will forfeit his standing among his American confrères if his intellectual freedom is inhibited by his religious commitment. Consequently, the Church establishment would prefer that the intellectual wear an institutional lifesaver of apostolic fervor and dogmatic prudence as he leaps into the intellectual unknown. However, many of these younger thinkers are making the leap without the lifesaver. This risk-taking, more than anything else, characterizes the significant Americanization of intellectuals who are also Catholics.

CHAPTER 15

◇◇◇◇◇◇◇◇◇◇◇◇◇◇◇◇◇◇◇◇◇◇◇◇◇◇◇◇◇◇◇◇◇◇◇◇

The Worshiper

THE CANDLES on the altar and around the catafalque in the center aisle flickered in the Gothic dimness of an overcast morning as three priests—celebrant in the center, deacon on the right, subdeacon on the left—chanted the closing prayers of the requiem mass. From the rear of the church the six pallbearers, led by the funeral director in formal attire, had already started walking down the side aisles to converge and genuflect in front of the altar. The two unseen singers in the choir loft sang the final funereal hymn, now in English, "May the Angels Bear You into Heaven," and the celebrant sprinkled holy water, uttering the last priestly wish, "May you rest in peace." In a dark corner of the church an elderly parishioner, her lips moving at high speed as she completed her recitation of the rosary, kissed the crucifix attached to her beads, dropped the holy instrument into her purse, and left the church by a side door.

That final liturgical ceremony was appropriately focused on the mass, the central act of Catholic worship and the embodiment of the central act of faith in the real presence of Christ in the sacrament of the eucharist. It affirms the abiding and core element in Catholicism as a Catholic enters into eternity. But this side of eternity, a Catholic worships in a variable context of cult and culture. The little old lady with her rosary beads, for instance.

There is within the community of Catholics the centripetal force of the Church, both as institution and as house of worship, drawing believers toward the eucharist.* The eucharist is the heart of all Catholic liturgical service and the focal point of the six other sacraments. At baptism the believer is given title to be admitted to the eucharist and the other sacraments. Confession restores the sinner to the state of grace necessary for receiving the eucharist. Confirmation *establishes* him in his faith. Matrimony provides the formal religious sanction for raising children to be citizens of a heavenly kingdom, and extreme unction prepares those who are on the threshold of entering that kingdom. Holy orders confer the priestly power to consecrate the eucharist and to administer or officiate over the other sacraments.

The eucharistic core of Catholicism involves religious worship with established time, place, ritual, and kind of participant. It is the corporate, official form of Catholicism, in its orientation traditional, conservative, and stable. Species of cults and influences of culture swirl around this nucleus—in America as everywhere else in the world. They are centrifugal, frequently distracting the faithful from the eucharistic core (for instance, toward the mother of God instead of God), often debasing the coin of Catholicism (by way of phosphorescent statues, moving-eyes pictures, dashboard medals, "sure-fire" intercessions for favors).

American Catholicism is a complex of such centrifugal forces. As a Church of immigrants, it has a proliferation of nationality variations and ethnic islands, each adding a flavor, a traditional devotion, a cultural deviation. Manifes-

* The operative word *transubstantiation* has been applied to the changing of the substance of bread and wine miraculously and truly into the body and blood of Christ. Recently, in one of the bold attempts to break the stranglehold of Thomistic philosophy upon Catholic theology, avant-garde Catholic theologians have proposed—in company with a number of Protestant theologians—the term *transignification*. Instead of a change in substance while bread and wine retain their "accidents" or appearances, these theologians focus on a change in the meaning of bread and wine. Regardless, the eucharist remains paramount.

tation of these national origins has tended to cut Catholics off from the rest of America and to reaffirm European ties, so that Catholics turn up different from other Americans.

Catholicism in this country has become a conglomeration of different religious styles: "the intensely sentimental Catholicism of Spain, the fiercely Puritanical Catholicism of Ireland, the relaxed and affectionate Catholicism of Italy, the reasonable and sophisticated Catholicism of France, the deeply devotional Catholicism of Hungary and Poland."[1]

At the same time, the Catholic's drive to conform with the American environment has tended to blur his differences from the non-Catholic. Except when each goes through his own church door, it is almost impossible to tell them apart. In summarizing "the indistinguishability of the Catholic in the ordinary activities of life," Father Wiegel has underlined the American emphasis on individual piety as a private affair:

In the office, in the factory, in the professions, and in social intercourse, the Catholic is rarely distinguished from his non-Catholic fellows. The behavior of both is the same. It is not rare for a Catholic to discover only after years of friendly relations that the man who works next to him is a Catholic also. This is inevitable, for piety should not be manifested and it is impolite to talk about it. What is worse, many Catholics, though quite strict in matters of domestic morality, and who see to it that their children are solidly grounded in ethical matters by giving a splendid example themselves, will in professional life be unscrupulous and sophistic in their evasions of public morality. Not a few Catholic figures in public life have been convicted of highly immoral action, though their sincere and devout adhesion to Catholicism was indisputably evident. The moral shortcomings of the total American community are shared by the Catholics with no notable resistance. The Catholic has striven so hard and so long to be accepted by the American community that he has taken on the color and habits of the general environment, keeping his piety well out of sight. Now that he is unquestionably accepted, he is very loath to do anything which would isolate him from his group, which in its outlook is not Catholic. Piety is invisible and conformity is visible.[2]

The process of ethical assimilation is like losing a foreign accent in the first generation and refusing to learn a parent's native language in the second. The Catholic values his sense of belonging in America and does not want to endanger this social treasure with religious aggressiveness. The result is the tension between the pressure to stand apart in religious behavior and the desire to blend into American pluralism. Within this tension and between these two tendencies, the Catholic in America believes and worships, influenced by both.

The two tendencies are also represented by the liturgical and ecumenical movements which have become fashionable among Catholics. The liturgical movement has stressed immersion in a Catholic communal framework, using Church ritual as the visible cement for a distinct religious identity and awareness. By contrast, ecumenism stresses religious similarities and cooperation rather than differences between religious denominations, blending Catholicism into American religious pluralism.

Ironically, the same liberal, dedicated American Catholics are likely to be in the vanguard of both movements. They will promptly deny any contradiction between the two movements and indeed will point out a compatibility. That may be the case intellectually, philosophically, and theologically—in those remote realms of justification which Catholics often mistake for the arena of social realities.* In fact, the social consequences of the two movements diverge.

---

* Few attempts have been made to bridge the gap between theological-philosophical complexities and social-political complexities. A particularly perceptive analysis has been made by theologian Robley Edward Whitson of Fordham University, who identifies a negative and a positive pluralism. "Negative pluralism presumes that one position at most can be valid and every other position is *totally* invalid." Positive pluralism recognizes different roads with the same destination—"the truth sought." It does not involve replacing diversity with uniformity, "but the elimination of divisive error so that unitive individuality can be realized." (See Rev. Robley Edward Whitson, "Religious Pluralism and Christian Authenticity," paper delivered at the Edward Gallahue Conference on Religious Convergence, Princeton Theological Seminary, Princeton, October, 1964. Conference papers are being published by Princeton University Press.)

The ethos of the liturgical movement tends to separate what it denotes as the People of God as Christian witnesses; the ecumenical movement tends to make common cause with other American believers and to blend religious groups together. The first consequence damages the Catholic image in America; the second complicates relations with Rome. Pointing out the differing social tendencies will unavoidably provoke the dialectics and the denunciations of the liturgical and ecumenical partisans.

Actually, the liturgical movement emulates ethnic Catholicism in attempting to create a communal sense among Catholics. When they were immigrants mixing nationality and religion, separateness came naturally. The national parish, the ethnic priest, and the distinctive ritual provided framework, leadership, and expression. The novena, nine days of special public or private devotions, is an example. Its spiritual aim has been nationality-oriented. The mother-dominated Irish have preferred novenas to the mother of God; the patriarchal Italians have a fondness for novenas to Saint Joseph or Saint Anthony. It is hardly an accident that in the flight to the suburbs and in the process of assimilation the novena is declining. There is probably no more depressing scene in contemporary American Catholicism than the evening novena in honor of the Immaculate Conception conducted by a resigned young priest in a decaying urban parish before a languid handful of elderly lower-middle-class ladies singing off key.

The nationalities have rallied around particular saints or particular attributes of the Virgin Mary. Saints as well as generals are useful historical heroes for all nationalities, and heroes are best honored with processions and parades. Through public demonstrations nationality groups show their strength within the community of Catholics. The Irish, of course, have set the standard with their Saint Patrick's Day parade, a statement of Irish as well as Catholic power. This mixture of nationality and religious devotion still pervades the remaining ethnic parades in America, with floats and marching clubs and fife-and-drum corps honoring hero-saints.

Therefore, it is not surprising that the cult of saints has thrived in America. By tradition, formal Church designation, and popular veneration, a patron saint is born. He can be the special sponsor of a country or of almost any conceivable role in modern society, for patron saints keep up with the growing division of labor and the list of new nations. In America the intellectual and the assimilated Catholic in a Protestant-oriented pluralistic culture has been uncomfortable with the cult of saints. But it is an important part of Catholic devotion and a source of considerable revenue to manufacturers and retailers of religious objects.

Limiting the list to the letter *A*, there are patron saints for Alsace (Saint Odile), the Americas (Our Lady of Guadalupe and Saint Rose of Lima), Argentina (Our Lady of Lujan), Armenia (Saint Gregory Illuminator), Asia Minor (Saint John the Evangelist), Australia (Our Lady, Help of Christians), accountants (Saint Matthew), actors (Saint Genesius), advertising (Saint Bernardine of Siena), alpinists (Saint Bernard of Menthon), altar boys (Saint John Berchmans), anesthetists (Saint René Goupil), archers (Saint Sebastian), architects (Saint Thomas the Apostle), armorers (Saint Dunstan), art (Saint Catherine of Bologna), artillerymen (Saint Barbara), artists (Saint Luke), astronomers (Saint Dominic), athletes (Saint Sebastian), authors (Saint Francis de Sales), automobilists (Saint Frances of Rome and Saint Christopher), and aviators (Our Lady of Loreto, Saint Thérèse of Lisieux, and Saint Joseph of Cupertino).[3]

By the 1960s, liberal intellectual Catholics were widely criticizing the excesses surrounding the cult of saints. The reaction against the European carryover amounted to a further Americanization of Catholic devotion. One of the boldest criticisms appeared in *The Critic,* which published

John Bellairs' satire on the "life and amazing times" of a fictional Saint Fidgeta, "patroness of nervous and unmanageable children." The saint "appeared in 1272 to Scintilla Sforza, who became Mother Latifundia, foundress of the Order of Faithful Fidgettines (O.F.F.)," and from this order the following candidates for patronage were produced:

St. Pudibunda, who on her wedding night decided that God had called her to a life of spotless virginity. The causes of her death that very night are not known, but the pious may guess at them. She was posthumously admitted to the order.

St. Adiposa, author of numerous anti-ascetic tracts. She decided that a life intentionally cut short by over-weight could be consecrated to God. Confined to her cell by immobility for much of her life, she wrote a long, strangely moving hymn to St. Fidgeta. . . .

St. Dragomira, the warrior nun of Bosnia. Converted from paganism by the Fidgettine missionary Anfractua, she spent her life in fomenting religious wars, and is usually credited with Christianizing Upper Bosnia. She was clubbed to death by her pagan brother, Bogeslaw, after a long and heated argument about Christian hate. Patroness of edged weapons.[4]

Spoofs aside, the liturgical movement is theologically more sophisticated than the ethnic devotions to saints, but its social thrust is still toward separateness. It seeks to crystallize an identity that will set Catholics apart. In social terms, a misconception and a misunderstanding underlie its approach. It looks out on an America which no longer exists and cannot be resurrected: an America with a style of living in tight-knit, cohesive communities. The community has been replaced by the city and the suburb, where there is more isolation than interaction, where there are lonely crowds and changing populations. The liturgical movement, in spite of this social reality, does not seek only to make worship more accessible to the Catholic by using the vernacular and increasing the congregation's participation. It seeks to create a sense of cohesion among Catholics by encircling them with a pervasive religious context that governs their lives as witnesses to the message of Christ.

Its spirit was summarily illustrated by Father John J. McEneaney, treasurer of the Liturgical Conference, which is the powerhouse of the movement. In June, 1965, he addressed the twenty-fifth annual Liturgical Week sponsored by the Conference, which has reached the height of its American success since the reforms it has promoted have recently been adopted in response to Council promulgation and papal order. Father McEneaney urged, "We must recapture the ancient Christian sense of the Mass as community, as the assembly of the People of God."[5] The term "People of God" has an obvious similarity to the Jewish self-designation as the "Chosen People." In aiming at total religious pervasion, the Liturgical Movement resembles Orthodox Judaism, which imbues every aspect of living with religious ritual and connotation and which isolates its members from their religiously different neighbors.

The Liturgical Movement can be cited as a characteristic Catholic movement, suffering from a lack of realism and yet attractive because of its idealism and its dramatic impact. Appropriately, the liturgical revival began under the aegis of the Benedictines, who embody the rural, corporate life of medieval times. Forty years ago the Benedictines provided some organization for the movement in the United States at their establishment in Collegeville, Minnesota, the largest Benedictine monastery in the world. There, in an isolated, self-contained environment with a men's college as an appendage, the Benedictines have created a liturgical world apart from the urban mainstream of America. But even at the Collegeville house, the obsessive war against outside encroachments is losing battles. It is obvious to anyone who has lived there[6] that the monks and their collegiate vassals have created not only an inspiration but also an anachronism. This is a lesson to apply to the ethos of the liturgical movement.

While winning a victory in gaining ritual changes, the

liturgical movement has by no means succeeded in renewing and expanding Catholic involvement in corporate devotion. For there is a difference between changing the mechanics of the liturgy and persuading Catholics to engage in a liturgy-inspired life. *The National Catholic Reporter* posed the problem succinctly in a June 30, 1965, headline—"Will Success Spoil Liturgy Reform?"

The Liturgical Conference, founded in 1940 and long in limbo, became the approved American center for information and service on liturgical matters. The reforms propounded in 1964 included stipulations that the vernacular be used in the celebration of the mass and administration of the sacraments, that the congregation give oral responses and join in the singing at mass, and that the priest celebrate mass facing the congregation. Externally, the reforms Americanized the American Catholic ritual. Some felt it had even become Protestant—a reaction illustrated by one outraged Chicago parishioner, who stalked up to his pastor after the congregation had sung Martin Luther's "A Mighty Fortress Is Our God" and snapped, "Thanks for leaving the holy-water fonts."[7]

The loudest protest was led by a suddenly audible, quickly silenced professor of moral theology, Father Gommar Albert De Pauw. In organizing the short-lived Catholic Traditionalist Movement in early 1965, he directed the writing of a manifesto which explicitly deplored efforts to "Protestantize" Catholics. Father De Pauw added that some of the changes had made the mass "no longer the sacrament of Calvary but a song fest with the overtones of a hootenanny."[8]

Though the changes have Americanized the liturgy, the spirit of the liturgical movement has a de-Americanizing import. In seeking a sense of community, it could produce tight little islands of self-conscious Catholics who are out in the world but maintain primary psychological contacts with their Catholicism. Edifying, but unrealistic and also divisive in contemporary mass society.

But despite this tendency, liberal Catholics are the leading proponents of the liturgical movement. They see it in terms of a Catholic renaissance. As the perceptive Catholic commentator James O'Gara wrote approvingly in *Commonweal,* the supporters of the movement "dare to suggest that participation in the liturgy could once more become the central and most formative force affecting all members of the Christian community, adults and children."[9]

The argument, even the terms, follows that of Mary Perkins Ryan in her controversial challenge to the parochial schools. Mrs. Ryan asserts that she does not plead for a return to medieval Christendom. Granted: but then she regresses farther in time—to the early Church—for her Rousseau-like inspiration. Her terminology may be vague and her distinctions confusing, but she remains an advocate of a self-conscious Catholic community:

With the example of the early Church in mind, we cannot dismiss as a wild fancy the idea that participation in the worship of the Church—understood in a far fuller sense than has been possible in recent centuries—could once more become the central and most important formative force affecting all members of the Christian community, and that around this focus other means of religious formation could be organized to supplement and extend it—without the need for also providing the Catholic young people with a general education.[10]

The same inclusive view is reflected in an essay jointly written by two religious active in the movement. They describe "the wonderful burgeoning out of the liturgical movement into all areas of life and action."[11]

As the supporters of liturgical renewal say, the goal of religious enrichment and devotional involvement extends far beyond hymn-singing in English on Sunday morning. The liturgy embodies a whole way of life. What they overlook is the reality of an urban mass society where the tight-knit corporate religious life is almost impossible to achieve. They cannot accept Will Herberg's celebrated insight that the religion of America is religion. Protestant, Catholic, and Jew—Americans belong to religious denominations in their process of self-identification and belonging. Except for a minority of diehards, American Catholics do not feel exclusive; in the first place this was impossible for an underprivileged minority, and in the second place it has become undesirable for an accepted group of middle-class Americans. The American tune is pluralistic. As Professor Herberg writes:

The most striking evidence of the Americanization of the Catholic Church in this country probably came when American Catholics began to regard their church as one of the three great American religious communities and themselves as devotees of religion in one of its three American forms. This did not at any point involve an explicit rejection of the church's claim to be the one true and universal church; rejection, or even questioning, of this claim would obviously be impossible for a Catholic. What it did involve was a deep-lying, though often unarticulated, conception of American social reality.[12]

A pluralistic style is gaining ground among both clergy and laity. Cardinals turn up at funeral ceremonies for prominent citizens—whether in Catholic church, Protestant church, or synagogue. Priests take their turn saying grace at chamber of commerce meetings. Laymen marry across religious lines with few inhibitions. Catholics share in the overwhelming American approval of the view that all religions should be tolerated: in a September, 1963, poll for *Redbook* magazine, Gallup found 88 percent of the Catholics approving "toleration of all religions," along with 86 percent of the Protestants and 85 percent of all those surveyed. A member of the hierarchy in the Midwest has summarized what is evident: "There is a tendency to look for points of similarity among various religious groups, and dialogue has replaced religious debate."[13]

A choice reminder of the pressure to harmonize Catholic religious rules and American realities is a gold-bordered card served up with the Friday steak on airplanes: "The Vatican has granted special dispensation to Roman Catholics on American Airlines from the obligation of abstinence on all Fridays and other days of abstinence. On future flights, should you prefer seafood, please make this known at the time of making your reservation. We will be glad to accommodate you." This is the voice of pluralism flying over America "on all Fridays and other days of abstinence." Both the airline and the Church are ready to accommodate the passenger. In the end, even Curial Rome nods to Americanization.*

From time to time, the irrepressible American touch is also added to Catholic devotions with innovations and statements that border on the bizarre. In Chicago, a parish church announced that the seat collection was being raised to 25 cents because "just as in any other business, a rise in overhead dictates an increase in the cost of the product." A church in Ohio once solved the seat collection problem by installing turnstiles. In New York an electronic system lights up in one church, cueing the congregation: SIT, KNEEL, STAND. In Joliet, Illinois, there is a church pulpit that saves the preacher from walking up stairs: the pulpit rises and descends like an elevator. And in Milwaukee there was the electronic pastor who recorded the Sacred Heart novena and played the tape back for the congregation.

Beneath these superficialities, the assimilation of Catholicism as a religion is proceeding on a profound level under the official policy of ecumenism. The unity of all Christendom is its ultimate goal, but here and now in America it operates as an official acceptance of American pluralism. The open-door policy clearly released the long-standing commitment of American Catholics to pluralism. By the

---

* This March 12, 1964, dispensation for United States airlines presaged wholesale liberalization of abstinence regulations.

end of 1964, about 75 dioceses had engaged in ecumenical activities ranging from joint clergy conferences and retreats to interdenominational meetings and parish open houses. Typical of the momentum was the action of the Santa Fe Archdiocese, which joined the New Mexico Council of Churches. Early in 1965 the seven-member Bishops' Commission for Ecumenical Affairs was operating and approving specific ecumenical projects.

In mid-1965, social and organizational contacts were brought to the sensitive level of the theological. The overtones were historic. Meeting officially in Baltimore, the traditional capital of American Catholicism, were descendants of the great protagonists of the Protestant Reformation —the Lutherans—and the Jesuit sons of Ignatius Loyola.* The thunder of past controversy and condemnation was reduced to a joint statement which rang as harmoniously as church bells, but which was unprecedented for Catholics and Lutherans in America: "We confess in common the Nicene faith. . . ."[14]

Clearly, the ecumenical movement is carrying the day and thereby placing pressure upon the liturgical movement to adjust to the demands of ecumenism. In effect, the liturgical movement must abandon the inner-directed style of the rural monastery and enter the pluralistic hurly-burly of urban America. Then, the liturgical movement would follow the pattern of those Catholic movements which become established; it would enter the mainstream.

On the popular level, belief in a future Christian unity was also growing, as was borne out by Gallup Poll findings, with Catholics more optimistic than Protestants. In March, 1959, some 23 percent of the Catholics and 13 percent of the Protestants said they thought that the day will come when all Christians are united into one church. In the September, 1963, poll for *Redbook*, Gallup found that the optimists

---

* Before the summer was over, there also were official Catholic meetings with Episcopalians, Presbyterians, and Greek Orthodox.

had increased to 29 percent among Catholics and 17 percent among Protestants.

Moreover, across the disappearing interfaith barrier, Catholics and Protestants have a matching view of each other's religions which indicates the directions ecumenism will take. When asked to list the churches most similar to theirs, Catholics select the Episcopalian and Lutheran.[15] According to Professor Milton Rokeach, Catholics and Protestants agree on which denominations have the closest resemblance. The breakdown ranges from Catholic through Episcopalian, Lutheran, and Presbyterian to Methodist and Baptist. He reports also that defections usually occur to similar churches.

In terms of religious participation, American Catholics certainly are a churchgoing phenomenon. One survey reports that 72 percent of American Catholics go to mass every Sunday, 45 percent receive communion at least once a month, and 66 percent go to confession at least twice a year.[16] In recent years Catholic churchgoing has held steady while the national pattern has declined from a 1958 peak, when Gallup reported that 49 percent of American adults attended church in a typical week. The figure slipped gradually to 45 percent in 1964 owing to a decline in Protestant attendance. In both 1961 and 1964, the Catholic figure was 71 percent; by comparison, the Protestant figures were 41 and 38 percent respectively.[17]

The portents invariably point to more rather than less religious involvement for American Catholics. Beyond the informed consensus that its expanding middle-class membership provides the strength of the Catholic community, there are pieces of statistical evidence. With assimilation and education, Catholic churchgoing increases. An estimated 89 percent of Catholics with college education attend weekly mass[18] compared with the overall Catholic figure of 71 percent. This confirms the figures cited earlier in connection with Catholic college students, which showed 83 percent weekly church attendance among Catholic graduates of non-Catholic colleges and 96 percent among graduates of Catholic colleges.[19] In his Detroit pocket study, Lenski found that third-generation Catholics had more "doctrinal orthodoxy" and "devotionalism" than the first and second generations, and the middle class was more active devotionally than the working class.[20]

In the alchemy of the American experience, the opposing tendencies to separate and to assimilate have pulled Catholics in two directions. Yet both have reinforced the religious participation of Catholics. As immigrants, Catholics found a protective home in a Church that safeguarded their national identity. As mobile middle-class Americans, Catholics go to church on Sunday as part of the American pattern. In the past, churchgoing has been a deep-seated American tradition, while today it is a social requirement. As Herberg argues persuasively, religion is vital to self-identification, adding social force to spiritual need. Moreover, the blend of the triple melting pot of Protestant-Catholic-Jew has been smoothed by the ecumenical drive, which encourages believers to stay where they are in affiliation while they come together in spirit. As with the Catholic joiner, the impact of America is partner to the embrace of Catholicism, producing the remarkably faithful Catholic worshiper.

PART IV

The Future

CHAPTER 16

◇◇

This Side of Eternity

THE DOUBLE IDENTITY of American Catholics is rooted in a conflict imported from Europe, a conflict obscured, overlooked, or ignored. The conflict is between Anglo-Saxon and Roman influences, and American Catholic ambivalence stems from these buried roots. The future character of Catholicism in the United States depends on how much of the Roman is uprooted and how much of the Anglo-Saxon (or American) is added.

The evolution involves the Church of immigrants in the nation of newcomers. The United States is dominated by an Anglo-Saxon orientation—which incorporates much more than the higher status accorded white Anglo-Saxon Protestants. The Catholic Church in America has been dominated by Romanism—which involves a more profound control than that of Italian pope and Roman Curia.

The conflict, at bottom, is between two fundamental points of view, two wholesale orientations, even two historical contexts. It is *not* a religious conflict concerning faith and morals, but a social, cultural, and intellectual phenomenon. American Catholics are caught between seemingly immovable Roman traits and irresistible Anglo-Saxon tendencies.

In Europe the Anglo-Saxon and Roman conflict has been evident both historically and geographically in the differences between northern protesting liberalism and southern compliant conservatism.

In the Roman tradition, the power to rule and legislate resides in the state; the emperor's (or pope's) will is law; the division between ruler and ruled is deep and wide; the duty to obey is paramount. The benefit of the Roman system is stability; the danger is obsolescence.

In the Anglo-Saxon tradition, consensus is the essence of legislation; the consent of the governed is paramount; the ruler receives his rights from the ruled; the responsibilities of freedom are cherished. The benefit is flexibility; the danger is chaos.

The adjective *Roman* before Catholic Church is the expression of a cultural straitjacket—which the church has struggled to remove since shortly after its founding. Indeed, the battle against cultural confinement is the oldest one in Christendom; the struggle has ever been to free essential dogma from accepted custom and to separate religious conversion from cultural conversion.

In the beginning the Church had to escape a Jewish monopoly. The first conservative-liberal struggle occurred between Peter and Paul, between the literal fisherman and the mystical tentmaker. Paul had "to withstand [Peter] to the face" (Acts 15:7) at what is commonly regarded as the first Ecumenical Council, in Jerusalem in A.D. 60. Simply stated, the issue was whether a convert needed first to become a Jew before he became a Christian. The answer was no. For the early Church, the death of circumcision as a precondition for conversion was the birth of universality.

A similar goal has been pursued in the Vatican Council of the 1960s: to liberate the Church from restrictive external forms. The reach for freedom from cultural and social traditions (which affect the intellectual, as well) is a direct link between John XXIII and Saint Paul, between 1962 and 60.

The early Church, unbound by cultural restrictions, burgeoned for 300 years as an inchoate, largely unstructured enterprise. It was a Church era of great saints, glorious martyrs, and horrendous heretics. It was an age of charisma and of turbulence. Winners became Church fathers, losers heretics. Then Rome prevailed.

Christendom took its outward shape from the Roman order, dividing into rigid castes of clergy and laity, into provinces and administrative units. Christianity became imperial as popes became "emperors" and emperors became Christians. The merger was embodied in the first Christian emperor of Rome, Constantine, in the fourth century. It was lavishly embellished by the crowning of Charlemagne as holy Roman emperor by Pope Leo III at Christmas mass in 800.

The alliance of emperor and pope became more intimate in the marriage of church and state which controlled the medieval communes. Religious and political leaders held power jointly, reinforcing each other, except during their periodic spats. Christianity became an inseparable thread in the cultural and national fiber; organized religion and organized government flourished side by side. For each particular nationalism there was a particular church—both culturally conditioned.

The major threat to Romanism emerged in northern Europe, in answer to the same urgency that moves American Catholic liberals today: to de-Romanize the Church. The threat was cultural, not religious. The protesters sought at the outset to change the style of the Roman Church, not to replace it. Luther's original protest focused on the abuses which had grown up around indulgences; his ninety-five theses had no argument with the validity of the "papal tickets" themselves. What ensued, however, was one of history's biggest surprises—the Protestant Reformation.

Out of the religious turmoil rose the conflict that would be exported to America. Romanism in southern Europe was threatened by the Anglo-Saxon North, which produced the founding fathers of the United States. The waves of immigrants who later joined them in the New World were heavily Catholic, and the dominant national group among these was the Irish.

Despite their northern origins, the Irish were standard-bearers of the Roman style, and they placed the Catholic Church in America at Rome's disposal. It was a supreme marriage of convenience. The tribal society of the Irish was attuned to the cultural peculiarities of the Roman Church, and the attachment was nurtured by political circumstance. Besieged almost constantly since Roman times by invaders from across the northern seas, the Irish held to their Catholic faith as a constituent of their unfulfilled sense of national destiny. The English left the Roman fold, but the Irish remained Rome's loyal island in the North.

In America, the Irish faced economic deprivation and social hostility, and they fought on—within the Catholic Church and for the Catholic Church. Not fenced in from the surrounding environment by a language barrier, the Irish needed their religion all the more to preserve their national identity. With numbers on their side, they rose to power in the American Catholic Church, maintaining a close alliance with the Roman matrix in self-defense against the Anglo-Saxons. The Irish ear heeded Rome eagerly, and Rome saw no reason to ignore the attention—for a whole new world was at stake.

The tactical alliance gave birth to the prevailing characteristics of the American Church. Other immigrants and other influences came afterwards, but they had not the strength to break the Irish-Roman merger. The Romanized community of Catholics reflected an emphasis on authority, a focus on privilege, a corporate context, and an other-worldly orientation. All four stood in ideological contrast with the familiar Anglo-Saxon qualities of freedom, egalitarianism, personal responsibility, and a this-worldly vision. Point by point, the cultural dialectic of the four contrasts would absorb the Church of Rome in America.

1. *Authority versus freedom.*   Emphasis on the Church as

supreme and all-inclusive lawgiver in faith and morals contrasts with emphasis on participation by the People of God in determining faith and morals. In the conservative view, Rome does not listen; it only speaks. By Roman enlargement papal infallibility has encompassed whatever the pope utters, making him the final authority on a wide range of issues. The attitude filters down through the ranks of the clergy so that free expression in the Catholic Church becomes confused with rebellion and disobedience.

In fact, papal infallability is so hedged by conditions* that it has been used only once since its formulation in 1870: in 1950, to proclaim the dogma of the Assumption of the Virgin Mary into heaven. Canon F. H. Drinkwater, an English authority who demonstrates characteristic Anglo-Saxon Catholicism, has pointed out the dangers of "creeping infallibility" and stressed that "the divinely appointed spokesman of the Church is infallible because the Church is infallible."[1]

Meanwhile, Archbishop Egidio Vagnozzi, apostolic nuncio to the United States, stands as the guardian of the Roman emphasis on centralized authority and on American acquiescence. He has even said that once the Vatican Council is over, things will return to "normal." The Archbishop's intrusions into the affairs of the American hierarchy reflect his Romanism, and the resulting resentment is typically American. Cardinal Spellman has reportedly suggested in a flash of anger that the Archbishop be sent on a diplomatic mission to Lapland.[2]

2. *Privilege versus egalitarianism.* Best expressed in terms of a social system, the word *privilege* invokes the

---

* "Papal infallibility means that the pope, when speaking 'ex cathedra' on a matter of faith and morals, cannot make a mistake and teach error. He speaks 'ex cathedra' when, in virtue of his office and apostolic authority as Supreme Shepherd, he intentionally and manifestly defines a revealed doctrine of faith or morals which must be held by all members of the Church." (See *1965 National Catholic Almanac*, ed. Rev. Felician A. Foy, O.F.M., Paterson, Saint Anthony's Guild, 1965, p. 163.)

Roman caste system, where ruler and ruled, teacher and taught are clearly separated and located in a rigid hierarchy. Its opposite is fraternal membership and full participation by all members. The American Catholic revolt against Romanism is well described by Daniel Callahan, whose egalitarian viewpoint is evident in the following:

> The whole Church is the People of God. That means the Church is a community, made up of people each with different gifts, vocations and functions, but each sharing a common humanity, equality and destiny in the eyes of God. Some will have the power of orders (priests); some will have the power of jurisdiction (bishops and popes); some will have neither of these powers (the laity). Nonetheless, these different functions do not disturb the Christian equality of each person; and that is a significant basis for personal freedom. Even amidst a hierarchical order, Christian equality implies a fraternal relationship of those teaching and those taught, of ruler and ruled. Those who rule can only do so by serving, and the spirit of service will be demonstrated by humility and openness.[3]

3. *Corporate versus personal responsibility.*   The corporate-personal conflict is evident in moral attitudes. In the United States, the parochial school has embodied the corporate approach to morality, stressing obedience to the establishment rather than self-direction. Parochial schools are obsessive on the subject of good behavior, though, as we noted in Chapter 4, their impact on internal moral development is not markedly different from that of public schools. Natural virtues, grounded in a commitment to moral behavior without recourse to supernatural orders, are neglected in parochial school education.

The existential responsibility of being your brother's keeper in larger dimensions than the local parish has thrived in northern Europe. In Rome, where social responsibility is ignored, Catholics have usually done as the Romans do. In America, the minority Catholic dissent against the corporate approach can be illustrated from a bold address given by a layman at an opening session of the National Catholic Educational Association convention in 1965. After noting that "obedience is not the highest virtue," Professor Paul Mundy presented this admonition:

There is another alternative to obedience which is not disobedience: the reasoned, free acts of an autonomous, morally responsible, free person who must not always be told what to do and what not to do.

Obedience in the family and in education as a legitimate reality has a declining relevance and a very brief life expectancy as childhood recedes. The human process of growth is to a large degree the process of learning *not* to obey, for childhood is not a permanent disadvantage. The larger portion of one's life is to be lived as a constantly thinking, critically evaluating, self-determining adult. Our humanity, our dignity, our rationality, our freedom are to be respected. And because this is so, our very autonomy requires the climate that encourages the progressive maturing of personal responsibility.[4]

4. *Other-worldly versus this-worldly orientation.* The other-worldly view proceeds from universals to specifics, from the abstract to the concrete. Its reflex action when confronting the here and now is to turn toward general principles. The this-worldly view is the opposite, taking the here and now as its concrete frame of reference and point of departure. It takes the pragmatic, existential, Anglo-Saxon approach rather than the Scholastic, Olympian, Roman approach.

Typical of the this-worldly view is a statement by the German Jesuit theologian Karl Rahner. He has called for "a theology of the mysteries of Christ, of the physical world, of time and temporal relations, of history, of sin, of man, of birth, of eating and drinking, of work, of seeing, hearing, talking, weeping, laughing, of music, of dance, of culture, of television, of marriage and the family, of ethnic groups and the state of humanity."[5]

In his commentary on American Catholic intellectuals, Msgr. Ellis describes the handicap of the other-worldly view when he speculates on reasons for "the absence of a love of scholarship for its own sake" among Catholics:

> I do not pretend to know precisely what the cause of this may be, but I wonder if it is not in part due to the too literal interpretation which many churchmen and superiors of seminaries and religious houses have given to St. Paul's oft-quoted statement that "Here we have no permanent city, but we seek for the city that is to come," and their emphasis on the question of the author of the "Imitation of Christ" when he asked, "What doth it avail thee to discourse profoundly of the Trinity, if thou be void of humility, and consequently displeasing to the Trinity?"[6]

The four ideological contrasts embody American Catholic tensions. The Roman traits, which crossed the ocean to dominate the development of the American Church, coexist uneasily with the American tendencies deriving from the Anglo-Saxon heritage. The Americanization of Catholicism means de-Romanization, which will recast the Church as an American institution. This is the past and present story of American Catholics in perspective. The future story is emerging from the changes taking place within the Catholic Church, particularly in America, and the changes taking place in America, particularly as they affect Catholics.

Many other labels might be used to describe the tensions between the Roman and Anglo-Saxon orientations, but they are adequately represented by the four just described. The polarities can be strung out in a litany of opposing cultural traits: the closed Roman system versus the open American system; space versus time; static versus dynamic; system versus process; papal primacy versus collegiality; essence versus existence; authority versus personal responsibility; family-tribe versus city; certitude versus search; monarchy versus democracy; unity versus pluralism; institution versus personal relationships.

The patterns of change in the American Church have given rise to catch phrases—the New Breed, the emerging layman, honesty in the Church—and have many manisfestations—criticism of the parochial school, complaints about anti-intellectualism, demands for involvement in current issues, even criticism of the hierarchy. These are social expressions of the revolt against Romanism; they are Anglo-Saxon expressions which have grown naturally in the pragmatic American environment. They also coincide with the decline (though by no means disappearance) of Irish power.

In America, Catholics have the opportunity to overcome Roman trammels and absorb Anglo-Saxon tendencies in a conducive environment. The American experience is on their side, with its freedom from European shibboleths and its impatience with inhibiting traditions. Moreover, America is not burdened with a holy city which prevents the harmonizing of various influences. What Rome did to Catholicism, Jerusalem did to Judaism and Constantinople to the Orthodox against the competing claims of Athens and Moscow. Such holy cities have been divisive and have nurtured spurious religious practices and claims, making religion culture-bound and nationality-dominated.

Significantly, Baltimore did not dominate American Catholicism. Indeed, the American Church is controlled by two complexes of urban power, New York–Boston–Philadelphia–Washington and Chicago–Saint Louis–Cincinnati–Detroit–Milwaukee, with the West Coast developing as a third complex. The Catholic dispersal in America reflects a multiple spread of nationalities, urban centers, power, custom, and influence. Catholicism in America does not have one shape or form, and that is why the Roman style of the American Church has become—over time and distance—dinosaurlike. Huge, impressive, even frightening to outsiders, up close this Roman structure is threatened with evolutionary extinction, unless it adjusts to the new and furiously changing American environment.

Adjustments are being forced upon the Catholic Church in America by social realities and by American Catholics themselves. By being Americans, Catholics are both consciously and unconsciously creating unrest, generating self-examination, and fomenting changes. If nothing else the split identity, the American Catholic ambivalence, is forcing religion to look to its essentials. That is the incredibly significant consequence of the Catholic experience in this country. It is the essential source of ecumenism and the main hope for the viability of religion in this technologically overwhelming and intellectually baffling modern world.

In the broadest terms, the notion of a religious man can be transformed to include atheists—and exclude some bishops and cardinals. The crucial test can be stated this way: is the individual concerned about life's ultimate problems? Instead of drawing the dividing line between churchgoers and nonchurchgoers, those with religious concerns would be separated from those without them.

In this vein, the French Dominican scholar Father Festugière has suggested that subscribing or not subscribing to an established religion is an irrelevant detail. He has written that ultimately there are only two kinds of men:

> Those for whom religious problems exist and those for whom they do not. . . . Some people may have religious faith, may practice that faith outwardly without experiencing the anguish of religious problems. They may attend mass, take communion at Easter, fulfill the varied obligations of Christian law through a feeling of tradition, or through the simple desire to fulfill what is due in respect to the divine, or even to liberate themselves from some disquietude, once for all, through observing the rites instituted by men for that purpose, so that, having observed them, they may no longer have to think about them. Conversely, one may adhere to no creed whatever, perform no religious practices, yet be tortured throughout one's life by the problem of God, of what He is, of the relations between God and man.[7]

While northern European Catholics have confronted the nonbeliever and the atheist and found the experience "purifying," American Catholics in the grips of Romanism have enthroned formal belief and external behavior. They refuse to learn from those who do not believe with them. The younger Catholic commentators who are in tune with American intellectual attitudes are reminding their fellow Catholics of the function of unbelief. Michael Novak, for instance, has upset Catholic traditionalists with statements like the following:

Finally, I'd like to suggest that many Americans have yet to live through the crisis of unbelief which has been experienced by our civilization generally in the great wars of our time. We ought in our own lives to recapitulate this history of the last several generations, the history of those generations which for one reason or another severely criticized and usually rejected religious belief. We ought to live through it until we understand it, until we sympathize with it, until we feel it, until it has become part of us: this critique of religion, this purification, if you will. We ought to do that in part so that we can make our own free choice, so that when we renew our baptismal vows, it's a real renewal, it's our commitment.[8]

A widespread reorientation toward religious commitment is hardly around the corner; indeed, the suggestion might even call for burning at a Roman stake. But there is a growing awareness of the great need to free religion from cultural accidentals and from sheeplike behavior by unconscious flocks. America offers a magnificent opportunity to do this, since it encompasses so many cultures, nationalities, and denominations, and subjects them to enormous pressures of technology, thought, and human reorganization. Instead of being a secular force, America could become a purifying force for religion.

Because of the tensions in the American Catholic identity, because of the Anglo-Saxon and Roman confrontation, American Catholicism is evolving and transforming itself. The influences which have been described and analyzed in this book are at work shaping an identity that will emerge in the concrete—existentially. In twenty-five years, we shall not recognize the Roman Catholic Church in America.

CHAPTER 11

The Voter

Notes

I. PAST AND PRESENT

1. DOUBLE IDENTITY

[1] Quoted in Theodore H. White, *The Making of the President 1960*, New York, Pocket Books, 1961, Appendix C, p. 471.

2. THE ETHNIC ACCENT

[1] Quoted in Rev. Robert I. Gannon, S.J., *The Cardinal Spellman Story*, Garden City, Doubleday, 1962, p. 131.

[2] Quoted in *ibid.*, p. 2.

[3] Quoted in A. V. Krebs, Jr., "A Church of Silence," *The Commonweal*, July 10, 1964, p. 467.

[4] Alexis de Tocqueville, *Democracy in America*, ed. and abr. Richard D. Heffner, New York, Mentor, 1956, p. 155.

[5] *1965 Catholic Press Annual*, New York, Catholic Press Association, 1965, p. 23.

[6] Report of the New York City Commissioner of Almhouses for 1837.

[7] Report of the New York City Board of Assistant Aldermen in 1847.

[8] *Niles Weekly Register*, July 16, 1831, quoted in Edith Abbott, *Historical Aspects of the Immigration Problem: Select Documents*, Chicago, University of Chicago Press, 1926, p. 566.

[9] *Life and Letters of Edward Lawrence Godkin*, ed. Rollo Ogden, New York, Macmillan, 1907, quoted in Abbott, *op. cit.*, p. 516.

[10] *Ibid.*

[11] Thomas L. Nichols, M.D., *Forty Years of American Life*, London, 1864, quoted in Abbott, *op. cit.*, p. 518.

[12] *Ibid.*

[13] Rev. James Francis Maguire, *The Irish in America*, London, 1868, quoted in Abbott, *op. cit.*, p. 522.

[14] Chambers' *Edinburgh Journal*, June 13, 1846, quoted in Abbott, *op. cit.*, p. 95.

3. UNTIL DEATH PARTS THEM

[1] Quoted in "Family Not Immune to Cultural Change," *The National Catholic Reporter*, July 14, 1965.

[2] Carle Zimmerman, *The Family and Civilization*, New York, Harper, 1947, p. 471.

294   *Notes*

[3] Cited in Nathan Glazer and Daniel Patrick Moynihan, *Beyond the Melting Pot: The Ethnic Groups of New York City*, Cambridge, M.I.T. Press, 1963, pp. 257–58.

[4] W. Lloyd Warner and Leo Srole, *The Social Systems of American Ethnic Groups*, Yankee City Series, III, New Haven, Yale University Press, 1945, pp. 129–30. "Yankee City" is Newburyport, Massachusetts.

[5] Glazer and Moynihan, *op. cit.*, p. 194.

[6] Rev. John L. Thomas, S.J., *The American Catholic Family*, Englewood Cliffs, Prentice-Hall, 1956, pp. 244–46.

[7] The evolution of the southern Italian peasant family has been systematically described by Paul J. Campisi in "Ethnic Family Patterns: The Italian Family in the United States," *American Journal of Sociology*, May, 1948, pp. 443–49.

[8] Judson T. Landis and Mary G. Landis, "Mixed Marriages—Research Findings," in Evelyn M. Duvall and Sylvanus M. Duvall, eds., *Sex Ways, in Fact and Faith: Bases for Christian Family Policy*, New York, Association Press, 1961, pp. 84–86, 87–89.

[9] Rev. John L. Thomas, S.J., "The Factor of Religion in the Selection of Marriage Mates," *American Sociological Review*, August, 1951, pp. 487–91.

[10] Jerold S. Heiss, "Premarital Characteristics of the Religiously Intermarried in an Urban Area," *American Sociological Review*, February, 1960, pp. 47–55.

[11] October, 1963, Gallup poll conducted for *Redbook* magazine, reported in Walter Goodman, "Striking Changes in the Way Protestants and Catholics Feel About Each Other," *Redbook*, March, 1964. Unless other sources are cited, as here, the Gallup poll figures in this book are taken from findings released periodically to subscribers by the American Institute of Public Opinion, Princeton, New Jersey, in its "Public Opinion News Service" bulletins.

[12] Albert I. Gordon, *Intermarriage*, Boston, Beacon Press, 1964, p. 17.

[13] *Ibid.*, p. 163.

[14] *Ibid.*, p. 159.

[15] This has been demonstrated in various studies, among them Gerald J. Schnepp's *Leakage from a Catholic Parish*, Washington, D.C., Catholic University of America Press, 1942, and Rev. Joseph H. Fichter's *Social Relations in the Urban Parish*, Chicago, University of Chicago Press, 1954.

[16] Quoted in *1964 National Catholic Almanac*, ed. Rev. Felician A. Foy, O.F.M., Paterson, Saint Anthony's Guild, 1964, p. 586.

[17] Cited in Donald J. Bogue, *The Population of the United States*, Glencoe, Free Press, 1959, p. 696.

[18] Leonard Gross, "America's Mood Today," *Look*, June 29, 1965, p. 17.

[19] Rev. John L. Thomas, S.J., *Religion and the American People*, Westminster, Newman Press, 1963, p. 77.

[20] *Population Bulletin*, Washington, D.C., Population Reference Bureau, Inc., June, 1960, pp. 76–78.

[21] Charles Westoff *et al.*, *Family Growth in Metropolitan America*, Princeton, Princeton University Press, 1961, p. 187, Table 43.

[22] *Statistical Abstract of the United States*, Washington, D.C., U.S. Bureau of the Census, 1958, p. 41, Table 40.

[23] See, for example, Franklin J. Henry and Hugh E. Brooks, *An Empirical Study of the Relationships of Catholic Practice and Occupational Mobility*

to *Fertility*, Washington, D.C., Catholic University of America Press, 1958, p. 40.

[24] Quoted in "Priest Tackles Fertility Cult Theory," *San Francisco News-Call Bulletin*, August 3, 1964.

[25] Rev. Raymond H. Potvin, "Responsible Parenthood and Family Planning," *Homiletic and Pastoral Review*, August, 1965, p. 146.

[26] Cited in "Birth Control: The Pill and the Church," *Newsweek*, July 6, 1964, p. 52.

[27] Quoted in *ibid.*, p. 53.

[28] Thomas Monahan and William M. Kephart, "Divorce and Desertion by Religious and Mixed Religious Groups," *American Journal of Sociology*, March, 1954, pp. 454–65.

[29] William J. Goode, *After Divorce*, Glencoe, Free Press, 1956, p. 36.

[30] Anne Collins, "New Help for Divorced Catholics," *The Sign*, January, 1965, p. 13.

[31] Msgr. George A. Kelly, *Birth Control and Catholics*, Garden City, Doubleday, 1963, p. 70.

[32] See Michael Novak, ed., *The Experience of Marriage*, New York, Macmillan, 1964, and William Birmingham, ed., *What Modern Catholics Think About Birth Control*, New York, New American Library, 1964. An indispensable survey of Catholic theory in this area can be found in John T. Noonan, *Contraception*, Cambridge, Harvard University Press, 1965.

4. "NEAR EACH CHURCH A PAROCHIAL SCHOOL"

[1] Mary Perkins Ryan, *Are Parochial Schools the Answer?*, New York, Holt Rinehart & Winston, 1964, p. 176.

[2] Figures reported in a release at the annual convention of the National Catholic Educational Association, New York City, April 21,1965, mimeo.

[3] Robert Hutchins, "Speaking Out," *Saturday Evening Post*, June 8, 1963, p. 6.

[4] Walter Lippmann, "CBS Reports, with Charles Collingwood," May 1, 1963.

[5] Quoted in Edward Wakin, "Outside the Catholic Classroom," *The Sign*, October, 1963, p. 47.

[6] Edward Wakin, "Richard's Double School Life," *The Sign*, March, 1965. For other articles by the same author on this subject, see "Experiment in Educational Sharing," *Religious Education*, January–February, 1965; and "The Shared Time Experiment—How It Operates," *Saturday Review*, February 15, 1964.

[7] Quoted in Rev. Colman J. Barry, O.S.B., *The Catholic Church and German Americans*, Washington, D.C., Catholic University of America Press, 1953, p. 11.

[8] Quoted in *The Catholic Church in Fort Wayne*, Fort Wayne, Public Library of Fort Wayne and Allen County, 1961, p. 59.

[9] Quoted in "Educators Urged to New Advances," *The Long Island Catholic*, April 9, 1964, p. 3.

[10] Quoted in Wakin, "Outside the Catholic Classroom," p. 47.

[11] Msgr. O'Neil C. D'Amour, "The Catholic Case," *The Commonweal*, January 31, 1964, p. 518.

[12] Quoted in Daniel T. Sullivan, "Suburban School Battleground," *New City*, March 15, 1963, p. 9.

[13] Reported in Edward Wakin, "Inside the Catholic Classroom," *The Sign*, September, 1963, pp. 16, 68.

[14] Quoted in Wakin, "Outside the Catholic Classroom," p. 49.

[15] Quoted in *ibid.*, p. 47.

[16] Donald McDonald, "Second Thoughts: Can We Keep On Paying for Catholic Schools?", *America*, March 26, 1960, p. 760.

[17] This appraisal was made by John K. Daly, Jr., who has covered the NCEA annual conventions for several years as correspondent of the National Catholic Welfare Conference News Service, in his postconvention release distributed to newspapers. See John K. Daly, Jr., "The Critical Barrage Lifts, Educators Ready To Move On," *The National Catholic Reporter*, May 5, 1965, p. 5.

[18] Gerard E. Sherry, managing editor, *Georgia Bulletin*, "To Whom the Schools Belong?", speech delivered before the Secondary School Department at the annual convention of the NCEA, New York City, April 22, 1965, mimeo.

[19] Rev. Andrew Greeley, Peter Rossi, and Leonard Pinto, *The Social Effects of Catholic Education*, preliminary report, Chicago, University of Chicago, National Opinion Research Center, October, 1964.

[20] Daniel Callahan, "The Schools," *The Commonweal*, January 8, 1965, p. 475.

[21] Rev. William J. McGucken, S.J., "Catholic Education: Its Philosophy, Its Fundamentals, Its Objectives" (pamphlet), New York, America Press, p. 16.

[22] Quoted in Wakin, "Inside the Catholic Classroom," p. 69.

[23] Rev. Joseph H. Fichter, S.J., *Parochial School: A Sociological Study*, South Bend, University of Notre Dame Press, 1958, pp. 109–131, 442–46, 452–53.

[24] Joshua A. Fishman, "Childhood Indoctrination for Minority-Group Membership," *Daedalus*, Spring, 1961, p. 337.

[25] Peter H. Rossi and Alice S. Rossi, "Some Effects of Parochial School Education in America," *ibid.*, pp. 300 ff.

[26] George Kelly, *Catholics and the Practice of the Faith*, Washington, D.C., Catholic University of America Press, 1946.

[27] Bay City, the name given a small industrial city in Massachusetts, was the subject of research conducted in the early 1950s by J. Leiper Freeman, James M. Shipton, Peter H. Rossi, and Alice S. Rossi, then at Harvard University. Findings from the study have appeared in James M. Shipton, "Reference Groups in the Formation of Public Opinion," unpublished Ph.D. dissertation, Department of Social Relations, Harvard University, 1955; Peter H. Rossi and Alice S. Rossi, "Background and Consequences of Parochial School Education," *Harvard Educational Review*, Summer, 1957; and the Rossis' later version of their 1957 article, published in *Daedalus*, Spring, 1961.

[28] Fichter, *op. cit.*, pp. 109–131.

[29] Rossi and Rossi, "Some Effects of Parochial School Education in America," p. 322.

[30] *Ibid.*, p. 324.

[31] These findings were summarized by Rev. Andrew Greeley, Peter Rossi, and Leonard Pinto in "The Effects of Catholic Education," *The Critic*, October–November, 1964, pp. 49–52.

[32] Rev. Richard Madden, O.C.D., "Today's Teen-Agers and Vocations," speech delivered at the annual convention of the NCEA, Saint Louis, April 16, 1963, mimeo., p. 4.

33 John D. Donovan, "The American Catholic Hierarchy: A Social Profile," *American Catholic Sociological Review*, June, 1958, pp. 98 ff.

34 Fichter, *op. cit.*, p. 222.

35 Poll results of a survey by the National Opinion Research Center, University of Chicago, reported at the annual convention of the NCEA, New York City, 1965; cited in Daly, *loc. cit.*

5. CATHOLICS ON CAMPUS

1 Rev. Andrew M. Greeley, *Religion and Career*, New York, Sheed & Ward, 1963, p. 41.

2 *Ibid.*, Chap. 3.

3 Edward Wakin, *The Catholic Campus*, New York, Macmillan, 1963, p. 2.

4 Richard J. Clifford and William R. Callahan, "Catholics in Higher Education," *America*, September 19, 1964.

5 Rev. Richard Butler, O.P., *God on the Secular Campus*, Garden City, Doubleday, 1963, pp. 180–81.

6 Quoted in Clifford and Callahan, *op. cit.*, p. 291.

7 Rev. William J. Dunne, S.J., "University Relations Through the President's Eyes," speech delivered at the annual convention of the American College Public Relations Association, Denver, July 3, 1961.

8 John Henry Cardinal Newman, *The Idea of a University*, Garden City, Doubleday Image Books, 1959, p. 7.

9 Rev. Theodore M. Hesburgh, "The Work of Mediation," *The Commonweal*, October 6, 1961, p. 34.

10 John D. Donovan, *The Academic Man in the Catholic College*, New York, Sheed & Ward, 1964, p. 197.

11 Wakin, *op. cit.*, p. 197.

12 Quoted in Donald Bremner, "The Maryland College Case: A Clear Test for School Aid?", *The Reporter*, February 25, 1965, p. 37.

13 Donovan, *op. cit.*, p. 42.

14 Reported in Dr. Gerald F. Kreyche, chairman of the Department of Philosophy, De Paul University, Chicago, "Catholic Higher Education and Academic Freedom," speech delivered at the annual convention of the National Catholic Educational Association, New York City, April 22, 1965, mimeo.

15 Donovan, *op. cit.*, p. 198.

16 Kreyche, *op. cit.*

17 "Progress Report of College and University Campaigns over $10,000,-000," New York, American Association of Fund-Raising Counsel, April 25, 1962, mimeo.

18 Professor Robert F. Byrnes, "American Education: Some of Our New Responsibilities," presidential address delivered before the American Catholic Historical Association, Washington, D.C., December 29, 1961.

19 Donovan, *op. cit.*, p. 204.

20 Greeley, *op. cit.*, p. 74.

21 *Ibid.*, pp. 75, 78, 112–13, 176, 178.

22 Butler, *op. cit.*, p. 137.

23 Rev. Robert J. McNamara, S.J., "The Interplay of Intellectual and Religious Values," unpublished Ph.D. dissertation, Department of Sociology, Cornell University, 1963.

24 Rev. Thomas Anthony Rogalski, C.P., "How Important Is Catholic Education?", *Verbum Crucis*, July, 1963, p. 26.

25 Rev. Richard Butler, O.P., "Catholic Education Redefined," *Ave Maria*, October 12, 1963.

26 Clifford and Callahan, *op. cit.*, pp. 290–91.

27 Lawrence Shaw (pseud.), "Georgeham: 1984," *America*, August 29, 1964.

II. INSIDE THE CHURCH

6. SHEPHERDS AND THEIR FLOCK: THE PARISH

1 Sacerdos Occidentalis (pseud.), "Should the Council Look at Celibacy?", *The National Catholic Reporter*, June 9, 1965, pp. 1, 7.

2 Figures reported in *Time*, August 21, 1964, p. 40; cited in Rev. Stafford Poole, C.M., *Seminary in Crisis*, New York, Herder and Herder, 1965, pp. 170–71, fn. 3. Father Poole comments: "Rather understandably, the editors of *Time* were unable to give the source of their estimate. . . . Because of information received from confidential sources which I consider reliable, I believe that *Time*'s estimate is generally accurate." See also Rev. Joseph H. Fichter, S.J., *Religion as an Occupation*, South Bend, University of Notre Dame Press, 1961, pp. 196–200, 204–210.

3 Rev. Joseph H. Fichter, S.J., *Priest and People*, New York, Sheed & Ward, 1965, p. 190.

4 *Ibid.*, p. 186.

5 Quoted in *ibid.*, p. 201.

6 *Ibid.*, p. 200.

7 Louis Thomassin, *Ancienne et nouvelle Discipline de l'Église*, Paris, Lagny, 1886.

8 Theodulf, "Capitulary," in Rev. Jacques-Paul Migne, ed., *Patrologia Cursus Completus, Series Latina*, Paris, 1844–55, 221 vols., CV, 196.

9 See Rev. Philip M. Hannon, "The Development of the Form of the Modern Parish," in C. Joseph Nuesse and Rev. Thomas J. Harte, eds., *The Sociology of the Parish*, Milwaukee, Bruce, 1951, Chap. 1.

10 Quoted in John H. Fenton, "Chapels for Transients Rising Across U.S.," *The New York Times*, March 3, 1965.

11 See Francis A. Cizon and Rev. Joseph F. Scheuer, C.PP.S., *Parishes in the Human Community*, Highland, Ind., Le Play Research, Inc., 1960.

12 François Houtart, *The Parishes of Chicago*, New York, Le Play Research, Inc., 1959, pp. 84 ff.

13 François Houtart, "A Sociological Study of the Evolution of the American Catholics," *Social Compass*, January–April, 1955, pp. 189–216.

14 Rev. Joseph F. Scheuer, C.PP.S., "This Metropolitan Parish Has Four Distinct Social Areas," *Catholic Management Journal*, March, 1957.

15 Will Herberg, *Protestant, Catholic, Jew*, rev. ed., Garden City, Doubleday Anchor Books, 1960, p. 41.

16 *Ibid.*, pp. 89–90.

17 Rev. Walter J. Ong, S.J., *Frontiers in American Catholicism*, New York, Macmillan, 1957, Chap. 3.

18 Rev. Joseph H. Fichter, S.J., *Social Relations in the Urban Parish*, Chicago, University of Chicago Press, 1954, p. 137.

[19] James M. Gustafson, "The Clergy in the United States," *Daedalus*, Fall, 1963.

[20] Rev. Joseph H. Fichter, S.J., *Religion as an Occupation*, South Bend, University of Notre Dame Press, 1961, p. 177.

[21] Rev. John Hugo, "Parish Financing: A Pyramid Set on Its Head," Part I, *Ave Maria*, November 21, 1964, p. 8.

[22] Quoted in "Parish for Tomorrow," *Ave Maria*, March 7, 1964, p. 5.

[23] Thomas Leclerc, "Restructuring the Parish," *The National Catholic Reporter*, July 7, 1965.

7. SHEPHERDS AND THEIR FLOCK: THE DIOCESE

[1] Peter F. Drucker, "The Management Audit of the Catholic Church," *America*, February 25, 1956, p. 582.

[2] See Frank A. Santopolo, "The Interdependence of Priests and Laity in the Early Christian Church," unpublished research paper, Department of Sociology and Anthropology, Fordham University, 1953. Henry G. Beck's *The Pastoral Care of Souls in South-East France During the Sixth Century*, Rome, Gregorian University, 1950, gives a detailed portrait of the social and cultural determinants of religious practice and government in France in the Dark Ages.

[3] John D. Donovan, "The American Catholic Hierarchy: A Social Profile," *American Catholic Sociological Review*, June, 1958, pp. 98 ff. The information on the following pages of this book is drawn from the same source.

[4] Rev. Raymond Bosse, A.A., Ethna O'Flannery, and John J. Macisco, "The Monsignors of the New York Archdiocese: A Description and Analysis of Some Factors of Promotion," Fordham Sociological Research Laboratory, Working Paper No. 2, presented before the Sociology of Religion Seminar conducted by Dr. Thomas F. O'Dea, Fordham University, New York, 1958.

[5] *The Official Catholic Directory*, New York, Kenedy, 1964, p. 11.

[6] Archbishop Paul J. Hallinan, "The Myth of the Monolith," *Continuum*, Winter, 1964–65, p. 593.

[7] "What Would Happen if All U.S. Bishops Retired at 70?", *The National Catholic Reporter*, July 14, 1965, p. 1.

[8] Quoted in John Leo, "The DuBay Case," *The Commonweal*, July 10, 1964, p. 482.

[9] *Ibid.*, p. 478.

[10] See Rev. William T. Anderson, S.M., "A Study in Line and Staff in Five Dioceses," unpublished research paper, New York, Fordham Sociological Research Laboratory, 1960.

[11] Quoted in Edward R. F. Sheehan, "Not Peace, but the Sword," *Saturday Evening Post*, November 28, 1964, p. 40.

[12] "Changing Roles," *The Commonweal*, May 15, 1964, p. 238.

8. ISLANDS IN THE CHURCH

[1] See E. K. Francis, "Toward a Typology of Religious Orders," *American Journal of Sociology*, March, 1950, pp. 437 ff.

[2] See Edward Wakin, *A Lonely Minority: The Modern Story of Egypt's Copts*, New York, Morrow, 1963, Chap. 12.

[3] See Jacques Maritain, "The Christian and the World," *True Humanism*, New York, Scribner, 1938, for a penetrating analysis of the antinomies be-

tween the world and the spirit in theological, philosophical, and historical perspectives.

[4] Quoted in "Benedict, St., the Holy Rule of," in *A Catholic Dictionary,* ed. Donald Attwater, 3rd ed., New York, Macmillan, 1958, p. 51.

[5] Quoted in *ibid.,* p. 200.

[6] The figures are taken from the *1965 National Catholic Almanac,* ed. Rev. Felician A. Foy, O.F.M., Paterson, Saint Anthony's Guild, 1965.

[7] Francis, *op. cit.,* p. 449.

[8] Gustav Gundlach, *Zur Sociologie der katholischen Ideenwelt und des Jesuitordens,* Freiburg im Breisgau, Herder, 1927, p. 104.

[9] *1964–65 Catholic Press Directory,* New York, Catholic Press Association, 1964.

[10] "Newman Press/Paulist Press" (catalogue), New York, n.d.

[11] "Religion," *Time,* May 21, 1965, p. 80.

[12] "Industry," *Time,* January 20, 1961, p. 84.

[13] *Jubilee,* May, 1965, p. 55; *The Sign,* February, 1964, p. 77.

[14] *The Sign,* February, 1964, p. 77.

[15] *Sacred Heart Messenger,* March, 1965, p. 64; *The Sign,* March, 1965, p. 77.

[16] *The Sign,* February, 1964, p. 76.

[17] *Ibid.,* December, 1964, p. 74.

[18] *Ibid.,* p. 75.

[19] *Ibid.,* February, 1964, p. 69.

[20] *Ibid.,* December, 1964, p. 78.

[21] *Jubilee,* October, 1965, p. 33.

[22] Reported in John Cogley, "Unlikely Stories," *The New York Times,* May 23, 1965.

9. BRIDES OF CHRIST

[1] Rev. Godfrey Poage, C.P., Introduction, in Rev. George L. Kane, ed., *A Seal upon My Heart,* Milwaukee, Bruce, 1956, p. vii.

[2] "Give the Bride a Veil," in Kane, *op. cit.,* pp. 86–87.

[3] "Why I Am a Sister," *Jubilee,* October, 1964, pp. 18, 16, 20.

[4] Sister Bertrande Meyers, D.C., *Sisters for the Twenty-First Century,* New York, Sheed & Ward, 1965, pp. x–xi.

[5] See Robert A. Broenen, "Sister Formation," in Joan M. Lexau, ed., *Convent Life,* New York, Dial Press, 1964, p. 191.

[6] Leon Joseph Cardinal Suenens, *The Nun in the World,* tr. Geoffrey Stevens, Westminster, Newman Press, 1963, pp. 17, 18, 25, 33.

[7] Sister Charles Borromeo, C.S.C., "Can Sisters Be Relevant?", *The National Catholic Reporter,* March 31, 1965, p. 11.

[8] Sister Mary Gilbert, S.N.J.M., "By Rule, by Custom, by Unwritten Law," in Lexau, *op. cit.,* p. 80.

[9] Borromeo, *loc. cit.*

[10] Quoted in Meyers, *op. cit.,* pp. 80–81.

[11] John B. Wain, M.D., "Psychological Problems in Religious Life," *Review for Religious,* March, 1961, pp. 81–88.

[12] Sister M. William Kelley, I.H.M., "The Incidence of Hospitalized Mental Illness among Religious Sisters in the United States," *The American Journal of Psychiatry,* July, 1958, pp. 72–75.

[13] Dom Thomas Verner Moore, O.S.B., "Insanity in Priests and Religious,

Part I: The Role of Insanity in Priests and Religious," *The Ecclesiastical Review*, November, 1936; and "Part II: Detection of Prepsychotics Applying for Admission to Priesthood or Religious Communities," *ibid.*, December, 1936.

[14] Kelley, *loc. cit.*

[15] Rev. Herbert Thurston, S.J., *The Physical Phenomena of Mysticism*, Chicago, Regnery, 1952.

[16] Walter J. Coville, Ph.D., "The Personality Assessment of Candidates for the Priesthood and the Religious Life," paper delivered at the annual convention of the National Catholic Educational Association, Atlantic City, April 1, 1964, mimeo.

[17] Bishop John R. Hagan, "Some Factors in the Development of Religious Vocations of Women," *Journal of Religious Instruction*, March, April, and May, 1945.

[18] "Why I Am a Sister," *loc. cit.*, p. 16.

[19] Sister Ritamary Bradley, C.H.M., "The Notion of Authority," *The National Catholic Reporter*, June 30, 1965.

[20] Wain, *op. cit.*, p. 84.

[21] *Ibid.*, p. 85

[22] "Education," *Time*, July 17, 1964, p. 43.

[23] Suenens, *op. cit.*, p. 141.

III. IN MANY ROLES

10. THE PRESS

[1] Dan Herr, "Stop Pushing," *The Critic*, April–May 1963, p. 87.

[2] John O'Connor, "A Question of Purpose," *The Commonweal*, February 15, 1963, p. 538.

[3] John G. Deedy, Jr., in Martin E. Marty, John G. Deedy, Jr., David Wolf Silverman, and Robert Lekachman, *The Religious Press in America*, New York, Holt, Rinehart & Winston, 1963, p. 91. Mr. Deedy's contribution to the book is the most succinct and authoritative summary available on the Catholic press, past and present.

[4] *Ibid.*, p. 69.

[5] *Ibid.*, p. 75.

[6] Donald McDonald, "The Catholic Press," *The Commonweal*, October 18, 1957, pp. 63–64.

[7] O'Connor, *op. cit.*, p. 539.

[8] *Ibid.*, p. 540.

[9] Dan Herr, "Stop Pushing," *The Critic*, June–July, 1964, p. 2.

[10] O'Connor, *loc. cit.*

[11] *Ibid.*

[12] Dan Herr, "Stop Pushing," *The Critic*, December, 1962–January, 1963, p. 10.

[13] Deedy, *op. cit.*, p. 91.

[14] Norma Krause Herzfeld, "Catholic Press on Foreign Aid," *America*, November 23, 1957, pp. 241, 242.

[15] Rev. Albert J. Nevins, M.M., "Breast-Beating in the Catholic Press," *The Catholic Journalist*, September, 1963, p. 11.

302 *Notes*

[16] "Hooray, Thanks a Lot and Some Reasons Why" (editorial), *The National Catholic Reporter*, February 3, 1965, p. 3.

[17] *Ibid.*

[18] John Cogley, "Religion: Church Press," *The New York Times*, August 15, 1965.

[19] Quoted in Deedy, *op. cit.*, p. 81.

[20] *Ibid.*

[21] "Cross-Section: The Publication Explosion in the Catholic Press," *The Critic*, April–May, 1963, pp. 52, 53, 56.

[22] Rev. James W. Whalen of the College of Saint Thomas in Saint Paul has described the success story of *Catholic Digest* in the Summer, 1964, issue of *Journalism Quarterly*.

[23] *Ibid.*, p. 345.

[24] *Ibid.*

[25] Deedy, *op. cit.*, p. 104.

[26] *Ibid.*

[27] Edward Wakin, "A Sociological View of the U.S. Catholic Press," *1965 Catholic Press Annual*, New York, Catholic Press Association, 1965, p. 46.

[28] Msgr. S. J. Adamo, "Debate: The Priest as Reporter," *The Catholic Journalist*, March, 1964, p. 6.

[29] Robert G. Hoyt, "Freedom in the Catholic Press," *ibid.*, November, 1963, p. 6.

[30] *Ibid.*, p. 5.

11. THE VOTER

[1] Quoted in "A Cordial Affair," *Newsweek*, July 20, 1964, p. 27.

[2] Quoted in Gerhard Lenski, *The Religious Factor*, Garden City, Doubleday Anchor Books, 1963 (originally published 1961), pp. 135–36.

[3] John M. Fenton, *In Your Opinion*, Boston, Little, Brown, 1960, p. 207.

[4] Seymour Martin Lipset, "How Big Is the Bloc Vote?", *The New York Times Magazine*, October 25, 1964.

[5] Quoted in William V. Shannon, *The American Irish*, New York, Macmillan, 1963, p. 411.

[6] Based on the Gallup Poll releases of December 3 and 6, 1960.

[7] Shannon, *op. cit.*, p. 410.

[8] Samuel Lubell, *The Future of American Politics*, Garden City, Doubleday Anchor Books, 1956, p. 75.

[9] Angus Campbell, Gerald Gurin, and Warren E. Miller, *The Voter Decides*, Evanston, Row, Peterson, 1954, p. 77.

[10] Quoted in Lincoln Steffens, *Autobiography*, New York, Harcourt, Brace, 1931, p. 236.

[11] Quoted in *ibid.*, p. 618.

[12] Nathan Glazer and Daniel Patrick Moynihan, *Beyond the Melting Pot: The Ethnic Groups of New York City*, Cambridge, M.I.T. Press, 1963, p. 223. The section on the Irish in New York City presents descriptions and analyses which are applicable on a wider scale.

[13] *Ibid.*, p. 226.

[14] Florence E. Gibson, *The Attitudes of the New York Irish toward State and National Affairs, 1848–1892*, Studies in History, Economics, and Public Law, No. 563, New York, Columbia University, 1951, pp. 17–18.

[15] Quoted in Shannon, *op. cit.*, p. 154.

16 Cited in Edward J. Richter and Berton Dulce, *Religion and the Presidency: A Recurring American Problem*, New York, Macmillan, 1962, pp. 96–97.

17 Quoted in Reinhold Niebuhr, "Catholics and the State," *The New Republic*, October 17, 1960, p. 15.

18 Quoted in "Catholics Oppose 'Balancing' Ticket," *The New York Times*, August 8, 1964.

19 Quoted in "Bishop Raps Church Vote Tactic," *New York Herald Tribune*, August 9, 1964.

20 Quoted in "Johnson-Humphrey," *The New Republic*, August 8, 1964, p. 4. Brackets are *The New Republic*'s.

21 "A *Life* Poll by Elmo Roper: People's Choice for L.B.J.'s V.P.," *Life*, August 14, 1964, p. 70.

22 The analysis was conducted by the Office of Public Opinion Research at Princeton University for the Federal Council of Churches, and used four polls taken by the American Institute of Public Opinion during 1945 and 1946. Cited in Liston Pope, "Religion and the Class Structure," *The Annals of the American Academy of Political and Social Science*, March, 1948, pp. 84–91.

23 *Ibid.*, p. 88.

24 Quoted in Shannon, *op. cit.*, p. 412.

25 Bernard Lazerwitz, "A Sociological Comparison of Major United States Religious Groups," *Journal of the American Statistical Association*, September, 1961, pp. 568–79.

26 Bernard B. Berelson, Paul F. Lazarsfeld, and William N. McPhee, *Voting*, Chicago, University of Chicago Press, 1955, p. 70.

27 Quoted in Glazer and Moynihan, *op. cit.*, pp. 271–72.

28 *Ibid.*, p. 271.

29 Lubell, *op. cit.*, p. 224.

30 As Anthony Lewis wrote in *The New York Times* of November 4, 1964, "The unpopularity of Goldwater transcended all the usual ethnic and regional and economic categories of voters."

12. THE JOINER

1 *1965 National Catholic Almanac*, ed. Rev. Felician A. Foy, O.F.M., Paterson, Saint Anthony's Guild, 1965. This is the authoritative source used in this chapter in citing the goals and membership figures of Catholic organizations.

2 William J. Whalen, "The Knights of Columbus: Are They Obsolete?", *U.S. Catholic*, December, 1964, p. 8.

3 Quoted in Ed Grant, "A Passing Parade—Few Regrets," *The Advocate* (Newark), March 11, 1965, p. 3.

4 Rev. Gustave Weigel, S.J., "An Introduction to American Catholicism," in Rev. Louis J. Putz, C.S.C., ed., *The Catholic Church, U.S.A.*, Chicago, Fides, 1956, p. 17.

5 Edward Wakin, "The American Daydream, Part I: Business, Then Virtue," *The Sign*, November, 1962, p. 20.

6 An authoritative account of the problem has been written by Rev. Harold C. Gardiner, S.J., in *Catholic Viewpoint on Censorship*, rev. ed., Garden City, Doubleday Image Books, 1961.

7 The phrase as well as the theme was the subject of a book by Donald Thorman, *The Emerging Layman*, Garden City, Doubleday, 1962.

8 Weigel, *loc. cit.*

9 Henry J. Browne, "A History of the Catholic Church in the United States," in Putz, *op. cit.*, p. 35.

10 Daniel Callahan, *The Mind of the Catholic Layman*, New York, Scribner, 1963, pp. 110–11.

11 Rev. Robert F. Marrer, letter to the editor, *The National Catholic Reporter*, March 3, 1965, p. 8.

12 Garry Wills, "Brainwashing . . . for God's Sake?", *The National Catholic Reporter*, February 17, 1965.

13 Quoted in "Sees Fanatics in Cursillo's Ranks," *The National Catholic Reporter*, May 19, 1965, p. 7.

14 Quoted in Irwin Ross, "A *Post* Portrait: Cardinal Spellman," *New York Post*, September 24, 1957, magazine section, p. M-2.

15 Edward Marciniak, "The Catholic Church and Labor," in Putz, *op. cit.*, p. 270.

16 John Cort, "Are We Missing a Bus? Why Not Support the Murray Industry Council Plan?", *The Commonweal*, August 14, 1942.

17 Aaron I. Abell, *American Catholicism and Social Action: A Search for Social Justice, 1865–1950*, New York, Hanover House, 1960, p. 267.

18 Charles J. Tull has written an excellent summary of the Coughlin episode in *Father Coughlin and the New Deal*, Syracuse, Syracuse University Press, 1965.

19 Michael Harrington, *The Other America*, Baltimore, Penguin, 1963, p. 5.

20 Rev. John F. Doherty, S.J., "A Study of Change in the Religious and Social Attitudes of Eighty-five Members of the Christian Family Action Movement in a Suburban Parish," unpublished Ph.D. dissertation, Department of Sociology and Anthropology, Fordham University, 1963, 2 vols.

21 Rev. John M. Joyce, "Would Catholic Education Have Spoiled JFK?", *The Critic*, October–November, 1964, p. 22.

13. THE NEGRO

1 See James Truslow Adams, *The Epic of America*, Boston, Little, Brown, 1931, pp. 62–64.

2 Rev. John T. Gillard, S.S.J., *Colored Catholics in the United States*, Baltimore, Josephite Press, 1941, p. 41.

3 Quoted in "Cry Pax," *The National Catholic Reporter*, February 17, 1965, p. 1.

4 Rev. Rollins E. Lambert, "Negro Priests Speak Their Mind," *The Sign*, November, 1964.

5 *Ibid.*, p. 11.

6 Joseph R. Washington, Jr., *Black Religion*, Boston, Beacon, 1964, p. 235.

7 *1965 National Catholic Almanac*, ed. Rev. Felician A. Foy, O.F.M., Paterson, Saint Anthony's Guild, 1965, p. 524.

8 St. Clair Drake and Horace R. Cayton, *Black Metropolis*, rev. ed., New York, Harper Torchbooks, 1962, II, 413, 415, fn.

9 Gene Currivan, "Harlem Catholic Schools Cool to Transfers," *The New York Times*, December 9, 1963.

10 Drake and Cayton, *op. cit.*, I, 196–97.

[11] Gordon W. Allport, *The Nature of Prejudice,* Garden City, Doubleday Anchor Books, 1958, p. 417.

[12] "Bishops' Statement on Race Relations," reprinted in *1964 National Catholic Almanac,* ed. Rev. Felician A. Foy, O.F.M., Paterson, Saint Anthony's Guild, 1964, p. 115.

[13] Quoted in Edward R. F. Sheehan, "Not Peace, but the Sword," *Saturday Evening Post,* November 28, 1964, p. 32.

[14] "The Church and the Negro," *Ave Maria,* August 1, 1964, pp. 16, 18.

[15] "Detroit and St. Louis Use Vast Church Funds To Insure Fair Housing," *The National Catholic Reporter,* May 19, 1965.

[16] "Religion," *Time,* May 28, 1965, p. 88.

[17] Quoted in Terry Link, "Fair Housing Act Beaten but Is Still an Issue," *The Advocate* (Newark), November 12, 1964, p. 2.

[18] Quoted in *ibid.,* p. 1.

[19] Rev. Niels J. Andersen, S.J., "Proposition 14 and the Liturgy," *America,* November 21, 1964, pp. 658–59.

[20] Quoted in "Racism Denounced at Mass for Rights," *The New York Times,* November 15, 1964.

[21] Dennis Clark, "Catholic Laymen Are Failing in Interracial Relations," speech delivered at the annual convention of the National Council of Catholic Men, Atlantic City, April 25, 1963; quoted in *1964 National Catholic Almanac,* p. 61.

[22] Quoted in Joseph Michalak, "Priest Assails Catholic 'Racists,'" *New York Herald Tribune,* April 22, 1965, p. 13.

[23] Quoted in "Religion," *Newsweek,* August 30, 1965, p. 57.

[24] "Catholics Participate in March on Washington," *1964 National Catholic Almanac,* p. 76.

[25] Quoted in "Prelate Attacks 'Eager Beavers' in 'Holy Cause,'" *The National Catholic Reporter,* March 24, 1965, p. 1.

[26] Quoted in "A Different Drummer," *The National Catholic Reporter,* March 24, 1965, p. 9.

[27] Quoted in "Religion," *Newsweek,* March 29, 1965, p. 76.

[28] Quoted in "Catholic Dispute Stirs Milwaukee," *The New York Times,* October 24, 1965, p. 73.

[29] This statement, made in a paper read at Tufts University, is quoted in Milton Rokeach, "Paradoxes of Religious Belief," *Trans-action,* January–February, 1965, p. 9.

[30] *Ibid.,* p. 10.

[31] Dorothy T. Spoerl, "Some Aspects of Prejudice as Affected by Religion and Education," *Journal of Social Psychology,* February, 1951, pp. 69–76.

[32] Gerhard Lenski, *The Religious Factor,* Garden City, Doubleday Anchor Books, 1963, pp. 71–73.

[33] Allport, *op. cit.,* pp. 420–25.

[34] Andersen, *op. cit.,* p. 664.

14. THE INTELLECTUAL

[1] These three examples, in company with many others, are found in Frank L. Christ and Gerard E. Sherry, eds., *American Catholicism and the Intellectual Ideal,* New York, Appleton-Century-Crofts, 1961, pp. 47, 107–108, 255.

[2] Msgr. John Tracy Ellis, *American Catholics and the Intellectual Life,*

Chicago, American Heritage Foundation, 1956, p. 57. Msgr. Ellis's discourse
by the same title was first published in *Thought*, Autumn, 1955.

³ Rev. Gustave Weigel, S.J., "American Catholic Intellectualism: A Theologian's Reflections," *The Review of Politics*, July, 1957, p. 299.

⁴ Speech delivered at the communion breakfast of the John Carroll
Society, Washington, D.C., December 15, 1957; reprinted (abr.) in Christ
and Sherry, *op. cit.*, pp. 227–29.

⁵ Thomas O'Dea, *The American Catholic Dilemma*, New York, Mentor-
Omega, 1962, pp. 127–37, 25.

⁶ Daniel Callahan, ed., *Generation of the Third Eye*, New York, Sheed
& Ward, 1965.

⁷ Rev. Andrew M. Greeley, "Anything but Marginal," in *ibid*, p. 82.

⁸ Rev. Andrew M. Greeley, "Sociology of Religion," *The Critic*, August–
September, 1962, p. 12.

⁹ Rev. Andrew M. Greeley, *Religion and Career*, New York, Sheed & Ward,
1963, p. 137.

¹⁰ Peter H. Rossi, Foreword, in *ibid.*, p. viii.

¹¹ James W. Trent, "Progress and Anxiety," *The Commonweal*, October
2, 1964, p. 40.

¹² John D. Donovan, "Creating Anti-intellectuals?", *ibid.*, p. 39.

¹³ Daniel Callahan, "An Autobiographical Introduction," in Callahan,
Generation of the Third Eye, p. 13.

¹⁴ Rev. William L. Doty, *Trends and Counter-trends among American
Catholics*, Saint Louis, B. Herder, 1962, p. 236.

¹⁵ John Leo, "Thinking It Over: Irreverence as a Style of Life," *The
National Catholic Reporter*, June 9, 1965.

¹⁶ O'Dea, *op. cit.*, p. 107.

¹⁷ Quoted in "Bishop Asks for Sane Criticism," *The National Catholic
Reporter*, May 26, 1965.

¹⁸ Weigel, *op. cit.*, p. 274.

¹⁹ Ellis, *op. cit.*, p. 45.

²⁰ Bishop John J. Wright, Preface, in *ibid.*, p. 9.

²¹ Morton White, "The High Price of Polemics," *New York Herald
Tribune Book Week*, July 19, 1964, p. 3.

²² John J. McDermott, "The American Angle of Vision," *Cross Currents*,
Winter, 1965.

²³ See Karen Horney, M.D., *The Neurotic Personality of Our Time*, New
York, Norton, 1937, Chap. 1.

15. THE WORSHIPER

¹ Thomas Sugrue, *A Catholic Speaks His Mind on America's Religious
Conflict*, New York, Harper, 1951, p 42.

² Rev. Gustave Weigel, S.J., "An Introduction to American Catholicism,"
in Rev. Louis J. Putz, C.S.C., ed., *The Catholic Church, U.S.A.*, Chicago,
Fides, 1956, pp. 16–17.

³ An alphabetical list can be found in the *1965 National Catholic
Almanac*, ed. Rev. Felician A. Foy, O.F.M., Paterson, Saint Anthony's Guild,
1965, pp. 300–304.

⁴ John Bellairs, "Saint Fidgeta," *The Critic*, June–July, 1965.

⁵ Quoted in "Will Success Spoil Liturgy Reform?", *The National Catholic
Reporter*, June 30, 1965, p. 3.

[6] See Edward Wakin, *The Catholic Campus*, New York, Macmillan, 1963, Chap. 5, "St. John's Collegeville: Living Life Whole."

[7] Quoted in "Religion," *Newsweek*, December 28, 1964, p. 38.

[8] Quoted in George Dugan, "Priest Continues To Score Reform," *The New York Times*, April 3, 1965.

[9] James O'Gara, "Back to the Schools," *The Commonweal*, April 30, 1965, p. 183.

[10] Mary Perkins Ryan, *Are Parochial Schools the Answer?*, New York, Holt, Rinehart & Winston, 1964, pp. 43–44.

[11] Sister Jane Marie Murray, O.P., and Paul Marx, O.S.B., "The Liturgical Movement in the United States," in Putz, *op. cit.*, p. 310.

[12] Will Herberg, *Protestant, Catholic, Jew*, rev. ed., Garden City, Doubleday Anchor Books, 1960, p. 151.

[13] Quoted in Edward Wakin, "The American Daydream, Part 2: A View from the Patio," *The Sign*, December, 1962, p. 34.

[14] See John Cogley, "Churchmen Hail Baltimore Talks," *The New York Times*, July 8, 1965.

[15] This was confirmed in studies in Lansing, Michigan (see Milton Rokeach, "Paradoxes of Religious Belief," *Trans-action*, January–February, 1965), and in a Midwestern county (see W. Widick Schroeder and Victor Obenhaus, *Religion in American Culture*, New York, Free Press, 1964).

[16] "Religion," *Time*, August 21, 1964, p. 36.

[17] Gallup polls released December 21, 1961, and December 27, 1964.

[18] Bernard Lazerwitz, "Some Factors Associated with Variations in Church Attendance," *Social Forces*, May, 1961.

[19] Rev. Andrew M. Greeley, *Religion and Career*, New York, Sheed & Ward, 1963, p. 78.

[20] Gerhard Lenski, *The Religious Factor*, Garden City, Doubleday Anchor Books, 1963, p. 399, Table 57.

IV. THE FUTURE

16. THIS SIDE OF ETERNITY

[1] Canon F. H. Drinkwater discusses infallibility in Chapter 4 of his book *Birth Control and Natural Law*, Baltimore, Helicon, 1965.

[2] See F. E. Cartus, "The Vatican Council Ends," *Harper's Magazine*, September, 1965.

[3] Daniel Callahan, "Seven Paths to Freedom," speech delivered at Georgetown University, December, 1964; reprinted in *The National Catholic Reporter*, July 21, 1965.

[4] Paul Mundy, "Changing Educational Patterns Required by Changes in Society and the Church," speech delivered before the College and University Department at the annual convention of the National Catholic Educational Association, New York City, April 20, 1965, mimeo.

[5] Quoted in Desmond Fisher, "The Men Behind the Council," *The Sign*, September, 1965, p. 14.

[6] Msgr. John Tracy Ellis, "American Catholics and the Intellectual Life," *Thought*, Autumn, 1955, p. 377.

[7] Quoted in Henri Peyre, "Camus the Pagan," *Yale French Studies* (semiannual), Spring, 1960, p. 25.

⁸ The quotation is from a talk Michael Novak delivered before students from twenty-two colleges at a meeting in the summer of 1964. An article based on a tape recording of the talk was published in *The National Catholic Reporter*, May 12, 1965. The theme is developed at length in Novak's book *Belief and Unbelief*, New York, Macmillan, 1965.

Index

◇◇◇◇◇◇◇◇◇◇◇◇◇◇◇◇◇◇◇◇◇◇◇◇◇◇◇◇◇◇◇◇◇◇◇◇◇◇◇